Michael K. Salemi, Ph.D.

Professor of Economics
and Chair of the Department of Economics
University of North Carolina at Chapel Hill

Professor Michael K. Salemi is Professor of Economics and Chair of the Department of Economics at the University of North Carolina at Chapel Hill. He has been a member of the faculty there since 1976 and a Professor of Economics since 1987. He has held three distinguished term professorships at UNC–Chapel Hill: Zachary Smith Professor of Economics from 1993 to 1996 and Bowman and Gordon Gray Professor of Economics from 1987 to 1990 and again from 2005 to 2010.

As an undergraduate, Professor Salemi studied Economics at St. Mary's College in Winona, Minnesota, and received his bachelor's degree in 1968. He earned master's degrees in Economics from Purdue University in 1969 and from the University of Minnesota–Minneapolis in 1973, and he earned his doctorate in Economics from the University of Minnesota–Minneapolis in 1976.

At UNC–Chapel Hill, Professor Salemi has taught a wide variety of undergraduate courses, including Money as a Cultural, Economic, and Social Institution, a first-year seminar he created. He routinely teaches Principles of Economics and has taught Intermediate Macroeconomic Theory and Money, Banking, and Financial Markets. To graduate students, Professor Salemi has taught Advanced Macroeconomic Theory, Monetary Theory, and advanced seminars in Macroeconomic Policy and Research on Monetary Policy.

Professor Salemi has completed a variety of international assignments during his career. He was a Research Associate and Visiting Professor at The Graduate Institute in Geneva, Switzerland, from 1982 to 1983 and 1985 to 1987 and in 2001 and 2002. The Asian Development Bank selected him as a contributor to seminars on monetary policy for transitional economies in Beijing in 1991 and in Lao in 1992. Under the aegis of the Swiss State

Secretariat for Economic Affairs, he designed and delivered a technical assistance and training program at the State Bank of Vietnam in Hanoi in 2004. More recently, he was a visiting fellow at the Hong Kong Institute for Monetary Research in 2007 and again in 2008.

Professor Salemi is the author of 2 books and more than 60 published articles in macroeconomics, domestic and international monetary theory, and economic education. He is the coauthor of *Discussing Economics: A Classroom Guide to Preparing Discussion Questions and Leading Discussion* and *Teaching Innovations in Economics*. His journal publications have focused on formulation and estimation of optimal monetary policies, explanations for high unemployment in Hong Kong, and strategies for effectively teaching economics to undergraduate students.

Professor Salemi has had a career-long interest in economic education. While a graduate student, he served as Assistant Director of the Center for Economic Education at the University of Minnesota–Minneapolis. In 1977, he created the Teacher Training Program for graduate student instructors of economics at UNC–Chapel Hill, a program that is widely described as one of the best of its kind in the world. Professor Salemi has taught in the program and has helped administer it throughout his career.

An acknowledged expert in economic education, Professor Salemi has served as an instructor, workshop director, and workshop program director for national programs in teacher education. He was co-principal investigator for "Interactive Teaching in Undergraduate Economics Courses: Bridging the Gap between Current and Best Practices," funded by the National Science Foundation from 2004 to 2010. The American Economic Association (AEA) selected him to serve on its Committee on Economic Education from1981 to 1988, 1990 to 2000, and 2001 to 2007 and to chair the committee from 1994 to 2000. More recently, the AEA chose him and William Walstad to design, administer, and teach a continuing education program in economic education.

Professor Salemi has been a featured speaker on the teaching of economics throughout his career. He has given talks at many colleges and universities,

Money and Banking:
What Everyone Should Know

Michael K. Salemi, Ph.D.

THE
GREAT
COURSES®

PUBLISHED BY:

THE GREAT COURSES
Corporate Headquarters
4840 Westfields Boulevard, Suite 500
Chantilly, Virginia 20151-2299
Phone: 1-800-832-2412
Fax: 703-378-3819
www.thegreatcourses.com

including the University of Notre Dame, Michigan State University, Stanford University, Wellesley College, University of Kentucky, and Baylor University. He has been selected as a featured presenter at many conferences devoted to economic education.

Professor Salemi has received numerous teaching awards. From UNC–Chapel Hill, he received the Tanner Award for Teaching in 1980, the Instructor Excellence Award of the Young Executive Institute in 1986, the Economics Undergraduate Teaching Award in 1994 and again in 2000, and the Economics Graduate Teaching Award in 2002.

The recipient of a number of national awards as well, Professor Salemi was awarded the Bower Medal in Economic Education in 1998 from the Council for Economic Education. The National Association of Economic Educators awarded him the Villard Award for Research in Economic Education in 2001. The Gus A. Stavros Center named him a Great Teacher in Economics in 2007. He is also listed in Marquis *Who's Who in America*.

Professor Salemi is married to Ariana Pancaldo and is the father of Benjamin, Caitlin, and Chiara Salemi. He is an avid squash player and also an amateur photographer and woodworker. He enjoys hiking, particularly in the American Southwest. ∎

Table of Contents

Table of Contents

Money and Banking: What Everyone Should Know

Scope:

Most of us like money and believe we should have more of it. Economists think of money as an agreement—a social contract—among individuals that, if kept, makes our economic lives better and allows our economies to grow more rapidly. In this course, you'll learn much more about money as a social contract, as well as such topics as inflation and hyperinflation; financial institutions; stocks, bonds, and derivative securities; and central banks, exchange rates, and monetary policy coordination among developed nations. The last lecture considers the challenges that confront our monetary and financial institutions in the coming years.

Perhaps the most important point you will encounter in this course is that economies require efficient and ever-evolving financial institutions and markets in order to maximize their potential. The first lecture is a preview of the ways in which you will come to understand the connection between financial matters and economic well-being, focusing specifically on the interdependent relationship between Wall Street and Main Street. The second lecture looks at the evolution of money over time and its importance as a social contract that lowers the cost of trading. Lecture 3 continues the history of money with a look at the money creation process, from its original backing with gold to our current system of fiat money that is not backed by any commodity. Lecture 4 takes up the monetary history of the United States and the debates that have taken place since the founding of our nation about the proper role of the federal government in monetary and banking affairs. Lecture 5 closes your introduction to money with some interesting examples of local currencies and nonstandard banks.

In Lectures 6 and 7, you explore the topics of inflation and hyperinflation. You'll learn why it is rational to fear high rates of inflation and volatile inflation histories and why economists say that hyperinflation is the ultimate repudiation by a government of its money. Lecture 8 looks at the connection between saving and investment and the importance of investment as a contributor to economic growth. Lecture 9 covers the concept of the real rate of interest and explore the connection between interest rates and inflation.

With Lecture 10, you begin a series of 3 lectures on financial firms and institutions, specifically, financial intermediaries, commercial banks, and central banks. You'll see that financial intermediaries—firms that channel funds from savers to investors and others—enable us to make financial provisions that we could not make on our own. You'll also learn how both commercial banks and central banks create money and look at the responsibility of central banks for the growth in the money supply of their nations.

In Lecture 13, you explore the process of moving money through time and the tool that allows us to compare the value of a dollar at 2 different dates: present value. Lectures 14 and 15 begin an investigation of decision making in the face of uncertainty, looking at the concepts of probability, expected value, and risk and risk aversion. These concepts also provide a background for investigating financial institutions, which routinely make decisions in the face of uncertainty when they decide whether to lend funds or to underwrite an initial public offering of stock

In Lectures 16 and 17, you get an introduction to bond markets, learn about the various types of government and non-government debt obligations, and see how bond markets determine interest rates. In Lecture 18, you zero in on interest rates, which we can think of as market-determined "prices" for a "good" we call "early use of funds." Then, in Lecture 19, you learn why interest rates tend to move together and look at the factors that account for differences in interest rates, including inflation and risk. Lecture 20 introduces us to a kind of crystal ball we can use to predict interest rates in the future—a combination of price information on Treasury securities and something called the "expectations hypothesis."

Lecture 21 begins a series of 3 lectures on the stock market. After an introduction to stock markets, we look at 2 models used by academics and professionals to study how stock prices should be connected to economic events. We also explore the phenomena of stock market bubbles, which provide important insights into the workings of markets. In Lecture 24, you turn to derivative securities, the "toxic assets" of the financial market crisis that began in our country in 2008. As you'll see, these can also be useful tools that allow decision makers to lower the risk of their business operations. Lecture 25 focuses on the problem of asymmetric information—a situation in which one party in a transaction has more information than another—and learn how this problem affects financial markets. Then, in Lecture 26, you apply the concept of asymmetric information to understand how and why financial firms are regulated.

Lecture 27 brings us to a topic touched on throughout the course: the subprime mortgage crisis of 2008. Here, we consider the causes of the crisis, specifically, the contribution of mortgage-backed securities, as well as how the regulatory reform that followed is likely to change the financial landscape in the future. Lecture 28 considers the actions the Federal Reserve has taken to accelerate economic recovery and compare the Fed's policy with that of the European Central Bank. Lectures 29 and 30 ask what the objectives of monetary policy should be and whether central banks should follow rules or use discretion in conducting monetary policy. With Lecture 31, you return to the Federal Reserve, examining what constitutes "normal" policy for the Fed, the extraordinary actions undertaken by the Fed in the wake of the crisis of 2008, and the question of whether or not the Fed went too far. Lecture 32 looks at the topic of central bank independence and asks whether greater independence is associated with desirable economic outcomes.

Before the final lecture on challenges for the future, lectures 33 through 35 look at international monetary and financial relationships, including an introduction to exchange rates, the roles of financial institutions in international trade and finance, and the case for coordinated monetary policy among the nations of the developed world. Finally, in Lecture 36, we outline 3 questions and related challenges that will greatly affect the world's economies in the future: Will the United States solve its long-run deficit problem? Will the euro survive? And will regulators find a solution to the "too big to fail" problem? The resolution of these questions will greatly affect future growth, inflation, and financial arrangements around the world. ∎

The Importance of Money
Lecture 1

E conomists are fascinated by the idea of money as a social institution— an agreement among individuals—that, if we keep it, makes our economic lives better and allows our economies to grow more rapidly. This contract is as important to modern society as the invention of the wheel, and in this course, you'll learn much more about this contract and what it means to keep it. By way of introduction to our study of money, this first lecture explores the intimate connection between Wall Street and Main Street; much attention has been focused on this relationship as the United States has attempted to recover from the subprime mortgage crisis and the Great Recession.

Wall Street versus Main Street

- Our nation's attempts to recover from the subprime mortgage crisis and the Great Recession were often discussed using the metaphor "Wall Street versus Main Street."

- On October 3, 2008, as the subprime mortgage crisis was going from bad to worse and the Great Recession was showing itself to be much worse than the typical downturn, Congress enacted the Emergency Economic Stabilization Act of 2008. That act created the **Troubled Asset Relief Program** (TARP), which provided funds for the bailout of troubled financial firms. Over the coming months, the Federal Reserve and the Treasury used TARP funds aggressively to keep banks and non-bank financial firms from failing.

- At the same time, there was a populist outcry that the federal government should do more for Main Street, that is, for the workers and firms that were suffering because of the Great Recession.

- The important lesson for us is that the "Wall Street versus Main Street" idiom is inherently flawed because the success of each of these entities is inextricably bound together. Neither can "win" without the other. Economies require efficient and ever-evolving financial institutions and markets in order to maximize their potential.

The Connection between Wall Street and Main Street
- Why is it that the fates of Main Street and Wall Street are so closely intertwined? The reasons for this connection between financial matters and economic well-being can be boiled down to four:

  o **Stable value money is essential to efficient trade:** Adam Smith, in his book the *Wealth of Nations*, argued that a nation becomes wealthy when it organizes its productive efforts to take advantage of specialization, but specialization is an inherently social activity. Producing an excellent product only makes sense if we can trade it for other things that we want but do not produce. Thus, trade is essential to wealth creation and improvement in the quality of life. Smith also tells us, however, that trade can be accomplished efficiently only in a society that has adopted money.

  o **Healthy banks are essential to the process of channeling funds from savers to investors:** At its core, a bank is an institution that channels funds from savers to investors. This process is fundamental to economic growth. If those with productive ideas had to wait until they accumulated sufficient funds from their own saving before they acted on their ideas, little growth would occur.

  o **Efficient asset markets are essential to establishing values for debt instruments, currencies, and shares of stock:** It's important to know the value of financial instruments. One of the key reasons for the subprime mortgage crisis that led to TARP and contributed to the depth of the Great Recession was the simple fact that banks held large quantities of mortgage-backed securities.

○ **A well-designed and well-executed monetary policy is essential for an economy to keep inflation low and steady and keep resources fully employed:** Monetary policy as we think of it today began with the creation of the Federal Reserve System in 1914. There is still, however, a great deal of disagreement, even among economists, about what constitutes a well-designed and well-executed monetary policy.

- In this course, you will learn how the Federal Reserve changes interest rates in order to pursue its policy objectives, and you'll see that sometimes, as in the years of the Great Recession, the Fed also loans directly to financial firms.

- In 2014, the Federal Reserve will celebrate its 100th anniversary. Some economists and politicians believe that the best thing we could do on that anniversary would be to eliminate the Fed or make significant changes to it.

- Some argue that the Fed wields too much power, and they are angered by the Fed's bailout of financial firms during the Great Recession. Others believe that the Fed has learned a lot about the proper conduct of monetary policy during its first 100 years, although even those who are champions of the Fed would like to see its operations fine-tuned.

- Upcoming lectures are devoted to creating a better understanding of central banks and central bankers, not only in the United States but also in the United Kingdom, China, and other developed nations. In this context, we will ask several important questions: What threatens the value of our money? Why is it important to preserve the value of money, and what can a central bank do to achieve that goal? And given that a central bank is committed to preserving the value of money, is there room for it to do more?

Troubled Asset Relief Program (TARP): Provided funds for the bailout of troubled financial firms after the subprime mortgage crisis during the Great Recession.

Suggested Reading

Cassidy, "Anatomy of a Meltdown."

Federal Reserve Bank of San Francisco, "The Economy, Crisis and Response."

Greider, *Secrets of the Temple.*

Paulson, *On the Brink.*

Questions to Consider

1. How would you have handled the money problem faced by the 19th-century farmer?

2. What recommendations would you have offered to the neighbors on the Great Plains who were thinking about pooling their funds to build a windmill?

3. Now that you have been introduced to this course, what are the questions that you hope the course will answer? You might want to make a brief record of these and come back to them later.

4. How reasonable do you think it is to describe Ben Bernanke as one of the most powerful men in the world? Why?

The Importance of Money
Lecture 1—Transcript

Hello, and thank you for joining me. I have been fascinated by money since the beginning of my career as an economist. Now, I know what you are thinking. We all like money and most of us believe we should have more. But what interests me is not the question of my income or yours. What fascinates me is money as a social institution, money as an agreement among individuals, money as a collective contract that if we keep it, makes our economic life much better and allows our economies to grow more rapidly. This course is about that contract and about what it means to keep it. The contract called money is important, as important to our modern society as the invention of the wheel. I will say that again: Money is as important to our modern society as the invention of the wheel. Thus, this course considers issues that are fundamental in their importance to our lives and well being. In the very last lecture, we will consider challenges that face our monetary and financial institutions in the coming years. I believe, and I think you will come to believe, that rising to these challenges is extremely important. Of course, there is a lot to learn before we consider these challenges.

You will remember that the nation's attempts to recover from the subprime mortgage crisis and the Great Recession were often discussed using the metaphor "Wall Street versus Main Street." That phrase "Wall Street versus Main Street" evokes for me a drama of the sort written by John Steinbeck, let's see, with Henry Fonda playing the role of the common man and Lionel Barrymore playing the greedy capitalist. In that drama, it's every man versus the plutocrats. On October 3, 2008, as the subprime mortgage crisis was going from bad to worse and as the Great Recession was showing itself to be far more damaging than any typical downturn we'd experienced in recent decades, Congress enacted the Emergency Economic Stabilization Act of 2008. That act created the Troubled Asset Relief Program, the TARP, which provided funds for the bailout of financial firms that were in trouble.

In September 2008, Federal Reserve Chairman Ben Bernanke and Treasury Secretary Henry Paulson had testified on Capitol Hill in favor of the Emergency Stabilization Act and the TARP fund. Congress voted in favor of the act, and President Bush signed it. Over the coming months, the Fed and the Treasury used TARP funds aggressively to keep banks and non-bank financial firms from failing. At the same time that funds were flowing to help threatened financial firms, there was a populist outcry. That outcry said that the federal government should do more for Main Street (for the workers and the firms that were suffering at the hands of the Great Recession) and less for [Wall] Street (for the banks and financial institutions and their management). During his campaign, Barack Obama condemned "greedy CEOs who are taking too much risk," although as President, he continued to support both the Treasury and Fed initiatives to rescue the financial sector. Nevertheless, throughout the time of the Great Recession, one frequently heard the view that the federal government supplied too much assistance to the financial sector and too little to the common man. If the government can help those big banks, they can help me keep my home.

If there is one idea, I hope you will take away from this course, and I hope it fervently, it is that the Wall Street versus Main Street idiom is inherently flawed. Sure, at any given time, if the federal government gave fewer dollars to help commercial banks, it would have more dollars to help the unemployed. But that very narrow truth misses a much larger and much more important truth: The success of Main Street and the success of Wall Street are inextricably bound together. Main Street cannot win without Wall Street, and Wall Street cannot win without Main Street.

The most important point that we will encounter in this course is that economies require efficient and ever-evolving financial institutions and markets in order to maximize their potential. We will encounter this idea many times in different ways and guises and in different contexts.

In this first lecture I would like to provide a preview of the ways in which we will come to understand the connection between financial matters and economic well being—the interconnectedness of Main Street and Wall Street. For the sake of specificity, I will give you 4 reasons why the fates of Main Street and Wall Street are intertwined.

The first reason: Stable value money is essential to efficient trade. A famous quote:

> It is not from the benevolence of the butcher, the brewer, or the baker, that we expect our dinner, but from their regard to their own interest. We address ourselves, not to their humanity but to their self-love and never talk to them about our necessities but of their advantages.

Those words are from perhaps the most famous economist and from that economist's most famous book. The man: Adam Smith. The book: *The Wealth of Nations*. The quote goes to the heart of Smith's argument that a nation becomes wealthy when it organizes its productive efforts to take advantage of specialization. But, Smith warns us, specialization is an inherently social activity. Producing lots of excellent beer, great quantities of tremendously good bread, or the best beef in your village will make sense only if we can trade a lot of it for other things that we want but that we do not produce. So, Smith teaches, trade is essential to wealth creation and to the improvement of the quality of life.

But Smith goes further. He warns again that trade can only be accomplished efficiently in a society that has adopted money. While I'll take this point up in great detail in coming lectures, the following story captures much of what is true about the importance of stable value money for trade—that creator of wealth.

I love stories; I hope you like this one. Suppose you were a homesteader in the first half of the 19th century in someplace like Kansas or Missouri. You engaged in subsistence farming but, despite your great ingenuity, you could not provide for all of your needs. So occasionally, you took the days required to travel to a town and purchase what you needed. But how would you pay? Let's say that you brought some wool from your sheep with you to market and your first stop was at the shop of a garment maker who had bought wool from you in the past. You are in luck. The garment maker will again buy your wool.

You agree upon a price and then are presented with bank notes drawn on a bank in Illinois. Immediately you wonder, are the notes any good? Will the owner of the general store accept them when I visit him tomorrow? And if not, will they keep their value until I find someone who is willing to accept them? Now, suffice it to say that your concerns are extremely legitimate and they represent an impediment to trade. Your sheep may produce the finest wool in the territory—the garment maker may agree that your wool is without equal in quality—but that will be cold comfort to you and cold comfort to the garment maker if you find it a risky proposition to sell that wool.

In this course, we will come to understand that money is a social contract, and we will study the evolution of that monetary contract from very early times when money was typically a portable, highly used commodity. And we'll continue that study to modern times when money is—let's face it—intrinsically worthless paper currency or, in many cases, balances in an electronic record book.

My second point for you: Healthy banks are essential to the process of channeling funds from savers to investors. Let's stay with our example of homesteading on the Great Plains. Some years have passed and now you have neighbors with whom you cooperate and socialize. At one of your gatherings, one of you mentions that it be a very great enhancement to your productivity if each of you had a windmill to pump water from the wells you have dug. But there's a problem: None of you has the funds necessary to purchase the pipe or the moving parts required. Each of you saves something each year for a rainy day, but none has enough to order the necessary from back East. After talking for awhile, you realize that collective action is possible. You realize that if you pool your funds with your neighbors, one windmill could be built immediately. You and your neighbors have just decided to create a bank.

At its core, a bank is an institution that channels funds from savers (those who save from their income in order to spend more than their income at a later time) to investors (windmill builders, those who wish to build productive equipment and buildings, which economists refer to as capital). Channeling funds from savers to investors is fundamental to economic growth. If those with productive ideas had to wait until they accumulated sufficient funds from their own saving before they acted on their ideas, little growth would occur.

Channeling funds from savers to investors is mutually beneficial. Savers earn interest on their savings. Investors gain the opportunity to enact their ideas sooner rather than later. You and your homesteader neighbors will come to learn that your decision to pool funds so that one of you can build a windmill sooner is not without its challenges. How will you decide which neighbor builds? How will you decide how much interest to charge? How will you ensure that the borrower will repay? In modern economies, many of these problems are solved by financial institutions such as banks and the markets for credit in which they operate.

Efficient asset markets are essential to establishing values for debt instruments like bonds, currencies, and shares of stock. Financial markets are essential. Remember our original homesteader problem? Our homesteader was offered payment for wool in the form of a paper bank note drawn on a bank in Illinois. One way to express the problem that our homesteader faced is to say that the homesteader did not know the value of that bank note in terms of some widely accepted payment medium, let's say gold.

Knowing the value of things is very, very important, even when those things are financial instruments. One of the key reasons for the subprime mortgage crisis that led to TARP and certainly contributed to the depth of the Great Recession was the simple fact that banks held large quantities of mortgage-backed securities. Of course, it was a problem that those securities lost value once house prices began to fall in 2007. But an even bigger problem was that banks and potential lenders to banks had no way of determining the value of those mortgage-backed securities once the housing crisis began. Why? Because there was no market in which those securities were traded. The value wasn't the face-value, and the value wasn't zero. Part of the job of markets would be to find out or discover what the value was.

Markets play essential roles in the functioning of our financial system. Bond markets provide a way for large and well-known businesses to obtain investment funds, funds to build their firms. Markets price financial securities so that borrowers, lenders, and financial institutions know what those securities are worth.

Contrast for a moment our homesteader's currency problem with what you might consider to be a similar problem today. Suppose you are traveling to Europe—it doesn't have to be France, or Italy, or Germany—the Czech Republic, for example. You know that you will need either euros or some other foreign currency to buy what you want to buy, but you do not have to guess the value of the euro; you do not have to guess the value of the Czech currency because many billions of euros are exchanged for dollars in foreign-currency markets every day. Indeed, many, many billions of financial currency units are traded every day for dollars—not just euros. We will study financial markets, bond markets, stock markets, and currency markets in detail in this course. We will come to understand what is traded in those markets, how to think about the prices that those markets set, and why those markets play an essential role in a modern economy such as ours. We will also come to understand the connection between those markets and important financial institutions such as the United States Federal Reserve, the European Central Bank, and the People's Bank of China.

I promised you 4 reasons; here is number 4: A well-designed and well-executed monetary policy is essential for an economy to keep inflation low and steady and to keep resources fully employed. Modern economies need well-crafted monetary policies. Here we have to leave our homesteader metaphor behind us. It makes no sense to talk about monetary policy in the first half of the 19th century. "Why?" you might ask. We had no monetary policy back then.

It's true that our nation made decisions about money and banks in the 19th century, and we will cover those decisions in our lectures. But monetary policy as we think of it today began with the creation of the Federal Reserve System in 1914. In fact, the requirement that the Fed promote low and steady inflation as well as full employment of our resources is an even more recent development as we shall learn.

But what is a well-designed and well-executed monetary policy? There is a great deal of disagreement about how to answer that question even among economists. We will learn how the Federal Reserve changes interest rates in order to pursue its policy objectives. We will learn that sometimes, as in the years of the Great Recession, the Fed does even more. It lends directly to financial firms, and we will learn why this is so.

In 2014, the Federal Reserve will celebrate its 100th anniversary. Some economists and politicians believe that the best thing we could do on that anniversary would be to eliminate or greatly change the Fed. They argue that the Fed wields too much power. They point to steps taken by the Fed during the Great Recession as evidence of that power, and they are angered by the Fed's bailout of financial firms during that period. Put another way, some critics hold that the Fed did too much for Wall Street and too little for Main Street.

Some critics go so far as to suggest we'd be better off returning to the gold standard. Others believe that the Fed has learned a lot about the proper conduct of monetary policy during its first 100 years. They argue that Fed policy under Paul Volker, Alan Greenspan, and Ben Bernanke has done an excellent job of conquering inflation in the United States, and we will take a look at the evidence that supports that view. But even those who are Federal Reserve champions would like to see the Fed revise and fine tune its operations. Some believe that the Fed should set a more explicit inflation target, like that set from time to time by the Reserve Bank of New Zealand. Ask yourself the question: Do you know what the target rate of inflation is? Of course you don't—the Federal Reserve does not announce one.

Some believe that the Federal Reserve has yet to find a way around the terrible incentives created by bailing out failing banks. (And, my goodness, we will talk about those incentives in great detail.) Those who look for improvement in this particular area are less motivated by the Wall Street/Main Street distinction and more motivated by the concern that the Federal Reserve creates terrible incentives when it bails out a failing bank. Economists call this problem the "too big to fail" problem, and we will study too big to fail also in some detail in this course.

Let's talk for a moment about powerful individuals. For the sake of argument, let me concede that the president of the United States is the most powerful single individual in the world. Who, in your view. is the second most powerful person in the world? Take a moment to think and write down your view, or if you are watching with someone else now, take a moment and exchange your views. Have you done it? OK.

Please permit me to share my humble opinion with you. The second most powerful person in the world is not a president, is not a general, is not an admiral, does not hold a cabinet post in our government or in another, and is not even elected. The second most powerful person in the world is Ben Bernanke, the Chairman of the Board of Governors of the Federal Reserve System. But why is Bernanke so powerful? A substantial portion of this course will be devoted to understanding central banks and central bankers, not only in the United States but also in the United Kingdom, in Europe (the euro area), in China, and in other developed nations. We will come to understand why central banks and central bankers are entrusted with the job of making sure our money retains its value; we will come to understand that it is the central bankers of the world that we hold responsible for keeping our monetary contract intact; we will come to understand that it is the central bankers in the world in whom we place the trust to keep this great invention working well.

In this context, we will ask and answer several questions: What threatens the value of our money? Many of you will say "inflation," but if I asked you, "why?" what would you say? Why, more basically, is it important to preserve the value of money? These are pieces of paper, after all. How can a central banker preserve the value of money? What can a central bank do to preserve that value? And, very, very, importantly, if we have a central bank that is committed to preserving the value of our money, is committed to keeping that social contract functioning well, is that all it can do, or is there room for it to do more?

Return again, please, for a moment, to the Main Street versus Wall Street theme we encountered earlier. Were the Stabilization Act of 2008, the TARP fund, and the way that our Treasury and the Federal Reserve used that fund essential to the Federal Reserve's job of preserving the value of the U.S. dollar? If you say, "yes," you should understand why. If you say, "no," you should likewise understand why.

Is it the case that Ben Bernanke—a non-elected individual—should somehow come more directly under the control of the voters, or is there wisdom in letting Ben Bernanke and the Federal Reserve latitude to pursue its policy? Part of this course is dedicated to answering all of these questions, and I look forward to the journey with you. Until next time, I wish you a very good day.

Money as a Social Contract
Lecture 2

This lecture, begins with a basic definition of "money" and traces the evolution of money through five stages: barter, commodity money, coined money, paper money backed by coins, and fiat money, which is what we use today. Throughout this evolution, you'll see that money operates as a social contract—members of society agree to accept money in exchange for goods and services. As we'll see, this contract has developed as it has because members of society have constantly sought to meet 2 competing goals: to lower the cost of trade while ensuring that money retains its value.

"Money" Defined

- The standard definition of **money** used by economists is something that can be used as a medium of exchange.

- Money is valued, not because it is intrinsically useful, but because it can be exchanged for useful things.

- This connection between money and exchange helps us understand the most important point in this lecture: Money is a social contract that lowers the cost of trading and has evolved gradually through time.

Barter

- **Barter**, defined as exchange without money, is the first stage in the evolutionary history of money.

- In *Money and the Mechanism of Exchange*, the economist William Jevons stated, "The first difficulty in barter is to find 2 persons whose disposable possessions mutually suit each other's wants … there must be a double coincidence, which will rarely happen."

- The search for a narrowly defined trading partner is costly because it takes time and the costs of locating trading partners and negotiating trades are disincentives to specialization.

- Primitive societies faced tremendous incentives to lower the cost of barter and often settled on successful schemes, including credit arrangements.

Commodity Money

- The next stage in the evolution of money is the development of commodity monies. A society uses **commodity money** when individuals typically buy and sell goods by exchanging a particular commodity that is agreed upon in the society to be acceptable for exchange.

- Commodity money has taken many different forms, including salt, cowry shells, large stones, and bricks of tea.

- Government has often played a role in deciding which commodity would function as money. For example, if a ruler or leader favored a certain kind of shell or feather, it might become money, although the commodity chosen as money must be scarce.

Coined Money

- As primitive peoples traveled beyond the borders of their homelands, they frequently found that their local money was not accepted and sought alternative ways to facilitate trade. Metals, especially gold, silver, bronze, and copper, were found to be valued in many societies, leading to the next stage in the evolution of money: the use of metals, in particular, metal coins.

- Several forces favored the use of metal rather than other commodities as money. Metal could be used to make a variety of goods, such as knives; it was durable; and it was typically more valuable (per unit of weight) than other commodities, which lowers the cost of transporting money.

Photos courtesy of Classical Numismatic Group, www.cngcoins.com.

Coining money provided governments with revenues because the government typically owned the mints that converted raw metals into coins and collected fees from those who sold metals to the mint.

- There were, however, 2 disadvantages to using lumps of metal as money: It was costly to verify the true metallic content and purity of a lump of metal, and it was costly to weigh the lump.

- By creating coins from metal, governments lowered the costs of using metal as money.

- The mint owner could also raise revenue by lowering the metal content of its coins. The word **seigniorage** denotes the revenue that a government obtains by deflating the value of its money. Seigniorage could be as simple as shaving metal from the edges of the coin or as complex as changing the price that the mint offers for metal to be coined.

Paper Money Backed by Coins

- The transition from coins to paper money is rooted in the practice of allowing citizens to deposit their goods in temples and palaces, which were relatively secure, well-guarded structures and were able to protect the citizens' wealth. The origins of paper money are the "warehouse receipts" received for deposits of precious metals and other commodities.

- The receipts themselves began to function as money when third parties traded them for commodities, rather than withdrawing their deposits. This practice represents the next step in the evolution of money: using money backed by a metal money, such as gold or silver.

- The use of this paper money lowered exchange costs because it was easier to exchange warehouse receipts than deposits.

- The managers of depositories soon realized that they could make loans to new parties by issuing new warehouse receipts. The scheme worked because on any given day, only a small fraction of deposits were withdrawn from the depository.

Fiat Money

- The final step in the evolution of money is the creation of **fiat money,** money that is valuable in exchange because a government declares it is.

- In 1844, the Bank of England established a rigid link between the amount of paper money in circulation and the gold reserves of the Bank of England. This meant that the supply of money in England would fluctuate with the gold reserves of the bank and with the availability of gold in general. Discoveries of gold in the New World led to rising prices of goods in terms of gold.

- For the next 130 years, it was typical for Western economies to back their paper money with gold. In most cases, paper money was convertible; that is, holders of paper money could demand gold in exchange at a rate set by the government.

- In times of national emergencies, for example, in World War I and World War II, nations abandoned the gold standard and suspended the convertibility of their currencies. Suspending convertibility allowed nations to finance some of the costs of war by issuing more currency than their gold stocks would have previously permitted.

- At the end of both World Wars, nations returned to the gold standard but quickly experienced problems. The supply of gold grew too slowly and erratically to allow the supply of money to keep pace with growth.

- For a time, the International Monetary Fund supplemented the supply of gold with "paper gold" called "special drawing rights." But the gold standard ended with President Nixon's decision in 1973 to permanently suspend the convertibility of the U.S. dollar into gold.

- In Western economies today, we use pure fiat monies that are backed by no commodity. The money is valued partly because governments declare it to be "legal tender for all debts public and private." Ultimately, however, money is valued because people agree it is valuable; people agree to accept money in exchange because they believe they can use money to purchase useful things whenever they wish.

Four Takeaways from the Evolution of Money
- Money is a social contract in that members of society agree to accept money in exchange for goods and services.

- This social contract has developed gradually through history because it has taken time to develop the trust necessary to exchange something of intrinsic value (a pound of nails) for something of no intrinsic value (a pound note).

- The contract has developed as it has because members of society have constantly sought to meet 2 competing goals: to lower the cost of trade while ensuring that money retains its value.

- Government is essential to the organization of monetary arrangements. Throughout history, government has played a crucial role in the development of the money contract. Today, it allows us to operate in a highly efficient fiat money exchange system. But our fiat holds its value only if our Federal Reserve keeps the supply of money from growing too rapidly. If the Fed fails, inflation results—and inflation is the modern counterpart to seigniorage.

Important Terms

barter: Exchange without money.

commodity money: A particular commodity that is agreed upon in the society to be acceptable for exchange.

fiat money: Money that is valuable in exchange because a government has declared it to be.

money: Something that can be used as a medium of exchange.

seigniorage: The revenue that a government obtains by deflating the value of its money.

Suggested Reading

Einzig, *Primitive Money*.

Jackson, *The Oxford Book of Money*.

Radford, "The Economic Organization of a P.O.W. Camp."

Smith, *The Wealth of Nations*.

1. What would be the relative advantages of a monetary system based on coinage of a precious metal, such as gold, over a fiat money system similar to what we have in the United States today?

2. Would the United States be better off with money backed by gold than with fiat money?

3. Why is it reasonable to describe inflation as the "modern-day equivalent of seigniorage"? The lord of the manor benefited from seigniorage in times past. Who benefits from inflation today?

Money as a Social Contract
Lecture 2—Transcript

Let me begin this lecture by telling you this story of how I came to own the interesting item that I am holding. Several years ago during the Christmas holiday, my family was visiting my wife's family in Great Barrington, Massachusetts. A baking frenzy was underway, and I have no skills, so I was sent to a specialty store to get some needed spices. While there, being a curious person and it being Christmas, I looked around and saw this item, and I asked the proprietor what it was. The proprietor came and looked at it and then answered, "It is a block of pressed tea. Tea." So I picked it up and looked at it carefully, and I turned it over and saw the repeated pattern that had been molded onto the back. And then it hit me. I recognized that I was holding a lot more than a block of pressed tea. I was holding money.

In today's lecture, I will trace the origins of money from its earliest uses until our modern day. I will argue that money has evolved substantially, and I will identify 5 stages in this evolutionary process. First, barter, where money is not used; then the earliest use of money using a commodity something intrinsically useful, but using it in a different way as money. And then, a form of money with which we are familiar, coins. Finally, we will come very close to the present day with phase 4 and take a look at paper money, but paper money somehow backed by coins. And finally, the fifth stage of the evaluation, fiat money: money that is valuable because the government says it is valuable.

But first we need a working definition of money. What does he mean, you might ask, when he says money? I will give you the standard definition used by economists. Money is something that can be used as a medium of exchange. So, what does that mean? When we make a trade, when we make an exchange, money is something that can be used in that trade and that exchange. But the most important idea of today's lecture is not the definition of money. That is easy. It is that a person values money not because it is intrinsically useful, but because it can be useful in exchange. It can be used to buy other useful things.

The connection between money and exchange will help us to understand the most important point of today's lecture: that money is a social contract that lowers the cost of trading and has evolved gradually through time. That gradual evolution is not an evolution that was too slow. It was necessarily slow because as the contract evolved, trust was built.

Let's talk about the first phase in the evolution of money, barter, which is no money at all. Jevons, in a famous book called *Money and the Mechanism of Exchange*, said, and I quote, "The first difficulty in barter is to find 2 persons whose disposable possessions mutually suit each other's wants." So, mutually suit each other's wants: "There must be a double coincidence, which will rarely happen." Double coincidence? What does that mean?

Well, you imagine 2 members of an early society. Let's call them Mark and George. Mark is a very skillful hunter who regularly comes back to his village with more meat than his family can eat. What about George? He is the best axe maker in the village. He is really good at finding and crafting the right kind of axe head and then lashing it to a good piece of wood, so that it works very well. The question is: Can Mark and George trade? Mark has meat to offer, but he may not want an axe. He may already have one. George probably wants meat, but he only has one thing to offer and that is an axe. That is what Jevons meant. Not only do I have to something to offer, but I have to have what the counterparty, in exchange, wants.

The search for such a narrowly defined trading partner—meat, axe, meat, axe—is costly because it takes time to find someone who wants an axe and has meat to trade. Indeed, an axe maker might trade his axes for, say, grain only because he thinks it will be easier to find someone who will trade meat for grain than someone who will trade meat for an axe. Wow, that is wasteful right? Not wanting grain, but buying some just because you can then trade it away?

The costs of locating trading partners and negotiating trades are disincentives to specialization. They lead George to be less willing to ply his trade as an axe maker, where he is really excellent. In fact, if the costs are high enough, the best axe maker in the world may decide to split his time between making axes and raising cattle. That is a waste, and you know what, economists hate waste.

Primitive societies face tremendous incentives to lower the cost of barter and often settled on successful schemes even including credit arrangements. Think about that. Primitive societies where there was no money, nevertheless, were able to come up with arrangements where someone would give their meat today, but receive payment a little bit in the future in order to facilitate the trades that made that society better off.

Well, Adam Smith, again in the *Wealth of Nations*, suggested the next state in the development of money when he said, and I quote, "Every prudent man in every period of society … must naturally have endeavored … to have at all times by him … a certain quantity of some one commodity or other, such as he imagined few people would be likely to refuse in exchange." As Smith suggested, the next stage was the development of commodity monies.

A society uses a commodity money when individuals typically buy and sell the goods they want by offering in exchange a particular commodity that is agreed upon in the society to be acceptable in exchange. Commodity money has taken many different forms. Salt was used in many societies and many different geographic locations. Cowrie shells were used—I have some—in Indochina and in Pacific regions. We do not know exactly why, but cowrie shells are beautiful, and they are available, but it takes effort to collect them. Economists would say that cowrie shells are scarce because of the effort it takes; and it may be that cowrie shells were used as commodity monies in areas where the political leader, the chief, liked wearing cowrie shell necklaces.

There are other famous examples of commodity money. Pretty much everyone in school has seen these pictures of large stones on the Island of Yap. That is an example of commodity money. Back to my tea brick, tea bricks were used as money in inner Asia. And that pattern that I pointed out to you on the back? Why was that there? It was there to make it easier to make change. It allowed that tea brick to be broken into smaller uniform pieces. It was a device that made that block of tea more efficient in facilitating trade.

Before we leave commodity money, I want to point out that government often played a role in deciding what commodity would function as money. Animals such as oxen or birds were more likely to be money in societies where live animal sacrifice was required. If the ruler favored a certain kind of shell or feather, it might become money. Keep in mind that the commodity chosen as money would have to be scarce. If anyone could pick up unlimited quantities of money from the seashore or the backyard, then no one in his right mind would give up something that he worked to produce in exchange for those shells or feathers.

Well, as we think about the evolution to the next phase of money development, we have to realize that primitive peoples traveled beyond their borders of their homelands. When they did, they frequently found that what they considered to be money at home was not accepted by potential trading partners in the new lands that they visited. But what they did observe was that metal, especially gold, silver, bronze, copper, and iron, were valued in other lands. Indeed, Captain Cook on his voyage was able to give iron nails from the Endeavour to the peoples he visited. They liked to have those nails. So, the next stage of the evolution of money was the use of metals and the coining of those metals.

Several forces favored the use of metals rather than other commodities as money. Metal was more likely to be useful in trade in other lands because it could be used to make a variety of useful goods such as knives that were used throughout the world. Metal was durable, and typically, metal was more valuable, per unit weight, which made the cost of transporting it on a trade mission sufficiently more efficient. But, there were 2 important disadvantages to the use of lumps of metal as money. It was costly to verify the true metallic content of a lump and that purity of that lump. Remember all that glitters is not gold. It was also costly to weigh the lump.

But by creating coins from metal, government again played an important role. They lowered the cost of using metal as money. Coins are very old. The earliest known coins are from Lydia, which is in modern Turkey, from the 7th century B.C. Copper, bronze, silver, and gold coins are widely found in ancient Greece and in ancient Rome. Words in use today trace their origins to early coins. We have heard of the phrase "the pound sterling." But a sterling was originally a silver penny used in England by the Normans at around 1300. Today, sterling has a technical meaning, an alloy that is 92.5% silver. How about the word "dollar"? The word "dollar" derives from the German word "Thaler," which was a minted in Bohemia in the early 16th century.

We have already argued that governments play an important role by coining money. It is solving the problems of weight and measures, and governments typically derived important revenues from its coining operations. The governments owned the mints that converted raw metals into coins, and they collected fees from those who sold metal to the mint. Ah, ha! But the owner of the mint, the government, could also raise revenue by lowering the metal content of its coins.

The word "seigniorage" denotes the revenue that a government obtains by deflating the value of its money and that word, "seigniorage," derives from the French word for "lord." Now, when I say "lord" here, I mean lord of the manor, the seignior. How does seigniorage work? It could be as simple as shaving metal from the edges of the coin, or it could be as complicated as changing the price that the mint offered for metal to be coined. It was a big deal, this seigniorage revenue, a big deal for government.

In 1542, Henry VIII earned—this is a staggering statistic—6 times the normal annual crown revenue by lowering the silver content of English coins. Six times. Every day, we handle quarters and dimes minted in the United States and every day, if we think about it, we realize that those quarters and dimes are fluted. They have fluted edges. Why? Was it the coin maker's art? Not at all. It was a very practical reason. The ridges in our quarters and dimes derive from the early attempts to assure the coin owner that the coins had not been shaved. Well, there is no silver in our quarters and dimes anymore, so it is no longer necessary, but that is why those ridges are there.

The transition from coins to paper money is rooted in the practice of allowing citizens in many civilizations to deposit their goods in temples and palaces. This is a very old practice. Temples and palaces were not only places of worship. They were not only places to which you came to offer sacrifice, but they were places that were secure and well guarded, and they evolve to take on the role of protecting the wealth of their citizens. In Babylon, by 1000 B.C., private deposits were accepted at the Babylonia temple. Even the Code of Hammurabi set out the rules for those deposits. Officials issued receipts to depositors and allowed them to transfer their deposits to third parties.

So the next step in the evolution of money is the use of money that is backed by metal such as gold or silver, but itself takes on paper form. The origins of this paper money are the warehouse receipts that we just talked about. Those receipts are receipts given by depositors for the precious metals that their customers left or their temple worshipers left in their possession. The warehouse receipts began to function as money, not when the metal was deposited, but when third parties traded them for commodities rather than withdrawing their deposits. Let's think of an example here.

So, I have deposited, let us say some gold, at my temple. I have received a paper receipt. I now, say weeks later, wish to make a purchase for my home. I go to the individual who is going to sell me what I desire, and instead of first going back to the temple to get the gold, I simply present my warehouse receipt. I, in a sense, sign it over to the person from whom I am buying. When that third party, the person who is selling me goods, takes my warehouse receipt and thinks of it as her own, or his own, that is when those receipts begin circulating as money.

Marco Polo found money printed on mulberry bark in China in the 13th century. In the west, London goldsmiths gave receipts for gold deposited with them, and those receipts functioned as money in the 17th century. The use of paper money lowered exchange costs since it was a heck of a lot easier to exchange warehouse receipts than the actual deposits. For one thing, the receipts were for a particular quality and quantity of gold, and the receipt actually said that. If you handed over the gold, you would have to weigh and it and assay it again.

Ah, and here is a very subtle, but very, very important step in the evolution. Think about the people who are managing the depository: the London goldsmith. We will talk about that London goldsmith in detail in another lecture, but let's just get a highlight. Those goldsmiths soon realized that they could make loans to new parties by issuing new warehouse receipts. The scheme worked because on any given day, only a very small fraction of the people who had deposited gold with those goldsmiths actually tried to get it back. So, here we are with money as gold or silver or copper coins. But we know that that is not our money today, so what happened? The final demise of the gold standard, according to Angelo Redish, occurred in 2 steps. In August 1971, United States President Nixon temporarily suspended the convertibility of the U.S. dollar into gold and made that suspension permanent in 1973.

So we come then, to the final step in the evolution of money from barter where there is no money, through commodity money, through gold coins, to fiat money; money that is valuable by fiat. It is valuable because the government declares that it is valuable. So, let's do a kind of experiment here. Pause for a minute, reach into your pocket, and take out a dollar bill. This is a little bit like a scavenger hunt. Search on that bill for evidence that that bill is not just money, you knew that, but fiat money. You're doing it? Well, you will not have to search for long before you find the words, "This note is legal tender for all debts, public and private." Folks, that is the clear declaration that our money, the U.S. dollar, is valuable because the U.S. Government says it is.

In 1844, the Bank of England established a rigid link between the amount of paper money in circulation and the gold reserves of the Bank of England. This meant that the supply of money in England would fluctuate with the gold reserves of the bank and with the availability of gold in general. For example, discoveries of gold in the new world led to rising prices of goods in terms of gold. As gold became more plentiful, its value decreased.

It was typical for the next 130 years for western economies to back their paper money with gold. In most cases, paper money was convertible. Holders of the paper money could demand gold in exchange at a rate set by the government. So they could bring their paper money to the government and get the predefined amount of gold whenever they wished. Ah, ha. But in times of national emergencies, obviously World War I and then again, World War II, nations, United Kingdom among them, abandoned the gold standard, and it suspended the convertibility of their currencies into gold. Why would they do that?

Well, suspending convertibility allowed nations to finance some of the costs of the war by issuing more currency than their gold stocks would have previously permitted. They wished to buy more munitions, buy more soldiers, and buy more of all the other war goods that were required, and they did not want to be limited by the amount of gold in their repositories. But, at the end of World War I and again at the end of WWII, nations did return to the gold standard. But they quickly experienced problems, problems that they had not had before.

The supply of gold was growing too slowly and also too erratically to allow the supply of money to keep pace with growth in the world's developed economies. Money in the form of gold was not growing as rapidly as production in the post-World War II economies of the nations of the world. So for a time, the International Monetary Fund, and we will talk about them in a future lecture, attempted to keep the gold standard working by supplementing the supply of gold with paper gold that were called special drawing rights. But, the gold standard ended, as Redish reminds us, with President Nixon's decisions to suspend convertibility, to make a break between the number of U.S. dollars and the quantity of gold held by the United States.

Today, in western economies, we have pure fiat monies that are backed by no commodity at all. The money is valued partly because governments declare the money to be "legal tender for all debts public and private." But ultimately, money is valued because people agree it is valuable. It is valued because people agree to accept money in exchange. It is valuable because people believe they can accept money and then turn around and purchase useful things whenever they wish.

Four important themes have emerged from our examination of the evolution of money. First, money is truly a social contract in which the members of a society agree to accept money in exchange for goods and services. It is an act of faith for me to give something that is truly useful, an axe or a pound of meat, in exchange for a piece of paper that really would not even do a very good job of lighting a cigarette or starting a fire. It is true that the words "In God We Trust" are printed on the back of our bills. But if we want to understand why the dollar has value, we would be far better off with the words, "In One Another We Trust."

Second, the social contract that is money has developed gradually through history because it has taken time to develop the trust necessary to exchange something of intrinsic value, a pound of nails, for something of no intrinsic value, a British pound note. That trust had to be developed very slowly and had to be developed in the context of the codes, the laws, and the belief of the society that began to accept different forms of money.

Third, the contract has developed as it has because members of society have constantly sought to meet 2 goals. I have always found that those goals to be in competition with one another. They have constantly sought ways of changing the money contract to lower the cost of trade. We want trade to be efficient and inexpensive, so that we could do more of it. But at the same time, we have wanted to make sure that we adopt a money that holds its value. Throughout history, government has played a crucial role in development of the money contract. From coordinating the choice of a particular commodity, to ensuring that the contracts made by goldsmiths were honored so those goldsmiths did not just renege, to setting up rules for the coining of precious metals, to developing laws that define the powers and responsibilities of the Federal Reserve.

So, government is essential to organization of monetary arrangements, and that is not surprising. We are government. A fiat money system is highly efficient. Valuable metals such as gold and silver are not tied up as backing for money but are released to alternative uses in electronics, jewelry, and many other purposes. The Federal Reserve can allow the supply of money to keep pace with the growth in our nation. But our fiat money holds its value only if our Federal Reserve keeps the supply of money from growing too rapidly. If the Fed fails, inflation results, and inflation is the modern counterpart to seigniorage.

Thank you very much.

How Is Money Created?
Lecture 3

There was a time when producing money meant mining a metal, such as gold. But that process has evolved to the point that today, money is created out of thin air by the central banks of the world, including the U.S. Federal Reserve. Many public figures believe that the United States should return to the gold standard—an arrangement in which governments agreed to peg the value of their paper money to gold. In this lecture, you'll gain a better understanding of how that system worked and why it ended, as well as the costs and benefits of our modern money-creation mechanism.

T-Accounts and London Goldsmiths

- In thinking about the creation of money, it is helpful to use the **T-accounts**, which is a graphical representation of the balance sheet of an economic entity. The T-account lists assets on the left and liabilities on the right. **Net worth**, also listed on the right, is the value of assets minus the value of liabilities.

- Recall from the last lecture that warehouse receipts for gold were the earliest forms of paper money used in Western civilization. In London, individuals deposited their gold with goldsmiths for safekeeping. In return, the goldsmiths issued gold receipts, which people then used as a convenience when buying and selling goods. The receipts for gold were paper money backed by gold deposits.

- Under this system, goldsmiths quickly realized that, on any given day, they held more gold in their safes than they needed either for their work or to satisfy customers who wished to trade back their receipts for gold. They concluded that they could create new warehouse receipts and lend them at interest to other customers.

Joe's Balance Sheet

Assets:		Liabilities:	
Automobile	$4,000	Credit card Balance	$750
Checking	200		
Savings	500		
		Net Worth:	
		$4,700 - 750 = $3,950	

Source: Michael Salemi.

- The creation of warehouse receipts did not increase the net worth of the goldsmith until the amount borrowed was paid back with interest.

- The gold warehouse receipts are an example of a gold-backed paper currency. The warehouse receipts circulated as money as long as the goldsmith/bank continued to redeem the receipts for gold whenever customers demanded gold. In this scenario, each goldsmith/bank held its own gold reserves.

- Banks in the United States continued to make loans with paper backed by gold well into the 19th century. Each individual bank held its own warehouse receipts and issued its own currency, although individual banks and their currencies often failed.

The Gold Standard

- The **gold standard** was an agreement among participating countries to fix the price of each country's currency in terms of an ounce of gold. England adopted the standard in 1819, and the United States adopted it in 1834.

- Under the gold standard, the government promises to buy and sell gold in exchange for its currency in order to keep the currency price of the gold at the promised value.

- Under a credible gold standard, the national currency is "as good as gold" and banks hold it in reserve.

The Bank of England

- The typical English bank operated in much the same way under the gold standard as it did after the gold standard was eliminated.

- The bank held British pounds in reserve so that depositors could convert their deposits to pounds whenever they wished. Depositors

The Bank of England is the central bank of the British system, the equivilant of the U.S. Federal Reserve.

rightly thought of the deposits as equivalent to pound notes because the bank stood ready to redeem deposits for currency.

- The bank used its **excess reserves** to make new loans by creating new deposit accounts for borrowers. Excess reserves were those calculated to be beyond the amount required by law or prudence.

- The real difference between the period of the gold standard and earlier times, when each bank held its own gold reserves, centers on the role of the Bank of England, the central bank of the British system.

- Under the gold standard, the Bank of England held the gold that backed the British pound, and its gold holdings placed an upper limit on the supply of British pounds.

- How did the Bank of England fulfill its promise to fix the price of gold in terms of pounds so that the pound remained as good as gold? If the value of the pound began to fall in terms of gold (that is, if the pound price of gold began to rise), the Bank of England raised the interest rate it charged on loans to other banks, which raised interest rates in England and tended to create a gold inflow. This inflow made gold more plentiful in England, reducing the price of gold and increasing the price of the pound in terms of gold.

- If the value of the pound began to increase in terms of gold (that is, if the pound price of gold began to fall), the Bank of England lowered the interest rate it charged on loans to other banks, which lowered interest rates in England and created a gold outflow from England to other counties. The gold outflow made gold less plentiful in England, increasing the price of gold and reducing the price of the pound in terms of gold.

The Current System of Monetary Creation

- Under our current system, it is the law of the land that currency is a valid form of payment for all debts. As you recall, the paper money issued by the central bank of the nation is valuable by fiat, that is, by government declaration.

- For the individual bank, the T-account is unchanged because each bank continues to hold the national currency in reserve for deposits.

- The difference is that after the gold standard ended, the Bank of England no longer fixed the price of gold in terms of the British pound. Therefore, it no longer had to increase gold reserves to levels sufficient to make credible its promise to buy pounds with gold.

- The Bank of England was free to create currency by making loans to banks without increasing its gold holdings. Banks in England that received the increases in currency through the deposit process were, in turn, free to create new deposits by making new loans to customers.

- There were—and are—no limits on the creation of money beyond the self-imposed limits set by the Bank of England.

The End of the Gold Standard

- During World War I and World War II, the Bank of England (and the central banks of most other combatants) left the gold standard temporarily in order to finance war expenditures by issuing new currency.

- After World War II, under the so-called Bretton Woods system, the United States fixed the dollar price of gold at $35.00 per ounce. Other nations held the dollar as reserves.

- Led by the United States, the world finally left the gold standard on August 15, 1971, when President Nixon announced that the United States would no longer redeem U.S dollars for gold.

- The United States left the gold standard because it placed tight restrictions on our ability to increase the supply of paper money. These restrictions were incompatible with other U.S. policy objectives, such as financing the Vietnam War.

Costs and Benefits of Returning to the Gold Standard

- There appears to be only one benefit to returning to the gold standard: On average, inflation was lower under the gold standard than it was in periods when central banks could create money without adding to gold reserves.

- In contrast, a return to the gold standard brings with it numerous costs. For example, U.S. prices were more volatile during the gold standard period than after it. It is also expensive to maintain a gold reserve; Milton Friedman estimated this expense to be as much as 2.5% of GNP.

- Further, under a gold standard, central banks are not free to undertake counter-cyclical policies, and nations fix the values of their currency to gold, implying that all exchange rates are constant and do not adjust to market forces.

- Finally, gold discoveries are random events, and the United States accounts for only a small share of them. At the same time, the real price of gold is highly variable. If the United States were still on the gold standard, it would have been trying to keep the price of gold constant while world market forces dictated that it should be changing significantly.

- Consider what has happened to the price of gold since the United States and the world abandoned the gold standard: The dollar price of gold hit an all-time high in 2010 at more than $1230 per ounce. Compare that to the real price of gold in 2010 as seen in Figure 3.1

- The real price of gold has been highly variable; this is not a surprise: World demand and supply for gold varies a lot, and the real price of gold adjusts accordingly.

Figure 3.1

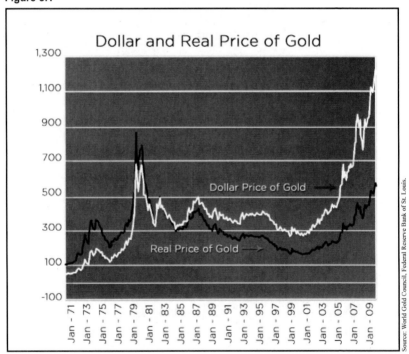

excess reserves: Reserves that were calculated to be beyond the amount required by law or prudence.

gold standard: An agreement among participating countries to fix the price of each country's currency in terms of an ounce of gold. England adopted the standard in 1819, and the United States adopted it in 1834.

net worth: Is the value of assets minus the value of liabilities.

T-account: A graphical representation of the balance sheet of an economic entity. The T-account lists assets on the left side and liabilities and the asset's net worth on the right.

Suggested Reading

Bordo, "Gold Standard."

Krugman and Obstfeld, *International Economics*.

Redish, "Anchors Aweigh."

Questions to Consider

1. During the gold-standard years, were British pounds and U.S. dollars "as good as gold"? Why or why not?

2. Does the dramatic increase in the price of gold documented in the last chart of the lecture constitute an argument for the gold standard or against it?

3. During the gold-standard years in the United States, it was illegal for a U.S. citizen to own gold bullion. Today, it is legal. Why do you think the U.S. government forbade citizens from owning gold during the gold-standard years?

How Is Money Created?
Lecture 3—Transcript

Just how is money created? Well, there was a time when producing money meant mining a metal like gold, getting dirty and sweaty. Indeed, one of my favorite movies of all times is *Treasure of the Sierra Madre*, which focuses a lot of attention on exactly how gold is mined. But the process evolved until today [where] it is true that money is created out of thin air by the central banks of the world, including are own United States Federal Reserve.

While it is true that the United States owns gold and stores that gold in Fort Knox, we will see that the gold at Fort Knox is no closer to money in the United States than the oil in our strategic petroleum reserve. One important point to keep in mind as we study the period of history in which money was backed by gold is that gold discoveries are random events, just like in *Treasure of the Sierra Madre*. After all, Columbus came to the New World hoping to find gold, as did many Europeans who followed him, and it would be surprising if a gold discovery that significantly increased the world supply of gold had no disruptive effect when money was backed by gold.

Nevertheless, there are today public figures who believe that the United States should and eventually will return to the gold standard. The U.S. could return to the gold standard within 5 years, according to magazine publisher Steve Forbes. The former GOP presidential candidate told the conservative newspaper *Human Events* that a gold standard would stabilize the dollar and restore confidence in the U.S. Treasury bonds among foreign investors. "If the dollar was as good as gold, other countries would want to buy it," Forbes said. Steve Forbes is not alone in his view. Texas Congressman Ron Paul suggests that our Federal Reserve System, where someone can "push a button and create new money" is flawed and that a return to the gold standard would be preferred.

By the end of this lecture, you will have a better understanding of the costs and benefits of our money-creation system. You will have a better idea of the costs and benefits of returning to the gold standard. Now, why is this important? As I have said before, money is an invention as important to the development of mankind as was the wheel. Without money, there would be very little trade. Without trade, according to Adam Smith, there would be very little specialization and specialization is, according to Smith, the source of the wealth of nations. So it makes sense, both in the context of this course and in the context of our citizenship, to ask whether we have the right system in place to manage the creation of money.

Today, we will learn how paper money was created during the era when money was primarily gold and other precious metals or backed by gold and other precious metals. We will see how the gold standard, an arrangement where governments agreed to peg the value of their paper money to gold— and I will explain what peg means—how that system worked and why it ended.

In thinking about the creation of money, it is helpful to use T-accounts, and these T-accounts are called "T-accounts" because they have the shape of the capital letter T. So, what is a T-account? A T-account is a graphical representation of the balance sheet of an economic entity, a household, a bank, whatever. The T-account lists assets on the left side and liabilities on the right-hand side. It also lists the entity's net worth on the right-hand side. By definition, a balance sheet must balance and to accomplish balance, net worth is always defined as the value of assets minus the value of liabilities.

Let's do an example in order to make sure that this is well understood. So Joe has just graduated from College and is taking stock of his life. Joe owns an automobile worth $4000 and has $200 in his checking account and $500 in his savings account. Joe went to State College and graduated with no student-loan debt, lucky Joe. But he does have some liabilities. He currently has a $750 balance on his only credit card. The T-account you're looking at depicts Joe's assets, Joe's liabilities, and Joe's net worth. Under the assets, auto $4000, checking account $200, savings account $500. Under the liabilities, credit card debt $750. His net worth is $4700 in assets minus $750 in credit card debt, his liability, his net worth $3950.

Recall that an early example of the creation of paper money revolves around London goldsmiths. The earliest uses of paper money in Western civilization were warehouse receipts for gold. Goldsmiths had good safes, and it became customary for their customers to leave gold for safekeeping with the goldsmiths. In return for depositing their gold with the goldsmiths, the goldsmith would issue receipts to their customers. The customers learned that it was more convenient and safe to buy and sell goods using the receipts themselves than returning to the goldsmith and reclaiming the gold. Viola. The warehouse receipts for gold became paper money backed by gold deposits. How could we use a T-account to explain the creation of paper money by a London goldsmith because indeed that happened?

Let's do an example. Let's imagine a goldsmith who has initially gold holdings of 1000 pounds, and by that I mean not weight, but 100 pounds sterling, and in exchange, the goldsmith has issued 1000 pounds sterling of warehouse receipts. Assets have $1000; liabilities have $1000, net worth of 0. In a minute, we are going to have our goldsmith make a change. But what is that changed based on? Well, goldsmiths, and ours in particular, quickly realized that on any given day, they held more gold in their safes, their vaults, their safekeeping places, than they needed either for their own work or to satisfy whichever customers wanted to reclaim the gold and re-present their receipts.

Goldsmiths were a clever folk, and they quickly concluded that they had a great opportunity. They could create new warehouse receipts without more gold, and they could lend those warehouse receipts to additional depository customers. Let's return to our T-account. After making such a loan, the balance sheet of our goldsmith would look something like the following. Now under the assets, the goldsmith would have 1000 pounds sterling worth of gold and a second asset, a loan of 1000 pounds. What would the goldsmith have as liabilities? Two thousand pounds sterling of warehouse receipts. Net worth would still be 0.

You're curious. Why would the goldsmith create new warehouse receipts if doing so did not increase net worth? When the borrower paid off the loan, the borrower would pay back principal, what was borrowed, plus interest. At that point, the net worth of the goldsmith would increase. If though, goldsmith had used modern accounting rules, net worth would increase at the time of the loan because it would reflect anticipation of the future interest payment, but that is not important to our story.

These gold warehouse receipts are an example of a gold-backed paper currency. The warehouse receipts circulated as money as long as the goldsmith bank continued to redeem the receipts for gold whenever customers demanded gold. Each goldsmith bank held its own gold reserves. So think about that for a minute. Each goldsmith bank had created new receipts, and yet the system would continue to function provided the goldsmith bank was never called upon to repay more gold than they were able to repay.

Banks continued to make loans with paper backed by gold well into the 19th century in the United States. Each individual bank held its own warehouse receipts and issued its own currency. That is, each individual bank had its own store of gold and created their own kinds of currencies. Keep in mind that those banks and those currencies could fail and often did. So, recall in our first lecture that our Kansas homesteader was legitimately worried about whether those notes from a bank in Illinois would continue to be honored. While this is a valid early stage in the gold standard, it is not what most economists mean by the gold standard, as we shall now see.

The gold standard, as occurred in most of the 20th century in the United States, was an agreement upon participating countries to fix the price of each country's currency in terms of an ounce of gold. To understand the origins of this version of the gold standard, the modern version, we have to again inquire about England, because England officially adopted the gold standard in 1819, although truth be told, the English mint had been fixing the value of the pound sterling in terms of gold since much early, 1717.

The United States adopted the gold standard in 1834 when it fixed the price of gold at $20.67 per ounce and kept it there until 1933. Under the gold standard, the government promises to buy and sell gold in exchange for its currency in order to keep the currency price of the gold at the promised value. So the gold standard is a promise. If the promise is credible, that is if the government's actions are as good as its word, then the national currency is as good as gold, and banks will hold that national currency in reserve.

The following balance sheets for an English bank and for the Bank of England explain how the gold standard worked. Keep in mind now, we are looking for a transition here. We are looking to understand how the modern gold standard, where the Bank of England promised to buy and sell gold at a fixed price, is different from the original gold standard when each bank held its own deposits of gold. So let's use this tool that we have taken the trouble to learn about in order to understand how the gold standard worked.

What about the typical English Bank? What did its balance sheet look like? Well, its assets included currency, pound notes, and loans. Other things as well, but most importantly currency and loans, promises to repay by the bank's customers. What about its liabilities? Deposits with the bank. Okay? Notice there is no gold there. What about the balance sheet of the Bank of England? What did it look like? Well, its assets included gold and any loans it had made to banks, and its liabilities had predominately one item: pound notes, the currency of England. The typical English bank operated under the gold standard in much the same way as it did when it held its own deposits of gold. The bank held, instead of gold itself, British pound notes in reserve so the depositors could convert their deposits to pounds whenever they wished.

The customers, that is the depositors, rightly thought of their deposits as equivalent to pound notes, and therefore, as good as gold, since the bank stood ready to redeem them for currency whenever the customers wanted. The banks used their extra or excess reserves to make new loans, like the goldsmiths did, by creating new deposit accounts for borrowers. Now, what is this term "excess reserves"? Well, the bank reckoned its extra or excess reserves to be reserves beyond the amount required by law or by prudent behavior.

Sometimes banks would hold no more than the legally required amount of reserves. They would loan every Sue they could. But sometimes, banks found it prudent to hold more reserves than required by law. In that regard, the banks were behaving a lot like the goldsmiths would behave, right? It was important to be able to redeem a depositor's demand for gold when the depositor made it. Today, banks want to make sure that they can give currency back for their deposits when a customer, a depositor, wishes. So in that regard, the banks behavior is not very much different. The real difference between the gold standard and earlier times when each bank held its own gold reserves centers on the role and the behavior of the Bank of England.

The Bank of England is the central bank of the British system. It is the equivalent of our Federal Reserve although it is very much older, and we will talk about that. Under the gold standard, the Bank of England held the gold that backed the British pound. Remember the balance sheet. Did this fix the money supply? You bet. The gold holdings of the Bank of England placed an upper limit on the supply of British pound notes. They limited the amount of currency. How did the gold standard work? How did the Bank of England fulfill its promise, to peg the price of gold in terms of its currency?

How did the Bank of England behave, so that the pound remained as good as gold? It did the following: If the value of the pound began to fall in terms of gold, how would we know that? Well, if the price of gold began to rise in terms of the number of pounds it took to buy an ounce, then the Bank of England would do one very simple thing. It would raise the interest rate it charged on loans to banks, and that would raise interest rates in England. What would happen? So what. Oh, but people are selfish. If England is playing higher interest rates, gold would flow into England in order to take advantage of those higher rates. Gold holders would want to deposit their gold in England where interest rates were now higher. What would that do? Well, that would make gold more plentiful in England. The price of gold therefore would fall and the price of the pound in terms of gold would rise back toward the promised level.

Let's do the opposite case. Suppose the value of the pound began to rise in terms of gold, so, the pound price of gold began to fall. The Bank of England would then lower interest rates and gold would flood away from England. That is called a gold outflow. The gold would leave England headed for other countries where interest rates were higher and the gold outflow would make gold less plentiful in England and make the price of gold rise in England and the price of the pound in terms of gold fall.

We come now to the transition from the gold standard to the current system of monetary creation. Please recall that under our current system, it is the law of the land that currency is a valid form of payment for all debts. We said earlier that paper money issued by England, by the United States, by the euro zone, is valuable by fiat, by government declaration. Let's return to our T-accounts one additional time to see what that means.

For the individual bank, the T-account is unchanged because each bank continues to hold the national currency, the national money, in reserve for deposits. The difference is that after fiat money is established and the gold standard ends, the Bank of England or the Federal Reserve, no longer fixes the price of gold in terms of the British pound or the U.S. dollar. Therefore, it no longer has to increase gold reserves to levels sufficient to make credible its promise to buy pounds with gold. The Bank of England, the Central Bank of the European Union, or the Federal Reserve are now free to create currency by making loans of currency to banks without having the additional gold necessary to make an exchange of those dollars or pounds or euros for gold.

Banks in England that receive the increases in currency are in free turn to create new deposits for their customers and there were and continued to be no limits to the creation of money beyond the self-imposed limits set by the Bank of England and the Federal Reserve as it fulfills its responsibility to its people.

Why did the world leave the gold standard? The Bank of England and most other combatants left the gold standard temporarily during WWI and WWII because it wanted to finance British War expenditures, U.S. War expenditures, and French War expenditures by issuing new currency. The British Treasury, for example, created war bonds. It sold those bonds in the open-market place and used the proceeds to finance war-time expenditures. Ah, but the Bank of England issued new British pounds to buy some of those bonds, so that the interest rates on those bonds would not rise too high.

After World War II, under the so-called Breton Woods system, the U.S. fixed the price of the gold at $35 per ounce. Other nations held the dollar as reserve. So this was our last return to the gold standard. What happened is that the U.S. pegged the price of gold at $35 an ounce and the U.S.'s promise was grounds elsewhere in the world for central banks to hold the dollar as if it was gold. Notice that now, not every central bank is holding its own gold reserve. Everybody is counting on the United States to make the dollar as good as gold, and therefore, are holding dollars as if they were gold. Led by the United States, the world finally left the gold standard on August 15, 1971, when President Nixon announced that the United States would no longer redeem U.S. dollars for gold. The U.S. left the gold standard because the gold standard placed very tight restrictions on the U.S. ability to increase the supply of paper money.

So, what? you ask. Well, these restrictions were incompatible with other U.S. policy objectives, not the least of which was financing a new war, the Vietnam Conflict. Let us now come back to the challenge posed by those people who believe that the U.S. and the world should return to the gold standard and let us do what economists always should do and examine the benefits and costs of returning to the gold standard.

What would be the benefit of returning to the gold standard? I will signal one very important one, and that appears to be all. On average, under the gold standard, inflation was lower than it was in periods when central banks could create money without adding to gold reserves. Put another way, under the restriction imposed by the gold standard, under the promise by the central banks to exchange gold for paper money, central banks all over the world issued less paper money with the result that the average inflation rate was lower. Less seigniorage.

But, there were costs. Under the gold standard, U.S. prices were more volatile than in any other period, including the period since we left the gold standard. In addition, it is expensive to maintain a gold reserve. Milton Friedman famously estimated the expense at being as much as 2.5% of gross national product. Why? Well, it is expensive to maintain that gold reserve. Maybe the most important cost is that under a gold standard, central banks are not free to undertake so-called counter cyclical policies. Their hands are tied by keeping their promise. They do not have the freedom to raise the money supply to stimulate the economy when that appears to be warranted.

Under the gold standard, the nations, all fix the values of their currencies to gold. What does that imply? Well, the value of one currency to another is also fixed. It cannot adjust to market forces. We all must keep in mind that gold discoveries are random events, and the U.S. accounts for only a small share of gold discoveries. For example, in 2009, the United States produced how much do you think? Only 9.1% of the world's gold. China produced 13.1%; South Africa produced 8.1%; Russia produced 7.8%.

I close this lecture by considering what has happened to the price of gold since the U.S. and the world abandoned the gold standard. The blue line in the diagram you see shows the dollar price of gold. It hit its all-time high in 2010 at over $1230 per ounce. The red line shows the real price of gold. That is the price of gold in dollars relative to a bushel basket of the typical goods consumed by a household in the United States. So, I have defined that real price so that the nominal and real prices are equal in 1983, but that does not mean anything. Put another way, that real price of gold is adjusted for inflation that is all.

What do I want you see here? What would I like you to notice from the graph? The real price of gold has been highly variable. This is not a surprise. World demand and supply for gold varies a lot, and the real price of gold adjusts accordingly to make demand equal supply. If the United States were still on the gold standard, the United States would have been trying to keep the price of gold constant when world market forces dictated that it should have changed a lot.

Let me ask you a final question: Are Stephen Forbes and Ron Paul right? Should we return to a world in which new money could be created only if gold reserves were obtained? If gold production grew slowly, would the resulting slow growth in the money supply drag down economic growth in nations that used gold for money? Would the United States be better off entrusting growth of the U.S. money supply to the Federal Reserve than to world-wide demand for and supply of gold for which the U.S. produces less than 10%?

You be the judge.

Monetary History of the United States
Lecture 4

The proper role of the federal government in monetary and banking affairs was debated early and often in the history of the United States. The federal government tried twice in the 19th century—and failed both times—to create a central bank that would oversee banks and maintain a national currency. The question of whether or not a national bank would concentrate too much power in the hands of too few occupied the Founding Fathers as they wrote the Constitution and considered legislation in the first sessions of Congress. But others of our forefathers believed that creation of a national bank and paper money were essential to the development of our nation. In this lecture, we shall see that disagreements about financial arrangements in the United States were tantamount to disagreements between competing visions for our new nation.

The First Bank of the United States
- The first National Bank of the United States was authorized by the Senate and House in 1791. At the time the Bank was chartered, the forces arrayed in favor of it and opposed to it mirrored competing visions for the evolution of our nation.

- Some opposed the Bank on the grounds that the Constitution did not explicitly permit the federal government to create a bank or issue paper money. Some opposed the issuance of paper money itself, fearing that it would invariably lead to schemes in which debtors increased their wealth at the expense of creditors.

- Some opposition to the Bank stemmed from fear of allowing the federal government to set up perpetual institutions, which were considered to be a hallmark of British government and a threat to personal liberty.

© Photos.com/Thinkstock.

President Washington intended to veto the bill authorizing the Bank but was convinced by Alexander Hamilton not to do so. Hamilton argued that the United States, to fulfill its potential as a great commercial nation, required financial and monetary systems that would facilitate payments and trade.

- Finally, some, including Thomas Jefferson, argued that the Bank was a threat to the agrarian way of life that they believed was the best way forward for the United States.

- Those who favored the creation of the Bank, notably Hamilton, believed that it would promote the development of commercial activity in the United States.

- Others supported the Bank because they saw advantages in the creation of paper money. For many farmers, economic activity amounted to raising crops and bartering the surplus with neighbors. These farmers feared that they might lose their lands if taxes were specified to be paid in gold, to which they simply didn't have access.

The Early Years of the First Bank

- In 1791, when the Bank of the United States was established, there was no single banking system in the United States. Four isolated systems existed in Boston, New York, Philadelphia, and Baltimore.

- After the establishment of the Bank, these systems coalesced into a single system that exchanged one another's obligations and maintained ongoing debtor-creditor relationships.

- The Bank of the United States functioned a lot like a central bank. Because it was the main government depository, it became an important creditor to state and local banks, and because it was their creditor, the Bank had the power to regulate local banks by pressing them for payment.

- In 1811, the bill to extend the charter of the Bank was allowed to lapse. Clearly, the country remained divided on the question of the role of the federal government in banking and financial matters. Important constituencies continued to disagree about whether the bank was an appropriate source of financial discipline or whether it amounted to an infringement by the federal government on individual and states rights.

The Second Bank of the United States

- A Second Bank of the United States was established in 1816, but it had operational difficulties almost from the beginning.

- When a panic and recession swept the United States in 1818, the Bank, rather than extending credit to offset the recession, was forced by its lack of reserves to call in credit and intensify the recession.

- The demise of the Second Bank came at the hands of President Andrew Jackson, who believed that it was corrupt and wanted it to cease operations even before its charter expired in 1836.

- Jackson instructed the secretary of the Treasury to deposit federal tax receipts in state banks. The Second Bank began to run at a loss, was converted to a regular bank when its charter was not renewed, and went bankrupt several years later.

The National Bank Acts of 1863 and 1864

- The federal government did not resume control over the monetary system in the United States until the National Bank Acts of 1863 and 1864.

- At the beginning of Lincoln's presidency, Treasury Secretary Salmon Chase had on hand approximately $2 million, a tiny fraction of what Congress had appropriated for war preparations.

- In 1861, the U.S. government suspended payment in gold. In 1862, it issued new legal tender, paper currency called "**greenbacks**."

- The National Banking Acts of 1863 and 1864 created a system of federally chartered banks (national banks) that were supervised by the newly created Office of the Comptroller of the Currency. These national banks were required to purchase Treasury bonds and were allowed to issue greenbacks for up to 90% of their bond holdings.

- The banking acts also created a tax of 10% on banknotes issued by state-chartered banks, with the intent of driving these banks out of existence.

- The creation of the first U.S. dollar can be fairly said to be a byproduct of the federal government's desire for a source of revenue to finance military action during the Civil War.

The Gold Standard and the Coining of Silver

- In the last quarter of the 19th century, 2 important questions faced the United States: When would it return to the gold standard, and would it permit the coining of silver?

- A dual monetary standard had existed during the greenback period, with both greenbacks and gold circulating as forms of payment. But there was no fixed exchange ratio of one for the other because the government did not offer to exchange gold for greenbacks at a fixed price of gold.

- The price of gold in terms of greenbacks rose dramatically during the Civil War. Once the war ended, the greenback price of gold declined gradually, until by 1872, it was only about 10% higher than its 1861 level.

- As the United States paid off its war debt, the greenback price of gold came closer to its prewar level. This touched off debate about when the country would return to the gold standard.

- At the same time, there was debate about whether the United States should allow the coining of both silver and gold. Although both were legally money, only silver circulated as money because gold was too expensive. In 1834, new legislation ended silver's dominance as money and made gold the metal of choice for coinage.

- As the United States was poised to leave the greenback period and return to a metal standard, the question became: Which metal—gold, silver, or both? The issue was settled by the Coinage Act of 1873, which eliminated free coinage of silver and cast the die for the gold standard in the United States.

The "Crime of 1873"

- Although the Coinage Act caused little controversy when it was approved, it proved to be detrimental to the U.S. economy during the last quarter of the 19th century. Indeed, Milton Friedman termed the act the "Crime of 1873."

- As a result of the act, gold became scarce, with the price of gold to silver more than doubling between 1873 and 1900.

- The elimination of silver from the money stock cause caused the money supply to grow too slowly to keep pace with potential growth in real output.

- U.S. price levels fell from 1876 to 1896 at a rate of 1.5% per year, a development that hit farmers particularly hard.

- Friedman blames the Coinage Act for recessions that occurred in 1892–1894 and 1895–1896 and for the banking panic in 1893.

- Increasing the money supply more rapidly through the resumption of silver coinage was a crucial issue in the presidential campaign of 1896. William Jennings Bryan was a leading proponent of free silver but was defeated in the election by William McKinley.

The Federal Reserve Act of 1914

- The role of the federal government in monetary affairs was settled with the passage of the Federal Reserve Act of 1914.

- But debate on the proper limits of federal authority in monetary affairs is hardly over. The Federal Reserve broke new ground in expanding its role in monetary affairs during the Great Recession of 2007–2009, and many are still questioning whether or not the Fed did too much.

Important Term

greenbacks: Paper currency issued in 1862; it was used as legal tender after the U.S. government suspended payment in gold in 1861.

Suggested Reading

Friedman, "The Crime of 1873."

Friedman and Schwartz, *A Monetary History of the United States.*

Hammond, *Banks and Politics in America.*

Rockoff, "The 'Wizard of Oz' as a Monetary Allegory."

Questions to Consider

1. Why were the opponents to the Bank of the United States successful in blocking the renewal of its charter? Would those same opponents have been against the establishment of the Federal Reserve in 1914?

2. Why do you think the issue of whether or not to coin silver was so hard fought? Who would have been for "free silver"? Who would have been against it?

3. Do you believe the National Banking Acts of 1863 and 1864 were good policies or bad?

Monetary History of the United States
Lecture 4—Transcript

In the last lecture, we talked about the views of Steve Forbes and Ron Paul that the United States would be better off if it returned to the practice of backing currency with gold. Some of what motivates supporters of a return to the gold standard is concern about the power wielded by the Federal Reserve Bank of the United States and those who run it.

The proper role of the federal government in monetary and banking affairs was debated early and often in the history of the United States. The federal government tried twice in the 19th century, and failed both times, to create a central bank that would oversee other banks and maintain a national currency. The question of whether or not a national bank would concentrate too much power in the hands of too few occupied the founding fathers as they wrote the Constitution and considered legislation in the first sessions of Congress. The connection of this concern about the abuse of power to the use of gold as money is straightforward.

If gold coins are money, then anyone who has gold has money. While mints converted bullion to coins, citizens typically had the right and sometimes the obligation to trade their bullion to the mint for gold coins. If, on the other hand, a national bank was able to issue paper money, then those who controlled the bank could increase or decrease the quantity of money in circulation without reference to the availability of gold or any other scarce commodity. That ability is power, and it is power that some of our forefathers feared.

But others of our forefathers believed that creation of a national bank and paper money were essential to the development of our nation. Today, we shall see that disagreements about financial arrangements in the United States were tantamount to disagreements between competing visions for our new nation. Imagine it is December of 1790 and you are visiting the third session of the first Congress of the United States. The ink is barely dry on the Constitution, which was adopted on September 17, 1787, but not finally ratified by Rhode Island, the last state to do so, until May 29, 1790. What will you see? What you will witness as you visit Congress on this particular day is a debate on a proposal offered by Alexander Hamilton, Secretary of the Treasury, to charter a national bank, the Bank of the United States, which we now refer to as we will see, as the first bank of the United States.

The Senate passed Hamilton's bill authorizing the bank on January 20, 1791. The House, after much heated debate, approved the bank by a vote of 39 to 20 with most of the yes votes coming from New England, New York, New Jersey, and Pennsylvania. President Washington at first seemed to be convinced that the bill was contrary to the Constitution. He had gone so far as to instruct James Madison to prepare a veto. However, Hamilton counter argued that the purpose of the Constitution was to set up a workable government for the United States. Hamilton argued that government had the power and the right to employ "all means requisite and fairly applicable to the attainment of the ends of such power" provided that they were not precluded by the constitution itself and not, "contrary to the essential ends of political society." What Hamilton meant was that the United States in order to fulfill its potential as a great commercial nation required financial and monetary systems that would facilitate payments and trade.

Well, Washington was convinced by Hamilton's argument and signed the act incorporating the bank on February 25, 1791. The bank was located in Philadelphia. After a temporary location at the Carpenters Hall on Chestnut Street, the bank moved in 1797 around the corner to its permanent and present location on Third Street between Chestnut and Walnut in a building designed by Samuel Blodget. When you go to Philadelphia, take a look. It is still there. The forces arrayed in favor of and in opposition to the Bank of the United States mirrored, as I have said, competing visions for the evolution of our nation.

So what were some arguments in opposition to the bank? Well, some opposed the bank on the grounds that the Constitution did not explicitly permit the federal government to create a bank or issue paper money. The Constitution authorized the federal government to coin and forbade the states from doing so. The Constitution forbade the states from issuing paper money but was silent as to what the federal government might do. The Constitution forbade the states to make anything but gold and silver legal tender but omitted to say what the federal government might do. The Constitution, likewise, forbade the states from impairing contracts.

This latter prohibition is monetary in nature because the depreciation of legal tender paper money was thought to violate contracts. Some opposed the creation of a bank explicitly because they were opposed to the issuance of paper money. They feared that paper money would invariably lead to schemes where debtors increased their wealth at the expense of creditors. Indeed, the United States had ample experience with currency depreciation. The Continental Congress issued paper money—it was called Continentals— to finance the revolutionary war. By the end of the war, Continentals were essentially worthless. Some opposed creation of the bank because they were opposed to the federal government setting up perpetual institutions, which they considered to be a hallmark of British government and a threat to personal liberty.

An agrarian representative from Georgia, James Jackson, demanded "Was it not the ecclesiastical corporations and perpetual monopolies of England and Scotland that drove our forefathers to this country." Some opposed the creation of the bank because they thought that it was a threat to the agrarian way of life that they believed was the best way forward for the United States. Thomas Jefferson, in particular, argued for a self-sufficient way of life that eschewed trade, especially trade for European manufactured goods.

With all that opposition, could there be offsetting support? Yes, yes. Some, and notably, Hamilton, favored creation of the bank because they favored the development of a commercial United States. Indeed, one of the reasons that the Articles of Confederation proved unworkable was that individual states interfered with cross-state trade. In the Constitution, those committed to commercial activity sought arrangements that promoted trade and commercial growth.

Some favored creation of the bank explicitly because they favored the creation of paper money. Why? For many rural Americans, economic activity amounted to raising crops and bartering surplus crops with neighbors. While these individuals were industrious, they rarely exchanged their labor or its fruits for gold and silver. These farmers were frightened that if taxes were specified to be paid in gold that they might lose their lands because they did not have access to gold.

One of the complaints of Daniel Shays and those who participated in Shays's rebellion was that creditors demanded payment in gold and silver when there was not enough specie in Massachusetts to pay the claims. Some favored creation of the bank because they agreed with Hamilton's interpretation of the Constitution cited earlier. While Congress and President Washington allowed creation of the bank in 1791, a later Congress allowed its charter to lapse 20 years later in 1811.

In 1791, when the Bank of the United States was established, there was no banking system in the United States. There were 4 isolated systems centered in Boston, New York, Philadelphia, and Baltimore. But after the establishment of the Bank of the United States, the various systems coalesced into a single system that exchanged one another's obligations and maintained ongoing debtor-creditor relationships. The Bank of the United States functioned a lot like a central bank. Because the Bank of the United States was the main government depository, it ended up as an important creditor to state and local banks. It lent those state and local banks money, and because it was their creditor, the Bank of the United States had the power to regulate local banks by pressing them for payments. Do what I want or I will make you pay some.

Some important individuals did not like the discipline imposed by the Bank of the United States. Famously, John Jacob Astor of New York was furious because the bank had denied him credit. The third and fourth presidents of the United States, Thomas Jefferson and James Madison, had opposed the creation of the bank in the first place and had not changed their minds by the times their presidencies began. Some continued to dislike the fact that some of the shareholders in the Bank of the United States happened to be British.

There was a bill to extend the charter of the Bank of the United States, and it was tabled by the House in a vote of 65 to 64 and defeated in the Senate by a vote of 18 to 17 with Vice President George Clinton casting the deciding vote. Clearly, the country remained divided and closely divided at that on the role of the federal government in banking and financial matters. Important constituencies continued to disagree about whether the bank was an important and appropriate source of financial discipline or whether on the other hand it amounted to an infringement by the federal government on states' rights and individual rights.

The forces that favored a bank tried again and succeeded 5 years later to establish a second bank of the United States, in 1816. But this arrangement did not go well. Unlike the first bank that had been ably run by Albert Gallatin, the second bank had operational difficulties almost from its beginning. Essentially, and very importantly, the second bank behaved perversely. Here is an example. A panic and a recession swept the United States in 1818. But the bank, rather than extending credit to offset these recessionary forces was forced by its own lack of reserves to call in credit and intensify the recession. The exact opposite of what we would expect a central bank to do today.

The death of the second bank of the United States came at the hands of none other than President Andrew Jackson, who believed that it was corrupt and wanted it to cease operations even before its charter expired in 1836. Some political analysts likened Jackson's effort to those of a gallant knight doing battle with some monster. Jackson instructed the secretary of the Treasury to deposit federal tax receipts in state banks. Think about that, deposit their own receipts of the federal government, not in the federal bank, but in state banks. So, not surprisingly, the second bank began to run at a loss and was converted to a regular bank when its charter was not renewed and went bankrupt several years later.

So for a time, the federal government was not front and center in national financial matters, but it's said that necessity is often the mother of invention, and as we shall see the necessity in this case for government revenues brought the United States back into the business of banking. The time is the Civil War between the states and the need for revenue on the part of the federal government finally settled the debate about federal involvement in financial matters.

The federal government did not, in particular, resume control over the monetary system in the United States until the National Banking Acts of 1863 and 1864. At the beginning of Abraham Lincoln's presidency, Treasury Secretary Salmon Chase had on hand approximately $2 million, a tiny, tiny fraction of what Congress had appropriated to begin war preparations and an even smaller fraction of what he thought was necessary to prosecute the war. In 1861, the U.S. government suspended payment in gold. We have seen this before in our lectures. In 1862, it issued new legal tender paper currency that were called "greenbacks": Their backside was green.

The National Banking Act of 1863 and 1864 created a system of federally chartered banks called national banks that were supervised by the newly created office of the Controller of the Currency. That office still exists. National banks were required to purchase Treasury Bonds as a condition of their establishment. So, national banks were required to lend money to the federal government. What did they get in return? They were then allowed to issue greenbacks for up to 90% of their bond holdings. So we have a new national currency, and banks can issue it if they lend to the federal government. These 2 banking acts also created a tax of 10% on bank notes issued by state-chartered banks, and the intent plainly was to drive state-chartered banks out of existence.

Many of these state-chartered banks did convert to national banks, but some survived by accepting deposits rather than by issuing notes. According to Milton Friedman and Anna Schwartz in their *Monetary History of the United States*, $292 million worth of national bank notes were in circulation in 1867. The creation of the first U.S. dollar can be fairly said to be a by-product of the federal government's desire for a source of revenue to finance military action during the Civil War.

In the last quarter of the 19th century, 2 important questions faced the United States. When would it return to the gold standard and would it permit the coining of silver? One hundred years after Congress debated the question of whether to create the Bank of the United States, Congress continued to be divided on the appropriate role of the federal government in financial matters. Once again, the issue of what would be money was hotly contested. And once again, like in Andrew Jackson's time, a prominent politician became known for his stand on monetary issues.

During the greenback period, there was a dual monetary standard with both greenbacks and gold circulating as forms of payment. But, there was no fixed trading ratio or exchange rate of one for the other because the U.S. Government did not offer to exchange gold for greenbacks at some fixed price of gold. So, not surprisingly, the price of gold in terms of greenbacks rose dramatically during the years of the Civil War. Currency became less valuable in terms of gold and gold become more valuable in terms of the currency.

Once the war ended, the greenback price of gold did decline gradually and by 1872, it was only about 10% higher than it had been in 1861. So with those 2 prices coming close together it raised the question, when would the U.S. return to the gold standard? As the U.S. paid off its war debt, and the greenback price of gold came closer to its pre-war level, debate was touched off about when the U.S. would return to the gold standard, and there was debate about whether the United States should allow the coining of silver as well as gold. Let's reflect on this a little bit because this is important.

From the Coinage Act of 1792, either silver or gold was legally money in the United States. So from 1792, one could have gold coins or silver coins circulating in the United States. Until 1834, however, only silver circulated as money. Why? What is wrong with gold? Well, it is a simple answer. Gold was too expensive and people had an incentive to melt down gold coins in order to use the metal itself. Silver coins they left in the form of coins.

In 1834, there was some new legislation, and it replaced the 15:1 ratio of silver to gold, which had been set down in the 1792 Act with a new ratio, 16:1. What does that mean? Well, in 1792, a unit of value in silver had to have 15 times as much metal as a unit of value in terms of gold. So a dollar silver coin would have 15 times the weight of a dollar gold coin. In 1834, that was changed to a 16:1 ratio. That legislation ended silver's dominance as money and made gold the metal of choice for coinage.

So, as the U.S. was poised to leave the greenback and return to a metal standard, the question was which metal, gold, silver, or both. The issue was settled by The U.Ss Coinage Act of 1873, which eliminated free coinage of silver and cast the die for the gold standard in the United States. The Coinage Act caused little controversy when it was approved, but it proved itself to be very bad medicine for the U.S. economy during the last quarter of the 19th century. Indeed, Milton Friedman has termed the act the "Crime of 1873." Strong language. What was the nature of the crime?

Gold became very scarce with the price of gold to silver more than doubling between 1873 and 1900. The elimination of silver from the money stock caused the money supply to grow too slowly to keep pace with potential output growth in the United States. As a result, prices in the United States fell from 1876 to 1896 at a rate, on average, of 1.5% per year. Think about that for a minute. Twenty years of price deflation at 1.5% on average per year. This fall in prices hit farmers particularly hard as the price of their crops fell while the price of what they bought fell less rapidly.

Milton Friedman blames that Coinage Act for bad recessions that occurred in 1892 to1894. A second bad recession in 1895 to 1896, and he blames that act for the banking panic of 1893. Increasing the money supply more rapidly through the resumption of silver coinage was a crucial issue in the presidential campaign of 1896.

William Jennings Bryan delivered the famous cross of gold speech at the Democratic National Convention held in Chicago. Jennings said:

> If they dare to come out in the open field and defend the gold standard as a good thing, we shall fight them to the utmost, having behind us the producing masses of the nation and the world. Having behind us, the commercial interests and the laboring interests and all the toiling masses, we shall answer their demands for a gold standard by saying to them, you shall not press down upon the brow of labor this crown of thorns. You shall not crucify mankind upon a cross of gold.

William McKinley defeated Bryan in 1896 and again in 1900. But, the silver issue continued on even into the imagination of the American people. If you have read Frank Baum's book, *The Wizard of Oz*, you will know that it is a monetary allegory. What is the evidence? The slippers are not ruby. That was a device of Hollywood. Dorothy's slippers are silver, and Dorothy wears silver slippers as she trips her way toward Oz along a gold-covered road.

The role of the federal government in monetary affairs was, perhaps, settled finally with a passage of the Federal Reserve Act in December of 1913 and the establishment of the Federal Reserve in the following year. But I find it fascinating that the proper role of government in monetary and banking affairs was debated early and often throughout our history. The federal government tried twice, before the Federal Reserve Act, to create a central bank that would regulate banks and maintain a national currency. Debate on the proper limits of federal authority in monetary affairs is hardly over. The Federal Reserve broke new ground in expanding the role that it took upon itself in monetary affairs during the Great Recession of 2007 through 2009. Debate has raged on whether or not the Fed did too much.

Let me leave you with a final question. Suppose that you had not only visited Congress, but that you had been a member there in 1791 or in 1816 or in 1863 or in 1873. How would you have voted on chartering the first bank of the United States? How would you have voted on chartering the second bank of the United States? How would you have voted on allowing the federal government to create the greenback and how would you have voted on borrowing silver as a coin metal?

Thank you.

Local Currencies and Nonstandard Banks
Lecture 5

Money and financial arrangements in the United States were hotly contested in the 19th-century political arena. Part of the debate centered on whether the federal government had the right, under the Constitution, to create a central bank and issue paper money. In this lecture, we'll learn that the institution of money is so important to economic welfare that citizens sometimes take the matter into their own hands. We will look at local currencies and microfinancing, both of which help us to understand and appreciate how financial arrangements, including money, are important to the economic welfare of individuals.

The Story of Wörgl

- During the Great Depression, a village in Austria initiated a controversial financial arrangement in the hope that it would solve some of the economic woes experienced by both the village itself and its citizens.

- Like much of the world in 1932, Wörgl was experiencing high unemployment, reduced tax revenues, and deteriorating public facilities. As a solution to its problems, the village created 32,000 Austrian schillings worth of a new local currency that it called "labor certificates" and used them to hire workers for public projects. The town also paid civil servants a fraction of their salaries with the labor certificates.

- The labor certificates depreciated at a rate of 1% per month, giving their holders an incentive to spend them and stimulate the local economy. Businesses accepted the certificates in payment and paid taxes with the certificates.

- The town of Wörgl agreed to convert the labor certificates to official Austrian schillings at a 2% discount and kept a deposit in a local bank for that purpose.

- The experiment ended after about a year and a half, when outside authorities opposed it, but during the time that it was in effect, tax and fee revenues increased substantially as a result of improved economic activity, many worthwhile public works projects were completed, and no inflation occurred.

- By issuing labor certificates, Wörgl was able to coordinate improved economic activity. To assuage concerns about accepting the certificates in exchange, Wörgl provided for the conversion of the labor certificates into Austrian schillings and agreed to accept them in payment of taxes.

- The Wörgl experiment underscores the idea that money is a social contract. During the Depression, Wörgl and its citizens used a local currency to create mutually advantageous exchanges that would not have occurred otherwise.

- Wörgl also helps us appreciate the importance of financial arrangements for the functioning of an economy and understand the difference between successful and unsuccessful financial institutions.

Cigarettes as Currency

- Another example of a local currency can be found in the elaborate trading system based on cigarettes established by prisoners at Stalag VIIA during World War II.

- Red Cross parcels provided a somewhat regular supply of cigarettes and foodstuffs to the 50,000 prisoners at the camp, and prisoners began to use the cigarettes from the parcels as money. They were even accepted in trade by nonsmokers, who understood that they could later exchange cigarettes for food; thus, both smokers and nonsmokers had confidence that cigarettes would hold their value.

- A disadvantage of using cigarettes as money was that prices fluctuated. When Red Cross parcels first arrived and cigarettes were plentiful, prices would rise. When a time had passed without new Red Cross parcels, cigarettes became scarce and prices fell.

"Deli Dollars"

- In 1989, Frank Tortoriello, owner of a delicatessen in Massachusetts, wanted to move his deli and sought a loan from a local bank, but his application was denied. With guidance from the Schumacher Society, Tortoriello issued "Deli Dollars." These were sold for $8.00 but were good for $10.00 worth of merchandise at the deli.

- Through this scheme, Tortoriello raised sufficient funds to move the deli, and because the Deli Dollars had staggered redemption dates, he was not forced to redeem them all in a short period of time.

- This example is an interesting amalgam of a local currency and a microfinance scheme. Deli Dollars permitted Tortoriello to borrow from his future customers. The discount they received functioned like interest on the loan. The promise of future meals served as security that the customers valued more than the bank that had turned down Tortoriello's loan application.

"Ithaca Hours"

- In 1991, Paul Glover spearheaded the movement to issue "Ithaca Hours" in Ithaca, New York. Glover issued 2 free Ithaca Hours (each with a face value of $10.00) to people who agreed to accept them and to be listed in a publication called "Hour Town."

- The purpose of the project is to promote the local economy. Because Ithaca Hours are not accepted outside the town, anyone who accepts an Ithaca Hours certificate in exchange for a good or service commits to spending that certificate with another local merchant or service provider.

- Unlike Deli Dollars, Ithaca Hours are not sold by a firm trying to raise funds for its own use. Instead, Glover gave Ithaca Hours away to "subscribers," who agreed to spend them locally and accept them from others.

- Ithaca Hours function like a real currency, staying in circulation among local citizens and businesses.

Cooperative Arrangements

- In addition to local currencies, there is another type of nonstandard financial arrangement that addresses the desire of individuals to coordinate their economic activity through the process of lending and borrowing funds. Such an arrangement is captured in a scenario in which 10 village families would each like to buy a bicycle.

- If each family saves $10.00 a year to buy a $100.00 bicycle, then they will all wait 10 years before they own bicycles. If they pool their money, however, one family will be able to buy a bicycle each year.

- One potential flaw in such an arrangement is that families that have received their bicycles have an incentive to stop making their annual contributions to the pool. If families doubt that others will continue to make payments, they may judge the cooperative arrangement to be risky and prefer the go-it-alone solution. Clearly, some enforcement mechanism is necessary to ensure that all promised payments are made.

Alternative Lending Institutions

- As the story of the villagers and the bicycles suggests, there are many situations in which every member of a group could benefit from a coordinated arrangement to save funds and lend them out to group members.

- The story also underscores another important theme: There are many groups of individuals who, for a variety of reasons, do not have access to traditional lending institutions and must seek alternatives.

- Pawn shops, for example, have traditionally provided credit to those who could not obtain it from banks.

- Another mechanism for providing credit to an otherwise underserved population is the Rotating Saving and Credit Association (ROSCA), similar to our example of the villagers and the bicycles.

- Two important issues faced by a ROSCA are how to determine the order in which participants receive funds and how to ensure that individuals fulfill their promises to make contributions. Many ROSCAs use lotteries to determine who will receive funds and social consequences to enforce the contract.

The Grameen Bank

- In 1976, Professor Muhammad Yunus, head of the Rural Economics Program at the University of Chittagong, launched a project to provide banking services targeted at the rural poor. The result of his project was the Grameen Bank.

- The classic model of this bank relies on group lending. Grameen clients are too poor to offer collateral but tend to have close ties to a community; thus, borrowers form groups whose members monitor and support one another. Two members of the group may receive a loan at any one time. If a group defaults, it is barred from receiving future loans.

- Yanus realized that the marginal productivity of the investment made possible by a small loan is very high; that is, borrowers can repay because the loans lead to profitable investments.

- Another enforcement mechanism used by the Grameen Bank model is progressive lending, which makes available larger loans to groups or individuals who have successfully paid back smaller loans.

- The Grameen model has been hugely successful, although the bank has recently come under scrutiny from a variety of government agencies. Some critics question whether microfinance has the beneficial impact on poverty that the bank claims. Others are threatened by the growth of the bank and the power of Yanus. Still others criticize microfinance because some lenders charge high interest rates.

Financial Arrangements on Main Street
- As we have seen in this lecture, financial arrangements are not only the business of Wall Street. Citizens of Main Street understand the power of monetary arrangements to coordinate economic activity and, at times, have created monies to accomplish local economic objectives.

- Local currencies and microfinancing are 2 types of arrangements that thrive even amidst a multitude of highly financed traditional institutions.

Suggested Reading

Armendáriz and Morduch, *The Economics of Microfinance.*

E. F. Schumacher Society, "Local Currencies."

Glover, "A History of Ithaca Hours."

Unterguggenberger, "The End of the Woergl Experiment."

Questions to Consider

1. What is the difference between a store coupon and a local currency? Was the Deli Dollar a coupon or a currency?

2. In recent months, microfinance and the Grameen Bank have become very controversial? Why?

3. Is the establishment of a local currency a good tool to promote development of a local economy? Why or why not?

Local Currencies and Nonstandard Banks
Lecture 5—Transcript

In the last lecture, we learned that money and financial arrangements in the United States were hotly contested in the political arena during the entire 19th century. Would money be gold or paper? Would money be gold or silver? Part of the debate centered on whether the federal government had the right under the U.S. Constitution to create a central bank and to issue paper money. What we will learn today is that the institution of money is so important to economic welfare that citizens sometimes take the matter into their own hands. Today's lecture covers 2 sets of related ideas. Both sets help us to understand and appreciate how financial arrangements, including money, are important to the economic welfare of individuals. They also underscore the idea that money, in particular, and financial arrangements, in general, are cooperative arrangements—social contracts—as I have suggested before.

Let's start with a story. During the Great Depression, a village in Austria initiated a controversial financial arrangement in the hope that it would provide a solution to some of the economic woes being experienced both by the village itself and by most of its citizens. The town was Wörgl, and the man who came up with the idea was, and this is a mouthful, Michael Unterguggenberger, the city manager. Like most of the world, Wörgl was experiencing high unemployment, greatly reduced tax revenues, and deteriorating public facilities, such as roads. Wörgl created 32,000 Austrian schillings worth of a new local currency that it called "labor certificates" and used them to hire workers for public projects. The town also paid employed civil servants some portion of their salaries with the labor certificates. The labor certificates depreciated at the rate of 1% per month to give the holders of those certificates an incentive to spend them and stimulate the local economy.

Workers who otherwise would not have worked received the labor certificates and spent them with local businesses. Those businesses, which otherwise would not have sold goods, accepted the certificates, made sales and were able, in turn, to buy other local goods and pay taxes with the certificates. Before issuing the currency, Wörgl negotiated with the civil servants to accept some of their payment in labor certificates. Of course, newly hired workers understood in advance that they would be paid in these certificates.

Various shopkeepers participated in the agreement because they understood that it would stimulate business.

Wörgl also agreed to convert the labor certificates to official Austrian schillings, but at a 2% discount, and they kept a deposit of real Austrian schillings in a local bank for just that purpose. The experiment ended when outside authorities, including the Austrian State Bank opposed it. The entire experiment last about a year and one half.

In a final report, the city manager documented that tax and fee revenues increased substantially in Wörgl as the result of improved economic activity and that many worthwhile public works projects were completed. No inflation occurred. Ironically, some of the labor certificates never found their way back to Wörgl but were kept as souvenirs, which was another benefit to the local community. By issuing labor certificates, Wörgl was able to coordinate improved economic activity. To assuage concerns about acceptance of the certificates, Wörgl provided for a conversion of the labor certificates into Austrian schillings and agreed to accept them in payment of taxes.

During the Great Depression, Wörgl and its citizens used a local currency to create mutually advantageous exchanges that would not otherwise have occurred. Well, the city wanted work done on public projects but had no tax revenues. City workers were willing to work and wanted to buy goods with their earnings, but they had no earnings. City shops wanted to sell goods and were willing to pay their taxes with the currency. But none of these decision makers had the official Austrian schillings that would permit them to initiate what I call a cascade of activities. So Wörgl created a local currency that permitted local decision makers to coordinate their activities and permitted that cascade of activities to begin.

The Wörgl experiment underscores that money is a social contract and helps us appreciate the importance of financial arrangements for the functioning of an economy, and it helps us to understand the difference between successful and unsuccessful financial institutions.

Let us take a look at a few more examples of local currencies. They are very, very interesting, but they also can teach us quite a bit. This is one of my favorite stories about an event that actually did take place. During World War II, prisoners in Stalag VIIA, which was located at Moosburg in Bavaria, established an elaborate trading system in which cigarettes were used as money. The camp contained about 50,000 prisoners of many different nationalities and, of course then, many different tastes. Red Cross parcels provided a somewhat regular supply both of cigarettes and of foodstuffs to the prisoners in the camp. Very, very quickly, prisoners began to use cigarettes as money. Non-smokers were always willing to trade coffee, tea, and other foods for cigarettes knowing that they could use those cigarettes to buy goods and services they preferred. That bears emphasis here. Non-smokers accepted cigarettes even though they did not intend to smoke them because they knew that they could use them in turn to buy what they wanted.

So an advantage of the choice of cigarettes as money was that everyone, non-smokers and smokers alike, would always accept them in exchange for food. They understood that smokers would ultimately demand them, and that understanding led to confidence that cigarettes would hold their value. Now, there were disadvantages of using cigarettes as money. The most important disadvantage is that prices of goods in terms of cigarettes would fluctuate. When Red Cross parcels first arrived in the camp, cigarettes were very plentiful. What would happen then? Well, people were willing to give a lot of cigarettes in order to get say tin beef, and prices would rise. If a long amount a time had passed without new Red Cross parcels, smokers assured that cigarettes were coming relatively scarce, and then prices would fall. This variation in prices made camp life somewhat difficult.

But keep in mind that cigarettes really did function as money. They were accepted in trade not only by smokers, but by non-smokers alike who understood that they could later exchange them for things they wanted. This is not simply playing house. The cigarette money made a difference in the camp. Many more trades were accomplished because of this cigarette money, and those trades were very, very important to the imprisoned officers who made them.

Let's look for a more recent example. In 1989, Frank Tortoriello, owner of a delicatessen in Great Barrington, Massachusetts, wanted to move his deli and sought a loan from his local bank. Unfortunately, the bank denied his loan application leaving him without the means to move his delicatessen. But, with guidance from the Schumacher Society, Tortoriello issued Deli Dollars, which promised $10 worth of merchandise at the deli. Tortoriello sold the Deli Dollars for $8 each to individuals who gave them as gifts and purchased them for their own use. He raised sufficient funds to move his deli.

Deli Dollars were well-designed. They had staggered redemption dates so that the deli would not be forced to redeem them all in a short period of time. In this way, Tortoriello had an inflow of cash as well as Deli Dollars, and this example seems to me to be an interesting combination of a local currency and a kind of micro-finance scheme. Deli-dollars permitted Tortoriello to borrow from his future customers. The discount they received functioned like interest on the loan they made to him. The promise of future meals provided security that the customers valued more than the bank that had turned down Tortoriello's loan application.

While Deli Dollars resembled currency, there are no accounts that I know of, of third parties accepting them. That is, the Deli Dollars were created by the deli owner, sold to current and future deli customers, and then later re-presented to the deli owner in exchange for meals. But, I can find no accounts of the Deli Dollars being used to say, buy goods at the Great Barrington hardware store.

Ah, but I do have another example where a local currency certainly did and continues to circulate as money. In 1991, Paul Glover spearheaded the movement to issue Ithaca Hours in Ithaca, New York, the home of Cornell University. Glover issued 2 free Ithaca Hours, each with a face value of $10, to people who would agree to accept them and to be listed in a publication called *Hour Town*, nice play on words isn't it? H-O-U-R town. By 2000 according to Glover, thousands of Ithacans routinely accepted and spent Ithaca Hours. Now I can verify that. I was able to acquire Ithaca Hours myself on the one occasion when I happened to visit the farmers' market in Ithaca. Notice an important difference between Ithaca Hours and Deli Dollars. Ithaca Hours are not sold by a firm that is trying to raise funds for its own use. Glover gave Ithaca Hours away to subscribers who agreed to spend them locally and accept them from others.

Also, Ithaca Hours functioned like a real currency. They traveled between various Ithaca citizens and Ithaca businesses and stay in circulation. Deli Dollars made a single round trip: deli, customer, deli. Ithaca Hours keep traveling. So, what is that project all about? Well, the purpose of the Ithaca Hours project is to promote the local economy in Ithaca. Since Ithaca Hours are not accepted outside the town, indeed they are hardly known about outside the town, except for people like me who study them, anyone who accepts an Ithaca Hours certificate in exchange for some good or service is making essentially a commitment to spend that certificate with another local merchant or service provider, and indeed that is the point. Ithaca Hours is a scheme to promote the development of the local economy in Ithaca.

Closer to my home, Chapel Hill, North Carolina, we too have a local currency. It is called "the PLENTY," standing for Piedmont Local EcoNomy Tender. The PLENTY is widely accepted in Orange, Alamance, and Chatham County, and there is a catalog in which people and businesses who are willing to accept PLENTY can indicate their willingness to do so in the catalog and online. The PLENTY is a similar scheme to the Ithaca Hour. It is meant to stimulate the rural community just to the west of Chapel Hill.

In addition to local currencies, there is another type of nonstandard financial arrangement that addresses the desire of individuals to coordinate their economic activity, but now through the process of lending and borrowing funds. The motivation for this is easily understood, but I would like to capture the motivation in a parable. Imagine with me for a moment a remote village without any connection to a modern financial institution. It might be in Polynesia. It might be in Africa. You use your own imagination. Most likely the village is going to be located in an undeveloped country, or perhaps it was a village in a much earlier time. Now that we fixed our image, suppose further that in the village, there are 10 families. The number is arbitrary, but let's stick with 10. Each family would like to own a bicycle, and none has one. One family would use the bicycle to haul vegetables to market. Maybe a second family would convert the bicycle into a rickshaw and start a business. I imagine a third family would allow their 2 children to ride the bicycle to a town 20 miles away where they could attend a better school and so forth.

Left to their own devices, each of the 10 families could save up to buy their bicycle. Image a serviceable bicycle cost about $100 and imagine that in this rural area each family could scrap together about $10 of savings per year. Then all 10 families could have a bicycle, but all 10 families would have to wait 10 years, and all 10 families would end up buying the bicycle at about the same time. What a waste. Each family would hide its savings in a secure place waiting for the day when they had accumulated the price of a bicycle. For 10 years, all those funds would remain idle.

After the 10 years, the aggregated saving of the 10 families would be $1000, but only then would they be able to buy a bicycle. One year before, they would have an aggregate $900, but none of them would be able to buy a bicycle. That seems like a real waste to me. Is there a better arrangement? Well, maybe there is. Suppose the 10 families made an agreement. Each year the 10 families would meet in the village center perhaps sharing supper first, but certainly bringing with them the $10 they had saved in the past year. The families, perhaps, would draw lots, and the winning family would receive $100 to buy a bicycle, $10 from each of the 10 families.

After 1 year, one family would have a bicycle. After the second year, a second family would have their bicycle, and so forth and so on. Only one family out of the 10 would have to wait the full 10 years to buy a bicycle. Now, other ways to decide the order in which families obtained their bicycles would be possible. Perhaps the families would bid for the right to go next or perhaps there would be some sort of meritocracy where the village headman would say, ah, you have made an important contribution. You get to go next. Not important now. The important thing is that the accumulated saving of the 10 families would be put to work every single year. This is something they could do together and something they could not do family by family.

The cooperative arrangement seems clearly superior to the go-it-alone arrangement described at the outset where everyone waits. But will it work? One potential flaw is that the families who have already gotten a bicycle have an incentive to stop making their $10 annual contribution. That is important because if any family doubts that other families will continue to make payments, they may reach the conclusion that the cooperative arrangement is very risky and never participate. They would prefer to go-it-alone.

Can we solve this problem? What sort of mechanism could ensure that families would follow through, keep their promise, and make their payments every year, even though they already had gotten their bicycle? Well, there are lots of possibilities. One possibility would be that the village headman would ostracize any family that broke the commitment. A second possibility is that each family would agree in advance to forfeit the bicycle if they failed to make their promised payments. Other solutions are possible, and you can think of them, but it is clear that some enforcement mechanism would be necessary.

Sticking with this theme of cooperative financial arrangements of a nonstandard sort, let me point out that the benefits from providing even small loans to individuals are potentially very large, and institutions that embody the spirit of cooperation have sprung up to fulfill this potential. As the parable suggests, there are many situations in which every member of the group could benefit from a coordinated arrangement to save funds and lend them out to group members.

The story also underscores another important theme. There are many groups of individuals who, for a variety of reasons, do not have access to traditional lending institutions. Throughout the course of history, individuals who wanted to borrow but were unable to secure loans from banks and other standard lending institutions sought alternatives. I am going to ask you next time you drive through your city to keep your eyes open and think differently about something you may see, the pawn shop.

Pawnshops are very, very old institutions that have traditionally provided credit to those who could not obtain it from banks. How does a pawn arrangement work? Well to obtain credit from a pawnshop, the would-be borrower would bring some physical object to the shop such as a musical instrument, a piece of jewelry, a tool. In the southwest of the United States, Native Americans traditionally bring hand-made jewelry. The shop owner, the pawnshop owner, would lend the borrower an amount less than the estimated value of the object offered in pawn and retain the object as collateral. If the borrower paid back what was owed, the borrower would get the item back. If not, the pawnshop owner would sell the item to recoup the amount of the loan, and then we might have an opportunity to buy it as old pawn.

It follows that one mechanism for providing credit to an otherwise underserved population are these nonstandard arrangements popularly talked about as Rotated Saving and Credit Associations or ROSCA. There are lots of examples through history and across places of ROSCAs, including *tontine* in the Cameroon, and *tanda* in Mexico. These arrangements are alike in most respects. They are cooperative arrangements where people gather together and pool their savings. The way *tontines* are different from *tanda* and other ROSCAs are that the enforcement mechanism is different.

Two important issues faced by a ROSCA are how to determine the order in which participants receive funds and how to ensure individuals fulfill their promises to make contributions to the ROSCA. Many ROSCAs use lotteries to determine who will next receive the funds, and they use social consequences to enforce the contract.

Now I would like to turn to a far more organized nonstandard financial arrangement and tell you yet one more story. In 1976, Professor Muhammad Yunus, Head of the Rural Economics Program at the University of Chittagong, launched a project to examine the possibility of designing a credit delivery system to provide banking and lending services targeted to rural poor. Now you may know that Yunus won the Nobel Peace Prize for his activity in 2006. The result of Yunus's initiative is today called the Grameen Bank, and Grameen means "rural" or "village" in Bangla language.

The classic Grameen Bank model relies on group lending. Grameen clients are too poor to offer collateral but tend to have close ties to a community. So Grameen borrowers must first form groups whose members monitor and support one another, help one another to fulfill their repayment obligations. Groups number 5, and 2 members of the group can receive a loan at any one time. If a group defaults and does not repay what it borrows, every member of the group is barred from receiving future loans.

Yunus realized that the marginal value, the marginal productivity of the investment that was made possible by a very small loan to 4 people was very high. Borrowers, he believed, could repay because the loans, although small, led to very profitable investments, very valuable productive investments. Another enforcement mechanism used by the Grameen Bank model is progressive lending. What does that mean? Well, progressive lending makes available larger and larger loans to groups of individuals who have successfully paid back earlier smaller loans. Why is it an incentive? Well, someone who receives a small loan uses it and repays it finds him or herself in the position where their group can now seek bigger loans and undertake bigger profits.

The Grameen model has been hugely successful. For example, in Bangladesh alone, the Grameen Bank grew from nothing to one million members by 1991 and to 7.5 million members by June of 2008. Recently, the Grameen Bank has come under scrutiny from a variety of government agencies. Some critics question whether microfinance does have the beneficial impact on poverty that the bank claims. Other critics, especially those in government, are simply threatened by the growth of the bank and the power of Yunus himself. Still other critics claim that micro-finance arrangements are wrong because they charge high interest rates to their clients.

What we have learned here is that financial arrangements are not only the business of Wall Street. Citizens of Main Street understand the power of monetary arrangements to coordinate economic activity, and as our examples of local currencies have shown, they at times have themselves created monies to accomplish local economic objectives.

Finance is just not the business of the wealthy. The poor can benefit greatly from the ability to borrow and invest. The micro-finance model uses nontraditional ways to enforce agreements to repay and have proved successful arrangements throughout the world. Groups of individuals have sought ways to coordinate their economic activity that frequently transcends traditional models of money and banking. Local currencies and microfinance arrangements are 2 types of institutions that thrive even amidst a multitude of highly financed traditional institutions.

Thank you.

How Inflation Erodes the Value of Money
Lecture 6

Inflation is a lot like a snake: You know you're afraid of it but aren't quite sure why. Like snakes, some inflation is benign, some is poisonous, and it's important to know the difference. In this lecture, you'll learn that it is rational to fear high rates of inflation and volatile inflation histories, because high inflation rates erode the value of money and volatility makes planning for the future difficult. You begin by looking at the inflation history of the United States over the last 100 years. Then, you learn precisely what inflation is, investigate the connection between money growth and inflation, and discuss the reasons that inflation is costly.

The History of Inflation in the United States

- In the post-World War II period, the United States has had decades when inflation was very high and volatile and decades when it was low and steady.

- In the high-inflation decades, individuals spent substantial time and energy devising strategies that would protect them from unforeseen increases in inflation. For example, they bought larger houses than they otherwise would, reckoning that house prices would keep up with inflation.

- In low-inflation decades, individuals saved that time and energy and planned for the future as if the inflation rate would remain steadily between 1–3%.

- Before the end of World War I, there were large swings in the inflation rate—a high in 1920 of 24% and a low in 1921 of nearly −16%. Such an enormous change played havoc with many business and household decisions.

Figure 6.1

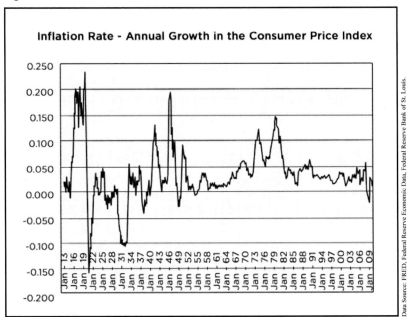

Graph of the inflation rate for the U.S. economy between 1913 and 2010 that shows our inflation experience has varied greatly.

- During World War II, when wage and price controls were in effect, and immediately after the war, inflation again varied greatly, swinging from about 13% in May 1942, to 0% in May 1944, to 18% in May 1947.

- After the 1940s, it appeared that inflation was under control. The inflation rate fell below 5% by the end of 1951 and stayed low for more than a decade. It rose gradually and was once more high and variable between 1970 and 1984.

- When the Volcker regime took hold at the Federal Reserve, inflation once more fell and fell quickly. Since 1985, the inflation rate has largely been captured between the band of 2–5%.

- Economists refer to the period since 1985 as the "Great Moderation" and the "Conquering of U.S. Inflation," but it never pays to assume that an enemy like inflation is vanquished forever.

The Consumer Price Index (CPI)
- **Inflation** is a persistent increase in the general level of prices. The **Consumer Price Index** (CPI) is an index of prices of goods and services (a bushel basket of goods) purchased by the typical household in the United States.

- The fact that the CPI is an index means that the bushel basket prices in each month are each divided by the bushel basket price in the base year, which is currently 1983. In the base period, the CPI is 100.

- The items in the bushel basket are determined by a survey of consumer purchasing behavior conducted by the Bureau of Labor Statistics. The contents of the basket change slowly, so that changes in the CPI are more attributable to changes in the prices of items already in the basket than to changes in the items themselves.

- The CPI is not truly a cost-of-living index. If the CPI grows by, say, 5% in a given year, the cost of living grows by a smaller percentage because savvy consumers will substitute away from items that have experienced high price increases and toward items that have experienced smaller price increases.

Computing the Inflation Rate
- Inflation is defined as the rate of growth in a price index, and there are many ways to compute an inflation rate. We can choose a different price index, a different period over which to measure changes in the chosen index, or perhaps, a different formula for computing the growth rate.

- The data presented at the beginning of the lecture used the CPI for all urban consumers and defined the inflation rate as the percentage change in the current month's index compared with the index 12 months earlier. By defining the inflation rate as the percentage change in the CPI over a 12-month period, we create a measure of the inflation rate that is less sensitive to temporary price changes.

- Note that a one-time price increase in an important commodity, such as oil, cannot cause inflation. Such an increase will cause the CPI to increase over a year or more as the increase in oil prices is incorporated into more of the items in the bushel basket.

- The OPEC price increases in the 1970s cannot explain the persistent differences in inflation rates observed in the data since that time. The OPEC cartel was able to raise the price of oil relative to other goods in the 1970s, but it was not able to continue to raise the relative price of oil as the years and decades passed.

"A Monetary Phenomenon"

- The well-known economist Milton Friedman said, "Inflation is always and everywhere a monetary phenomenon in the sense that it is and can be produced only by a more rapid increase in the quantity of money than in output."

- What Friedman meant is that growth in the money supply is both necessary and sufficient to explain inflation, but not all growth in the quantity of money causes inflation. Growth in money at a rate that just keeps pace with the growth in real output will not cause inflation, but growth in money in excess of the growth in real output will cause inflation.

- Two charts showing money growth rates and inflation rates for 79 countries for 2 different 5-year periods reveal a virtually 1:1 relationship between these 2 measures. Each 1% increase in excess money growth leads to a 1% increase in inflation (see Figure 6.2).

Figure 6.2

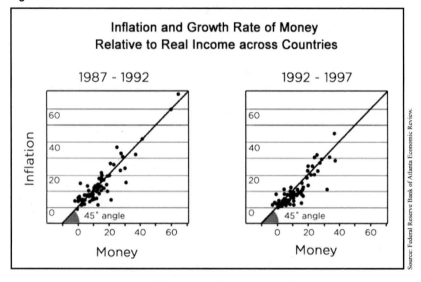

Source: Federal Reserve Bank of Atlanta Economic Review.

- The data strongly support Friedman's claim that inflation is always and everywhere a monetary phenomenon. Countries with high excess money growth have high inflation rates. Countries with low excess money growth have low inflation rates. Put another way, excess money growth of $n\%$ causes an inflation rate of $n\%$.

- Friedman explains the connection between money growth and inflation as follows: An increase in the growth rate of money puts additional purchasing power in the hands of potential spenders. For example, if the government increases defense spending, defense contractors and those who work for them will receive additional money. When they spend that money, they bid up prices on a wide variety of goods; thus, most prices increase and inflation results.

- Note that for this mechanism to work, the economy must be at full employment. If not, the increase in money could lead to higher employment without inflation or higher rates of output growth rather than higher rates of price growth.

The Costs of High and Variable Inflation

- High and variable inflation tend to occur together. Our original graph shows that bigger swings in the inflation rate occur when inflation is high (pre-World War II) than when it is low (post-1985).

- High and variable inflation makes it difficult for individuals to plan for the future, such as for retirement or a child's college education.

- Hedging inflation risk is costly in the sense that decision makers do things that they would not do if they could be sure that inflation would remain low and steady. In the 1960s, for example, young home buyers were often advised to buy as much house as they could afford because a house was considered a good inflation hedge.

- Individuals hold less money when they fear inflation. Money is a useful economic tool that facilitates trade, yet it loses value when inflation occurs. When inflation is high, people keep money holdings low and use other strategies for making transactions.

The Benefits of Low and Steady Inflation

- When inflation is low and steady, it is easier to plan for the future and to have confidence that our financial arrangements will work out as we planned. We also spend less of our resources hedging the risks associated with **volatile inflation** and use more of that wonderful invention, money.

- As we've seen, if inflation is high and variable, it is difficult to plan for the future, and we tend to invest more of our wealth in riskier assets in the hope that they will provide us some protection against inflation. We buy more house in the hope that house price gains will offset decreases in the value of our bonds and savings accounts. When inflation is high and variable, we also use less of that wonderful invention, money.

Consumer Price Index (CPI): An index of prices of goods and services (a bushel basket of goods) purchased by the typical household in the United States.

inflation: Persistent increase in the general level of prices.

volatile inflation: Inflation that oscillates between low and high rates.

Suggested Reading

Dwyer and Hafer, "Are Money Growth and Inflation Still Related?"

Friedman, *Money Mischief.*

Mishkin, *The Economics of Money, Banking, and Financial Markets.*

Questions to Consider

1. Given your current economic situation, would you be better off if the inflation rate suddenly increased to 10%? Why or why not?

2. Why is there a high positive correlation between the growth rate of a nation's money supply and the inflation rate experienced by the nation?

3. Of the reasons given in the lecture that inflation is costly, which is most important?

Lecture 6: How Inflation Erodes the Value of Money

How Inflation Erodes the Value of Money
Lecture 6—Transcript

Inflation is a lot like a snake. We know we are afraid, but we are not quite sure why. Naturalists explain that you can identify most poisonous snakes in the United States by the triangular shape of their heads. But who wants to get that close? Inflation is somewhat the same. Some inflation is benign. Some is poisonous, and it is really important to know the difference. In this lecture, we will learn that it is rational to fear high rates of inflation and, in particular, volatile inflation histories, when the inflation rate swings between high and low values. Why? High rates of inflation erode the value of money.

Farmers who store their grains in silos know that rot will claim some of their grain every month. Inflation is like rot. It erodes the value of our money by lowering the amount of goods, we can buy with it. Inflation is bad enough. Volatile inflation, inflation that oscillates between low and high rates, is even worse. Why? Volatile inflation makes planning for the future very difficult. We begin today's lecture with a report card of sorts, a look at the inflation history of the United States over the last 100 years. That history shows that there have been several periods where inflation caused real problems for U.S. decision makers. These are periods where economists and history and probably you too, give monetary authorities low marks, but there also periods from which we must learn.

We must learn in order to understand better how to control inflation in the future. After looking at some history, we zero in and ask precisely what inflation is, and we investigate the connection between money growth and inflation, and finally, we ask in some detail why economists say that inflation is costly.

In the post WWII period, the United States had decades when inflation was very high and very volatile and decades when inflation was low and steady. In the high-inflation decades, individuals spent substantial time and energy devising strategies that would protect them from unforeseen increases in inflation. For example, and I will talk about this more later, they bought larger houses than they otherwise would have, hoping that house prices would keep up with inflation. In low-inflation decades, individuals saved that time and that energy and planned for the future as if the inflation rate would remain steadily between 1 and 3%. When it did so, their decision to not use precious time and energy to hedge the risks of inflation was warranted.

The graph shows the inflation rate for the U.S. economy between 1913 and 2010. What does it show? It shows that our inflation experience has varied a lot. Before the beginning of WWII, there were very large swings in the inflation rate, a high in 1920 of 24% and a low in 1921 of nearly −16%. That is an enormous change over a very short period, a swing of 40% over a year or so. You can understand that that wide swing between high and low growth and the price level played havoc with many business and household decisions. During WWII, when wage and price controls were in effect, and immediately after the war, CPI inflation again varied greatly swinging from about 13% in May of 1942 to 0% in May of 1944 and then 18% in May of 1947.

After the 1940s, it appeared that calm had returned to the inflation history, and that inflation was under control. The inflation rate fell below 5% by the end of 1951 and stayed low for over a decade. But inflation had not been conquered. The inflation rate rose gradually in the '60s and was once more high and variable between 1970 and 1985. During that period, the consumer price index inflation rate once more hit a peak of 15% in 1979. When the Volcker regime took hold at the Federal Reserve, inflation once more fell and, in fact, fell quite quickly.

Since 1985, the inflation rate has largely been captured between the band of about 2 and 5%. Economists refer to the period since 1985 as the Great Moderation and some of them talk about it as a period in which U.S. inflation was conquered. But, as we will see in this lecture and later in the course, it never pays to assume that an enemy like inflation is vanquished forever.

So, what is inflation? Inflation is a persistent increase in what I will call the general level of prices. Now, right away, we need a standard for this term general level of prices, and I am going to use the standard, which is best known, known to you certainly. It is the consumer price index. But what is that? The consumer price index is an index of prices of goods and services, purchased by the typical household in the United States. Now it is very, very important for everyone to understand that the consumer price index is not the price of any one item, even an item as important as gasoline or heating oil or natural gas. Instead, the consumer price index is properly thought of as the index of the price of a bushel basket, a bushel basket full of the goods chosen by the typical family of 4 that lives in some city in the United States.

What do I mean when I say that the consumer price index is an index? What does that mean? Well, it means that the bushel basket prices in each month are each divided by the bushel basket price in some base year, and that base year is currently 1983, and we have a consistent agreement to set the value of the consumer price index to 100 in the base year. So, when you see, for example, that the CPI is 180, you know that prices are 1.8 times larger than they were in 1983. What is in the bushel basket? Well, that is determined by you. It is determined by a survey of consumer-purchasing behavior conducted frequently by the Bureau of Labor Statistics of the U.S. Department of Labor.

The items in the bushel basket are changed very, very slowly so that changes in the consumer price index are more due to changes in the prices of the items already in the basket and less due to changes in the items themselves. Now that makes sense. It is supposed to be a measure of prices, so we do not want to confuse things by having changes in composition of the basket, but that does have a downside. For example, it took awhile to get cell phones and cell phone services into the consumer price index. It is important for you to realize that the consumer price index is not truly a cost-of-living index and there is a good reason why, and it is important that we all understand it, but first let's make clear what that means.

If the CPI were to grow say by 5% in a given year, the cost of living would grow by a smaller percentage, 2 or 3% or something smaller. Why? Savvy consumers will move away from the items that have experienced high price increases and toward items that are good substitutes and have experienced smaller price increases. Let's do an example. Suppose there is a frost in Georgia and that greatly increases the price of peaches. I like peaches. You probably like peaches, but if the price of peaches goes very much higher, you and I and consumers in general are likely to substitute nectarines or some other fruit for the peaches that are now very expensive. Point is that the cost of eating fruit will not rise by the same percentage as the cost of eating peaches.

This is important not only to you as you manage your own budgets, but it is also important in a public policy sense. The Social Security Administration uses a different price index to compute cost-of-living increases that feed into increases in social security payments made to recipients and indeed, there is some talk, in political arenas, of further changing that formula to compute cost of living increases in social security payments.

So now we understand what the consumer price index is and it is time to ask exactly what is meant by the rate of inflation. Inflation is defined as the rate of growth in a price index. So the consumer price index is a number. It defines the cost of a bushel basket at a moment in time. The inflation rate explains how that number is growing, how high the growth rate is, how quickly those prices are rising. There are many, many ways to compute an inflation rate. One can choose a different price index, and there are many. One can choose a different period over which to measure changes in the chosen index, and for that matter, one can choose a different formula for computing the growth rate.

Recall that I presented some data to you about the history of inflation in the United States. What formula did I use, and what data did I use? Well, the graph that you saw used the consumer price index for all urban consumers, it defined the inflation rate as a percentage change in the current month's CPI index compared with that index 12 months earlier, so those were annual growth rates. By defining the inflation rate as the percentage change over 12 months, over than 1, 2, or 3 months, I created a measure of inflation that would be less sensitive to very temporary price changes.

I want to clear something up about the relationship between inflation and important prices, such as the price of oil. Let me say with no equivocation, a one-time price increase cannot cause inflation. It will certainly cause the CPI to rise, perhaps for as long as a year, but an increase in the price of oil cannot cause inflation. It will not simply visit itself within 1 month because many goods that we produce use oil, and those prices of those goods will rise as the price of oil is incorporated into them. But an increase in the price of oil, such, for example, as was caused by the OPEC price increases in the 1970s, cannot explain persistent differences in the inflation rates that we have observed in the data that we viewed. The OPEC cartel was able to raise the price of oil relative to other goods in the 1970s. But it was not able to continue to raise the relative price of oil as the years and decades passed. If you would like to convince yourself of that, all you need to do is to create some data of your own where the price of oil is divided by the CPI and then take a look at the graph.

What causes inflation? I have for you one of the most famous quotes in economics. "Inflation is always and everywhere a monetary phenomenon in the sense that it is and can be produced only by a more rapid increase in the quantity of money than in output." These are famous words and they were written by a famous economist, Milton Friedman, a Nobel laureate in economics and perhaps the most famous monetary economist of the 20th century. What Friedman meant is that growth in the money supply is both necessary and sufficient to explain inflation.

Friedman does not mean that all growth in the quantity of money causes inflation. Growth in money at a rate that just keeps pace with the growth in real output, with a growth rate of our economy, will not cause inflation. In fact, that growth in the money supply will facilitate the growth in real production. But Friedman does mean that growth in money in excess of the growth in real output will cause inflation. I have some evidence for you. The following charts show money growth rates and inflation rates for 79 different countries and for 2 different 5-year periods, 1987–1992 and 1992–1997. The data are from the International Monetary Fund, and the results depicted in the chart are similar to results reported by many other authors and economists who have studied cross-country variation in inflation and money growth. Let's begin by zooming in on the left panel, which covers the period of '87–'92. Along the horizontal axis is measured the excess growth in the money supply. That is Friedman's concept. And here access growth in money means the difference between the money growth rate and the growth rate in real income in the country. Along the vertical axis, is measured the inflation rate. Each point on the graph represents the 5-year inflation and money growth record of 1 of the 79 countries included in the study. So, if you could count the dots, there would be 79. The graph shows that there was a tremendous amount of variation in the inflation and money growth experience measured across the 79 countries. Most countries experienced inflation rates of say less than 10%, but some had inflation rates greater than 10%, some greater than 20%, and a few greater than 50%. The graph has a line, and that is the best-fit line, the line that fits the points better than any other line. When you look at that line, you notice that it appears to have a slope of about 1. What does that mean? Well, that means simply that every 1% increase in excess money growth is associated with a 1% increase in inflation. This is what Friedman meant: higher money growth, higher inflation and at about a 1-to-1 rate.

Now let's look at the right panel. Everything in the right panel is the same as in the left panel except that a different 5-year period, remember it is '92–'97 is used to gauge the money growth and inflation experience of the 79 countries. What one notices right away is that the best-fit line for the right panel looks identical to the best-fit line of the left panel. That was not arbitrary. The data say that it is identical. So, looking across countries, we see the same positive, virtually 1-to-1 relationship between money growth and inflation in '92 through '97 and in 1987 through 1992. The data positively and strongly support Milton Friedman's claim that inflation is always and everywhere a monetary phenomenon. Countries with high excess money growth have high inflations. Countries with low excess money growth have low inflation rates. Put another way, excess money growth of any percentage rate you want, call it n, is going to cause n% inflation.

But why? Why does money growth in excess of the rate of growth of a nation's productivity, cause inflation? Now, economists have lots and lots of models and lots and lots of explanations explaining why, but let's keep things simple. Let's focus on the explanation that Milton Friedman himself provided. What did Friedman say? Well, Friedman said that an increase in the growth rate of money puts additional buying power in the hands of potential spenders. For example, if the increase in money growth resulted from a decision by a government to buy additional defense-related products, defense contractors and those who work for them would receive additional money.

When the defense contractors and their employees spend the additional money that they have received, they bid up the prices of the goods, they buy. Since they buy a wide variety of goods and services, most prices rise and inflation results. For that mechanism, the mechanism that Friedman has in mind, to work as he says it does, an economy must be nearly fully employed. That means all of its resources must be put to use. If not, the increase in money could lead to higher employment without inflation because as people spend the new money they get, they could just call unemployed resources back to work. Friedman's rule 1-to-1 between excess money growth and inflation is meant to be a statement about an economy that is operating at its potential.

So, it is important now having explained what a price index is, having explained what inflation is, and having explained the connection between money growth and inflation, to explain something else and to explain it very, very clearly and convincingly. Why do I and most economists argue that high and variable inflation is very costly to the members of a society? It is important to note that high and variable inflation tend to come together. The original graph showed you that bigger swings in the inflation rate occurred when inflation was high on average than in post 1985 when it was low.

So what? Well, high and variable inflation, and this is very important, makes it difficult for individuals to plan for their future. Knowing how much one needs for retirement, for example, requires one to predict prices, my goodness, 30 years in advance. Imagine how hard that is. Imagine that you had planned for 2% inflation and then after 20 years of saving, you suddenly entered a period where you believe that inflation would grow during your retirement years at 5% per year. The dollars you had saved might simply be too few, and you may have, without deciding to, chosen for yourself a retirement income that wasn't as large to support a lifestyle that you had wished.

Another example, knowing how much to save for college requires one to predict college tuitions when a child is still very young. That is a difficult problem. Not only because inflation tends to drive up college tuitions, but also because college tuitions can grow more or less rapidly than general prices. Hedging inflation risk is costly in the sense that decision makers do things that they would not do if they could be sure, if they could be guaranteed, that inflation would remain low and steady, and I want to elaborate on an example.

In the 1960s, it was common advice to young homebuyers that they should buy as much house as they could afford, and maybe more, because a house was considered a good inflation hedge. Many companies would hold larger inventories of raw materials than they actually needed in order to hedge against the risk that those materials would grow in price. In addition, individuals hold less money when they fear inflation. Now, money, as I have argued several times already, is a very useful economic tool. It facilitates trade, but money loses value when inflation occurs and people fearing inflation may actually hold less money than they would if they were guaranteed that the inflation rate would be low. It follows that people use other strategies for transactions. Some economists describe these other strategies when they say that inflation leads people to bear shoe leather costs because it leads them to make more trips to the bank to move money between interest-bearing accounts and non-interest bearing accounts. That metaphor rings a little hollow in today's world because we do a lot of our banking electronically. But the basic point is still valid, although the shoe leather metaphor may not be. It takes time and effort to sweep out our non-interest-paying accounts. We need to do that less often when inflation is low, and more often when it is not and doing so costs resources.

As we near the end of today's lecture, let's reflect for a moment on why all of us are better off when the inflation rate is low and steady even though, as we will see later, there are some times when it makes sense to bear the risk of higher inflation. If inflation is low and steady, it is easier to plan for the future and have confidence that our financial arrangements will work out as we planned. We spend less of our resources hedging the risks associated with volatile inflation. We live, for example, in houses of a size justified by our desires rather than by our fears. We use more of that wonderful invention money.

On the other hand, if inflation is high and variable, it is very difficult to know how much to save for retirement, how much to save for college tuition, and so forth. If inflation is high and variable, we will invest more of our wealth in riskier assets in the hope that they will provide us some protection against inflation. We buy more house in the hope that house prices gain in value and offset the effects of inflation. We may buy more stocks and bonds than we are comfortable with. We use less of that wonderful invention money.

In the next lecture, we will study inflation in extreme situations and will learn just how damaging high inflation can be. In other lectures, we will study in greater detail the relationship between inflation and interest rates, and we will understand how and why our Federal Reserve treats as its most important job maintaining the inflation rate at a steady 2%.

Thank you.

Hyperinflation Is the Repudiation of Money
Lecture 7

H yperinflation is the ultimate repudiation by a government of its money. . When hyperinflation occurs, prices rise to such high levels that the outstanding stock of money issued by the government in earlier times will buy virtually nothing. Happily, the United States has never experienced a hyperinflation, but in this lecture, you'll see why our large national debt is a temptation to U.S. monetary and fiscal authorities to allow a massive inflation or, perhaps, even to cause one.

What Is Hyperinflation?

- Inflation is a sustained increase in the general level of prices. A one-time increase in oil prices, even a large one, is not, in and of itself, inflation. Inflation occurs when most items in a price index increase over time. The rate at which they increase is called the **inflation rate**.

- As we have seen, inflation is the modern-day counterpart of the ancient practice of seigniorage, whereby the monarch of a land would shave the coins he received in payment and use the shavings to mint new coins. The result is a decline in the value of the money held by private citizens—in effect, a transfer of wealth from citizens to the monarch.

- The term "**hyperinflation**" is used to describe episodes during which the monthly inflation rate exceeds 50%. At that rate, an item that cost $1.00 on January 1 of one year would cost $130.00 on the same day in the following year!

The Cause of Hyperinflation

- The ultimate cause of hyperinflation is a government's decision to finance large deficits by creating new money. The most well known instance of hyperinflation in the 20th century occurred in Germany between 1921–1923.

- On average, between August 1922 and November 1923, prices in Germany rose at a monthly rate of 322%. In the last days of German hyperinflation, the inflation rate was much higher—41% per day in October 1923.

- During the hyperinflation, the German government increased the money supply at an average rate of 314% per month. Why?

- As a result of the treaty ending World War I, Germany ceded equipment and territory and was required to pay substantial reparations. The treaty specified that the reparations must be paid in gold, which placed a great strain on Germany because its gold stocks were depleted and its export sector was operating at a very low level.

- The situation worsened in January 1923, when the French occupied the Ruhr Valley because German payments had fallen below treaty-specified levels. With the occupation, Germany lost access to both natural resources and the taxes that derived from their use.

- Germany responded to the occupation with a form of "passive resistance" that included direct payments to German citizens in the Ruhr. It paid its citizens not with gold but with paper money.

- The German government kept printing money to pay for expenditures in excess of those that could be financed by tax revenues. The connection between the high rates of money printing and ever-rising inflation rates was not acknowledged in Germany at the time.

- Of course, economists today see the causal role of money growth in hyperinflation. Once it becomes clear that the government has committed to printing money to finance a substantial deficit, people expect inflation to occur and are reluctant to hold paper money because they fear the loss of value that will result. Paper money is spent as fast as people get it.

- Of course, the increasing inflation rates that result from people bidding up the price of goods cause further damage to government finances and lead to even higher rates of money creation; thus, the hyperinflation spiral is underway.

- The result is a decrease in the ratio of money to prices as individuals rationally decide to hold less wealth in the form of money.

- Notice how causality works in hyperinflation: The belief that prices will increase ever more rapidly causes individuals to act in advance of actual price increases and lower the quantity of money they hold. People purposely lessen their money balances, thereby driving prices up all the more rapidly as they spend the money they have.

The End of Hyperinflation in Germany
- Hyperinflation ended in Germany with monetary reforms that occurred late in 1923. According to economist Thomas Sargent, the end was brought on by 3 simultaneous occurrences: "additional borrowing by the government from the central bank stopped, the government budget swung into balance, and inflation stopped."

- Notice how Sargent links the ends of hyperinflation to a change in government spending and borrowing. How can we square Sargent's view with Friedman's claim that inflation is "always and everywhere a monetary phenomenon"?

- Sargent points out that the root cause of hyperinflation is a government's decision to spend amounts far in excess of what tax revenues permit. In Germany, the government made direct payments to citizens as part of its "passive resistance" to the French occupation of the Ruhr.

- The government begins by borrowing funds through the issuance of bonds. Money growth occurs when the central bank buys the government bonds—perhaps in an attempt to keep their prices from falling and their yields from rising.

- Fiscal reform is necessary to end hyperinflation because without it, the government will continue to borrow and the central bank will have a strong incentive to continue to buy government bonds.

Other Cases of Hyperinflation
- The German hyperinflation may be the most studied, but it is not the only case of this phenomenon or the most recent. Argentina, Bolivia, Brazil, Chile, Peru, and Uruguay each experienced hyperinflations between 1970 and 1987.

- During hyperinflations in these Latin American countries, dollarization occurred as citizens used U.S. dollars in an attempt to avoid the loss of wealth inherent in holding their own currencies.

- The Bolivian hyperinflation is an interesting case that further illustrates Sargent's point. In 1982, Hernan Siles Zuazo took power as head of a leftist coalition that wanted to satisfy demands for more government spending on domestic programs but faced growing debt-service obligations and falling prices for the country's tin exports.

- The Bolivian government responded by issuing bonds that were purchased by the central bank of Bolivia. In effect, the Bolivian government (its treasury and its central bank together) printed money to finance the Siles-Suazo regime expenditures.

- Faced with a shortage of funds, the Bolivian government raised revenue through the inflation tax instead of raising income taxes or reducing other government spending.

- One of the reasons that dollars are held throughout the world is that citizens of many nations consider the dollar to be a more dependable store of value than the currency of their own nations. When citizens of other nations hold dollars, the United States collects a modest amount of seigniorage from them (an amount approximately equal to the rate of return on U.S. Treasury bills) because holding dollars is equivalent to making the U.S. government an interest-free loan.

Individuals around the world willingly pay that tax to avoid the risk of loss by holding their domestic currency.

- Although the German hyperinflation is better known, the current hyperinflation in Zimbabwe is actually worse. Between January 2007 and November 2008, Zimbabwe experienced an average monthly inflation of 1124%.

- Hyperinflation numbers are so staggering that reporting them presents a challenge. The danger is "zero dazzle" because there are so many zeros necessary to report, say, the monthly rate of inflation in a hyperinflation country. Another approach is to report the time necessary for prices to double.

The Damage and Temptation of Hyperinflation

- Hyperinflation destroys wealth that is held in the form of money or in any asset with a value fixed in terms of the depreciating currency.

- Hyperinflation destroys the efficiency that results from the social contract inherent in the use of paper money. In Germany, it reduced most people to barter.

- It also creates tremendous psychological costs as individuals worry about an uncertain future.

- Finally, hyperinflation allows a government to collect revenues outside of the political process.

- Perhaps some of the citizens and politicians in the United States who are currently worried about our federal deficits and our accumulated national debt see our debt as a temptation to create inflation in this country. Such a move would be a repudiation not only of our debt but also of the dollar.

Hyperinflation: Episodes during which the monthly inflation rate exceeds 50%.

inflation rate: The rate at which the price index increases over time.

Cardoso, "Hyperinflation in Latin America."

Hanke and Kwok, "On the Measurement of Zimbabwe's Hyperinflation."

Salemi, "Hyperinflation."

Sargent, "The Ends of Four Big Inflations."

1. Why would a nation ever allow a hyperinflation?

2. What is the connection between the end of a hyperinflation and a credible commitment by government to end deficit spending?

3. We have worried a great deal in recent history about our large government deficits. Is a hyperinflation in the United States a possibility?

Lecture 7: Hyperinflation Is the Repudiation of Money

Hyperinflation Is the Repudiation of Money
Lecture 7—Transcript

Hyperinflation is the ultimate repudiation by a government of its money. These are powerful words but they are literally true. If the inflation rate increases to a high enough level, the real cost to a nation's government of redeeming its money in terms of goods and services is nothing. What exactly does that mean? When hyperinflation occurs, prices rise to such levels that the outstanding stock of money issued by the government in earlier times will buy virtually nothing. We have all seen cartoons where someone flaunts his or her wealth by using a $100 bill to light his cigar. The idea of burning money is so shocking that we laugh in surprise, but the world has experienced inflations of such a magnitude that citizens came to realize that their best use of their currency was to burn it as fuel.

Prices in those economies had risen to such levels that a stack of currency could produce more heat by burning it than it could by using it to buy wood or coal. Happily the United States has never experienced a hyperinflation. We've experienced periods of high inflation, such as during the Revolutionary War when prices grew so rapidly and paper money lost value so quickly and completely that we gained an entry into the American phrase book, it's not worth a Continental. Remember that the Continental was the paper money of the Revolutionary War period.

Perhaps you would be tempted to discount the value of today's lecture because you believe that a hyperinflation could not happen in the United States. Hold on, please stay tuned. I will explain toward the end of the lecture why our large national debt in the United States is a temptation for us and for our government, for our monetary and for our fiscal authorities to allow a very large inflation and maybe even to cause one. Look, I'm not predicting hyperinflation in the United States, but incentives matter. That's a key tenet of economic belief and it's important as we think of our priorities as citizens to explain to ourselves why a large national debt is an incentive to cause or tolerate a large inflation.

So exactly what is and what isn't a hyperinflation? We know from the previous lecture that inflation is a sustained increase in the general level of prices. We know that a one-time increase in all prices, for example, even if it were large is not in and of itself inflation. Inflation occurs when most items in a price index rise over time, when most items in our consumer's bushel basket have price increases, and the rate of which the price of that bushel basket increases is called "inflation."

We have also seen that inflation is the modern day counterpart of the ancient practice of seigniorage, where the monarch of a land would shave the coins he received in tax payments and use the shavings to mint new coins. The result of seigniorage was a decline in the value of the money held by private citizens, a transfer of wealth from those citizens to the monarch, a tax that that monarch never explicitly declared or imposed.

Most economists believe that job one of the Federal Reserve Bank of the United States is to keep inflation low and predictable thereby preserving the purchasing power of our dollar. Helping you understand the causes and consequences of inflation is an important goal of this course. We study cases of extreme inflation because they're very interesting and because they have a cautionary element to them. They caution everyone to understand just how damaging to society inflation can be.

For the record, the term "hyperinflation" is reserved by economists to described episodes of inflation during which the monthly inflation rate is larger than 50%. I mean that, larger than 50%. So just how much inflation is that? At a monthly inflation rate of 50%, an item that costs $1 on January 1 would cost $130 on January 1 of the following year. That same item would cost $2,184,164 on January 1 the year after that. Yikes. It just couldn't happen you say. It can, and it has. The ultimate cause in hyperinflation is a government's decision to finance large deficits by creating new money. To fix ideas, let's consider the most studied and best known hyperinflation of the 20th century, that event occurred in Germany between 1921 and 1923.

On average between August of 1922 and November of 1923, so 15 months or so, prices in Germany rose at a monthly rate not of 50% [but of] 322%. This means that prices quadrupled each month during the 16 months of hyperinflation. Imagine that happening in your life, a pound of chicken that costs $2 at the beginning of May would, if inflation was occurring at the

German hyperinflation rate, cost $8 at the beginning of June. How would you run a household under those conditions? But things were going to get worse. In the last days of the German hyperinflation, the inflation rate went much higher, 41% per day in October of 1923. During the hyperinflation, the German government increased the supply of money by fantastic amounts at an average rate of 314% per month. Clearly, a hyperinflation causes great distress to the people who experience it. It would be bad enough for wage earners who received wage increases that never seem to keep pace with inflation, but it would be devastating for individuals, such as pensioners living on fixed, nominal incomes, incomes fixed in Marx in Germany. Imagine no increase in your income in response to these huge increases in the prices of things.

Why did the German government do this to its people? Well, there's a story. As a result of the treaty that ended World War I, Germany was forced to cede equipment and territory to the victors and was required to pay substantial war reparations in gold to the victorious nations. The fact that the treaty specified payment in gold placed great strain on Germany because its gold stocks were depleted. Germany had used those to prosecute the war and at the end of the war, its export sector was operating at a very, very low level. In short, Germany had little opportunity to gain gold to pay its reparations. The situation went from very bad to very much worse in January of 1923 when the French army occupied the Ruhr Valley because German payments had fallen below levels specified by the end of war treaty. What did Germany do?

After the Ruhr occupation, Germany lost access to both natural resources—gold fields, for example—and the taxes that derive from their use, and Germany responded to that occupation with what they called a passive resistance that included direct payments to German citizens in the Ruhr. It paid its citizens not with gold but with paper money.

The German government kept printing money to pay for expenditures in excess of the expenditures that could be financed by tax revenues. Tax revenues were very, very small relative to expenditures and the difference that the German government financed by printing money. Interestingly, the connection between the high rates of money printing, the high rates of money creation, and ever rising inflation rates was not acknowledged and, in many cases, was not understood in Germany at the time. Karl Helfferich, a prominent German economist of the time, said and I quote, "The increase in the circulation has not preceded the rise of prices and the depreciation of the exchange rate, but it followed slowly and at a great distance. It is not possible that this increase had caused the rise in prices of imported goods and the dollar."

So notice that Helfferich is making a timing argument. He is saying that money growth followed inflation rather than occurred in advance of inflation, and therefore money growth could not have caused inflation. Well, economists today including myself think otherwise about the causal role of money growth and hyperinflation.

Once it becomes clear that government has committed to printing money to finance a substantial deficit, people expect inflation to occur. They're smart after all, and they are reluctant to hold paper money for any period of time because they fear the loss of value that will result from inflation. A game of hot potato commences where individuals spend money as fast as they receive it. In fact in Germany, people would leave their workplaces during the noon hour asking for their morning's pay to rush to the stores to be able to convert that money to the things that they planned to eat for their supper. That's really a game of hot potato.

Of course the increasing inflation rates that resulted from people bidding up the prices of goods caused further damage to government finances and led to even higher rates of money creation. The hyperinflation spiral is underway. Money creation, rising inflation, even higher rates of money creation, still higher inflation. Well what results then is a decrease in the ratio of money to prices as individuals rationally decide to hold less wealth in the form of money. Think about that for a minute. They are lowering their desired levels of money holding even faster than prices are rising because they don't want to expose their wealth to the perils of future inflation. The money growth is causing inflation. Individuals are responding rationally by lowering the amount of money they use. Notice then how causality works in hyperinflation.

The people's belief that prices will rise ever more rapidly causes them to act in advance of the actual price increases and lower the quantity of money they hold. People purposely lessen their money balances thereby driving prices up all the more rapidly as they spend the money they have. To those who do not understand the process, like Karl Helfferich, it would appear that inflation was causing the growth in money because the timing indicated that, but in fact, the opposite was and is true. Current and anticipated future rapid growth in the money supply causes hyperinflation.

When and why did the hyperinflation in Germany end? According to Thomas Sergeant, the German hyperinflation ended with a monetary reform that occurred late in 1923, but Sergeant doesn't attribute the end of the hyperinflation solely to the monetary reform. He argues that 3 important things happened abruptly and simultaneously. "Additional borrowing by the government from the central banks stopped. The government budgets swung into balance and inflation stopped." Notice how Sergeant links the end of hyperinflation to a change in government spending and borrowing. Now how can we square Sergeant's view with Friedman's claim that inflation is always and everywhere a monetary phenomenon? Well Sergeant points out that the root cause of hyperinflation, the root cause, is a government's decision to spend amounts far in excess of what tax revenues permit. In Germany, the government made direct payments to citizens as part of its passive resistance of the French occupation of the Ruhr.

The government begins by borrowing funds through the issuance of bonds. Money growth occurs when the central bank buys the government bonds that the Treasury has issued, perhaps in an attempt to keep their prices from falling and their yields from rising. Fiscal reform is necessary, according to Sergeant, to end a hyperinflation because without it, everyone in the nation knows that the government will continue to borrow and the central bank will have a very strong incentive to buy the bonds issued by the government, that is to create the money of which Friedman speaks.

In a nutshell, Sergeant's view is simple. A nation cannot end a hyperinflation unless it tackles the root cause that led to the hyperinflation. So we are now in a better position to understand the behavior of those Germans who could produce a fire in their stoves more cheaply by burning money than by using the money to buy coal or wood.

The German hyperinflation had devastating effects on the German people. The German middle class was largely wiped out because they were unable to, by law, raise rents of the properties they owned fast enough to compensate for rising prices. The middle class owned apartments, and the value of those apartments fell as rents were not allowed to rise. On the other hand, companies that owned large stores of commodities improved their lot during the hyperinflation. You know the name of one of those companies. It was the Krupp family. Some historians go so far as to argue that the hyperinflation in Germany that raged until 1923 actually contributed to the rise of national socialism in Germany.

The German hyperinflation may be the most studied but it's not alone. And it's not the most recent. As we will see, it's not even the champion inflation producer. Argentina, Bolivia, Brazil, Chile, Peru, and Uruguay each experienced the hyperinflation between 1970 and 1987. During the hyperinflations in these Latin American countries, dollarization occurred as citizens used U.S. dollars in an attempt to avoid the loss of wealth in holding their own currencies. I myself experienced dollarization when I visited Kiev about 10 years ago in Ukraine. I could buy things as easily with U.S. dollars as I could with the local currency. Even local craftspeople who offered their handicrafts were willing to accept dollars and knew the prices they wanted to charge in dollars.

Among the Latin American inflations, the Bolivian hyperinflation is an interesting case that further illustrates what Thomas Sergeant had in mind. In 1982, Hernán Siles Zuazo took power as head of a leftist coalition that wanted to satisfy demands for more government spending on domestic programs but faced growing debt service obligations and falling prices for tin, an important export. The Bolivian government responded by issuing bonds that were purchased by the Central Bank of Bolivia. In effect, the Bolivian government, its Treasury and its Central Bank together, printed money to finance the regime expenditures. Faced with a shortage of funds, the Bolivian government raised revenue through an inflation tax instead of raising income taxes or reducing other government spending.

One of the reasons that dollars are held throughout the world is that citizens of many nations consider the dollar to be a more dependable store of value than the currency in their own nations. "U.S. currency is recognized as a symbol of stability and integrity around the world." That quote is from Michael Merritt, deputy assistant director of the U.S. Secret Service. It's not widely known that the Secret Service not only protects the president but also protects our currency from counterfeiters. The report, produced by the Treasury Department in which that quote appears, estimated that about $450 billion of the $760 billion U.S. dollars in circulation as of December 2005 is held abroad by citizens of a foreign nation. When citizens of other nations hold dollars, the U.S. collects a modest amount of seigniorage of them, approximately equal to the rate of return on U.S. Treasury bills because holding dollars is equivalent to making the U.S. government an interest-free loan. The stable value of our currency has real advantages for us. It's something worth protecting.

The rest of the world citizens willingly pay that tax in order to avoid the risk of losing much more by holding their domestic currency. They hedge their risks by holding the U.S. dollar. Again, while the German hyperinflation is better known than others, the current hyperinflation in Zimbabwe is actually much worse. Steve Hanke of Johns Hopkins University and the Kato Institute reports that between January of 2007 and November of 2008, Zimbabwe experienced an astounding average monthly inflation of 1124%. That is, prices rose by 11-fold every month on average. The highest monthly inflation rate during the period occurred, not surprisingly, in the final month and amounted to a daily inflation rate of just under 100%.

As a byproduct of his work, Hanke has created his own rogues gallery of hyperinflations that have occurred since 1923, the year of the famous German hyperinflation that we already talked about. Hyperinflation numbers are so staggering that we're reporting on them and the numbers that describe them present a very big challenge. I like to think of that challenge as zero dazzle because you have to add so many 0s before the decimal point in order to capture accurately the monetary increases and the increases in prices. But Hanke has developed an interesting table where he provides a different way to compare hyperinflations. Hanke reports the amount of time necessary for prices to double in several famous hyperinflations.

By Hanke's measure, Germany only ranks fourth among the hyperinflations. Zimbabwe ranks second. The all-time champion hyperinflation is Hungary where, at its worse, prices doubled every 15.6 hours. It would be frightening to take a nap. For Hungary, the hyperinflation occurred in 1946. Prices doubled in 15.6 hours. In Zimbabwe, in November of 2008, they doubled every day. In Yugoslavia, which experienced a hyperinflation in 1994, in January they doubled every 1.4 days. In Germany, that we've talked a lot about, in October of 1923 they doubled every 3.7 days. In Greece in 1944, 4.5 days, and in China in 1949, every 5.6 days.

Does the government of Zimbabwe understand that it is responsible for hyperinflation? It is hard to doubt that it does although I must say that it denies responsibility. According to the *New York Times*, Mr. Mugabe blames a Western plot for his nation's troubles. By now, however, you are well prepared to discount such self-serving claims.

Before we end this lecture, let's refocus for a minute on why hyperinflation is so damaging. Hyperinflation destroys wealth that is held in the form of money or in any asset with a value fixed in terms of the depreciating currency. Hyperinflation destroys the efficiency that results from the social contract inherent in the use of paper money. In Germany, it reduced most people to barter.

Hyperinflation creates tremendous psychological costs as individuals worry about an uncertain future. Hyperinflation allows government to collect revenues outside the political process. Perhaps some of the citizens and politicians in the United States who worry about our Federal deficits and our accumulated national debt are really worried because our debt is a temptation to create inflation in the United States.

Why would we ever want to create an inflation? To lower the pain of repaying that debt. Inflation in the United States would be a repudiation not only of our dollar but also of our debt. As I said at the outset, hyperinflation is the ultimate repudiation by a government of its money.

Saving—The Source of Funds for Investment
Lecture 8

B eginning in the summer of 2008, General Motors spent billions of dollars retooling its production facilities to manufacture an electric car—the Chevrolet Volt—which was rolled out in the fall of 2010. Some of the money for this venture came from GM's profits, but much of it came from ordinary American citizens. This lecture is about the connection between saving and investment—between decisions made every day by ordinary folks to put aside some of what they earn for future use and decisions by entrepreneurs to create new capital, such as the capital needed to produce an electric car. As you will see, saving makes investment possible. If there were no saving, there would be no investment, no new products, no technological advances in the workplace, and no growth.

A Definition of "Investment"

- When used by an economist, **investment** means the dollar value of increases to a nation's **capital stock**—its factories, equipment, software, and other durable goods used as part of the production process, as well as human capital.

- Many use the term "investment" to describe stocks, bonds, and other financial products that individuals purchase as part of a financial plan. Economists call such activity "**financial investment**" to distinguish it from economic activity that increases the nation's capital stock.

- A simple example explains why it is important to recognize the difference between investment and financial investment: Every day, millions of dollars worth of shares in GM are sold on the New York Stock Exchange; however, the ability of GM to retool its plant to manufacture the Volt is unaffected by these sales.

- Almost all of the sales are Peter-Paul transactions from which GM derives no funds. Still, both Peter and Paul would describe their purchases and sales of GM stock as part of their "investment strategies."

- At the same time, the value of GM shares is certainly important to GM. An increase in share prices indicates market approval of the company's decisions.

- A comparison of investment data for the years 2006 and 2009 shows a significantly lower share of U.S. gross domestic product (GDP) going to investment in the midst of our recession. This lower share was a serious indication of the pessimism with which business decision makers viewed the near-term prospects of the U.S. economy.

Capital Stock and Economic Growth

- A strong relationship exists between a nation's capital stock (which is a cumulative measure of all past investment activity) and economic growth (which makes it possible for each citizen to consume more and higher-quality goods).

- Cross-country data reveal a strong positive relationship between a nation's capital stock and its productivity. Simply put, nations with more capital are more productive; their workers have access to more and better "tools."

What Is Saving?

- **Saving** is the difference between a decision maker's income and consumption. Our economy saves when a household, firm, or government sector consumes less than the income that sector earns.

- Consider the Jones family. In a given year, the family earned after-tax income of $90,000 and spent $85,000 on food, clothing, rent, fuel, and other consumer goods. The Jones family saved $5,000, or 5.5%, of what it earned.

- Perhaps this is not the way you think of saving in your household. You may think about increases in the value of your assets, such as your retirement portfolio, as part of your saving.

- This is a case, however, where a valid point of view for one is not a valid point of view for all. It may be completely rational for you to count your capital gains when you consider your savings plans, but the economy as a whole cannot do that. The economy as a whole has funds for investment only if we save in the traditional way—by spending less than our income.

- Here's another example: Frank's Espresso Bar and Café has yearly after-tax profits of $150,000. Frank has decided to use $50,000 of those profits to purchase new kitchen equipment and the remainder to pay off some of the loans he obtained to start the company. In this situation, Frank is saving $150,000. It does not matter whether the business is using its savings to buy new equipment or to lower debt. Both actions constitute saving.

- Finally, let's look at the city of Whynot, North Carolina. The city has revenues from fees and sales taxes of $1.6 million and expenditures of $1.5 million in its most recent fiscal year. Whynot has decided to add the remaining $100,000 to the city's rainy-day fund. Again, Whynot is saving.

The Relationship of Saving and Investment
- One reason that economists study saving is that for the economy as a whole, saving makes investment possible. The amount of investment spending that an economy can undertake in a given period of time equals the sum of saving by firms, households, and governments in that economy plus any borrowing from the rest of the world.

- Every dollar's worth of goods produced in a nation generates a dollar's worth of income for someone. For the economy as a whole, total income in a year is just sufficient to purchase the goods produced. If every member of the economy spent all income on consumer goods and services, there would be nothing left over for investment.

- The only way that the economy can release resources for the production of investment goods is if consumers, firms, and government entities spend less than their income on consumer goods and services.

- Keep in mind that investment means the purchase of new capital. When households add funds to their 401(k) accounts, they are saving, but the act of adding to a 401(k) account does not in and of itself add productive capital to the economy.

Figure 8.1

Saving and Investment in the U.S.
(Billions of Dollars)

Year	Housholds	Firms	Federal Government	State and Local Government	Total Saving
2007	178.9	316.1	-236.5	21.7	280.2
2009	458.6	423.4	-1226.5	-19.2	-363.7

Year	Foreign Borrowing	Investment
2007	726.8	990.0
2009	428	278.6

Source: Federal Reserve.

Data comparison of 2007 and 2009 to illustrate how savings limits investment.

- Savings rates in the United States have varied significantly in the last 25 years. During the Great Recession, gross saving fell rapidly, reaching a 20-year low of just over 10%.

Figure 8.2

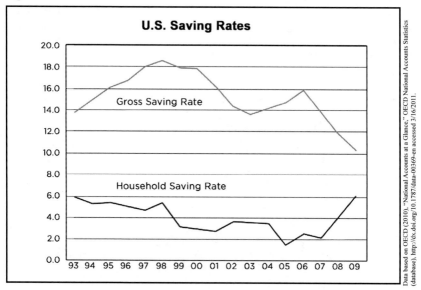

Data based on OECD (2010), "National Accounts at a Glance," OECD National Accounts Statistics (database), http://dx.doi.org/10.1787/data-00369-en accessed 3/16/2011.

Competition for Investment Funds

- Investors compete with households and government entities for funds.

- Federal government deficits use up savings that could be used for investment. Thus, government deficits curtail growth.

- A trade deficit means that the rest of the world allows us to "borrow" their productive capacity by sending to us a volume of goods and services of greater value than the goods and services we send back. In this sense, we are borrowing from foreign nations when we run a trade deficit.

- Foreign borrowing allows investment to be larger than it would have been otherwise. But foreign nations eventually expect to be paid back in goods and services, meaning that we will face a situation of negative foreign borrowing in the future.

- U.S. investment has averaged about 16% of GDP in the years since 1947. It has fallen dramatically during the Great Recession—far more than in other recessions.

Figure 8.3

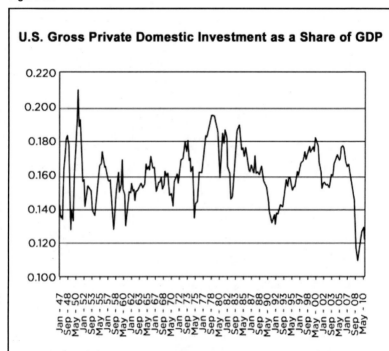

Savings Rates in Developed Countries

- Household savings rates vary a great deal across nations. For example, in 2010, while Belgium had a 12% household savings rate, Denmark's rate was −1.0. This negative rate means that Danish households consumed more than their income, with households borrowing to finance their extra consumption.

- Research suggests that this pattern was a response to a large increase in the price of the typical house in Denmark that occurred after financial markets there were liberalized. Danish households felt richer and spent some of their perceived wealth increase immediately.

- Denmark is not unique in this situation of dis-saving. Changes in the prices of assets held by U.S. households are frequently cited as one explanation for changes in U.S. saving rates.

Figure 8.4

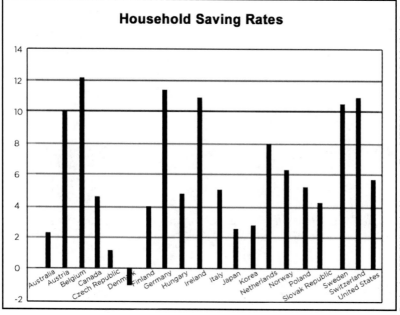

Data based on OECD (2010), "National Accounts at a Glance," OECD National Accounts Statistics (database). http://dx.doi.org/10.1787/data-00369-en accessed 3/16/2011.

- The household saving rate for the United States in 2010 was 5.7%, which was much higher than it had been prior to the Great Recession.

- Low household saving rates in the United States that are reinforced by large government budget deficits imply that our country faces an unpleasant choice: It can either borrow from the rest of the world to engage in investment projects, or it can allow investment to fall as a fraction of GDP, which means that both growth and standards of living in the United States will fall.

- No other alternative is possible because, for a nation, investment must equal the sum of saving by households, saving by businesses, and borrowing from other nations.

The Silver Lining in the Great Recession Cloud
- One legacy of the Great Recession may be that the American household rediscovers the virtues of saving. American consumers had come to believe that growth in the value of their homes provided a dependable source of growth in their wealth, enough growth that saving from their income was not necessary.

- The bursting of the housing bubble in 2007 may have taught American households that to provide for their futures, they must return to traditional forms of saving—setting aside something from every paycheck.

Important Terms

capital stock: The cumulative measure of all past investment activity.

financial investment: Stocks, bonds, and other financial products that individuals purchase as part of a financial plan.

investment: The value of increases to a nation's capital stock, such as its factories, equipment, software, and other durable goods used as part of the production process, as well as human capital.

saving: The difference between a decision maker's income and consumption.

Suggested Reading

Fisher, *The Theory of Interest*.

Mishkin, *The Economics of Money, Banking, and Financial Markets*.

Questions to Consider

1. How much does your household save? How would you go about deciding whether your household saves enough to meet its goals for the future?

2. Many economists believe that the increase in household saving that has occurred during the Great Recession is bad news in the short run and good news in the long run. Why can an increase in saving be both bad news and good?

3. Should the United States create additional tax incentives to promote saving?

Saving—The Source of Funds for Investment
Lecture 8—Transcript

Saving is the source of funds that makes investment possible. You will understand that expression very, very well by the time that this lecture is over. In June 2008, *Car and Driver Magazine* reported that General Motors was undertaking a strategic review of its Hummer brand. The very same article reported that GM had decided to go forward with production of the Chevrolet Volt, GM's plug-in electric car and would begin retooling the Detroit-Hamtramck plant. As events unfolded during the next 2 years, GM ceased production of the Hummer but rolled out the Volt in the fall of 2010. GM spent billions of dollars developing the Volt and retooling its production facilities to manufacture it. Where did all that money come from? Some of it came from GM profits but, you know, a lot of it came from ordinary folks like you and like me.

This lecture is about the connection between saving and investment, between decisions made every day by ordinary folk like you and I to put aside some of what we earn for future use and, on the other hand, decisions by entrepreneurs and managers of firms to create new capital such as the capital needed to produce an electric automobile. Along the way we're going to do what economists often like to do, we're going to take a look at some data that describes saving behavior in the United States and elsewhere. For most of the last 25 years, Americans have saved a very small fraction of their income but there may be a change underway. One of the side effects of the Great Recession and the subprime mortgage crisis has been a change in the saving behavior of American households. U.S. households are saving more now than they have in the past.

An increase in saving is typical during a recession but preliminary evidence suggests that the increased savings rate may continue after the recession ends. At this point, you're naturally asking what's the connection between the Chevy Volt and saving behavior of the American household. Well as we will see, the connection is very, very important and we need to understand it. While I will look at this connection in great detail, let me say at the outset that it's simply fair to say that saving makes investment possible. If there were no saving, there would be no investment, no new products like the Volt, no technological advances in the workplace, and no growth in the U.S. economy or in the productivity of the American worker. That is important to everyone. It is growth in the productivity of the American worker which, over the last 75 years, has allowed our households to raise their standard of living.

While those of us have put aside a few dollars every month for future plans and dreams have our eyes fixed on our own goals, taken together our savings decisions make the Chevy Volt possible. Without us, no Volt. Well the very first thing I need to do is to make very clear what I mean and what I do not mean by the word investment. That's very important both what I mean and what I don't. When used by an economist, investment means the value of increases to the nation's capital stock. What's that? Well a nation's capital stock are its factories, equipment, computers, and other durable goods used as part of the production process. A nation's capital also includes human capital: training, education, and the skills of the nation's workforce.

Many, many, many people use the term investment to describe the purchase of stocks and bonds and other financial products that they purchase as part of a financial plan. I will call those kinds of activities financial investment to distinguish them from the economic activity that increases the nation's capital stock. So I will use the term "investment," plain and simple, only to refer to increases in the nation's capital stock, but I'm going to defend my decision and a simple example helps me get that done because it explains why it's important to recognize the difference between investment and financial investment.

Every day millions of dollars worth of shares in General Motors are sold on the New York Stock Exchange. However, the ability of General Motors to retool its plant at Hamtramck is unaffected by these sales of GM shares. You're surprised. You should be, but the reason is that almost all of those sales are what I call Peter-Paul transactions from which GM derives no funds. Peter sells the share to Paul. Paul sells it to Jan. Jan sells it to Fred. Both Peter and Paul would describe their purchases and sales of GM stock as part of their investment strategy, but GM derives no direct benefit from the sale of those shares from Peter to Paul.

The value of GM shares in the market place is certainly important to General Motors. A rise in share prices indicates market approval of decisions made by General Motors, and that's a good thing for GM, for its managers, and for its workers, but a rise in the price of shares of General Motors does not in and of itself provide GM with the additional dollars that it can use to retool or for any other purpose.

Having defined investment, I naturally want to talk about how large it is. I want to do that by showing you data for 2 very different years, 2006 and 2009. In the first year, the U.S. economy was operating very near full employment. Workers were fully employed. Plants were working at capacity, but in 2009, as we all remember, the story was very, very different because the U.S. was mired in the midst of a serious recession and investment data for these 2 years is very, very different.

Let's think about 2006 first. Investment in 2006 was $2 trillion 327 billion. Gross domestic product, the measure of the total production of the United States, was $13 trillion, just under 400 billion. So as a fraction of GDP, investment was 17.4%, 17.4%. In 2009, investment was only $1 trillion, 589 billion. GDP was slightly higher, $14 trillion, 119 billion. That ratio, the share of investment in our GDP had fallen to 11.3%. Could we make sense of this? Sure.

In 2006, the United States was growing and investment accounted for a little over 17% of every dollar's worth of goods we produced. To explain that just say that every dollar's worth of goods produced in the United States had about 17% dedicated to the creation of new capital. In 2009, on the other hand, because the U.S. was mired in the midst of a serious recession, investment had fallen to only 11.3% of the United States gross domestic product. This lower share of GDP going to investment was a serious indication of pessimism, the pessimism that business decision makers experienced about the near-term prospects of the United States. After all, if you think that the economy will stay in recession you may, as a firm manager, not think it's the right time to invest in new tools and buildings, not the right time to grow your firm.

Why does preoccupation with investment, with growth in the capital stock? Well economists care about investment because they know that investment is an important contributor to economic growth. There's a very strong relationship between a nation's capital stock, which is a cumulative measure of all past investment activity and economic growth, which makes it possible for citizens to consume more in higher goods. If we were to look at data across different countries, we would see a very strong positive relationship between a nation's capital stock and its productivity. Simply put, nations with more capital are more productive. This just makes sense. It means simply that a nation where workers have access to more and better tools is a nation where workers are more productive. That's not surprising.

This is not simply a size effect. It's not simply a result driven by the fact that big economies are different from small economies. The data I have looked at controls for the size of an economy by measuring capital on one hand as a fraction of gross domestic product and productivity on the other hand as output per worker. So I correct for size and nevertheless find this strong, positive relationship between capital and productivity.

The bottom line? The bottom line is that investment and new buildings, new technologies, new equipment, new information makes nations more productive and increases our national growth rate. You should not find this surprising. An economy where the typical worker has more and better tools is an economy where that worker will produce more. Another example, in some economies we know that stevedores unloads cargo vessels by hand. In others, stevedores use winches, pallet trucks, and a variety of other cargo equipment. You're not surprised that the equipment makes a difference and that stevedores who use it move cargo faster. In economic terms, those folks are just more productive. I talked about saving being necessary for investment, and it now falls to me to explain what I mean by savings.

Saving is the difference between some decision makers' income and the decision makers' consumption. Our economy saves when some households, some business, or some sector of government consumes less than the income that that sector earns. Some examples, let's look at households first. The Jones family earned after-tax income let's say of $90,000. In the same year, the Jones's spent $85,000 on food, clothing, rent, fuel, and other consumer goods. We would say, economists would say, that the Jones family saved $5000 or 5.5% of what it earned. Perhaps this is not the way you think of a saving in your household. Why not?

Well, you may think about increase in the value of the assets you own. For example, your retirement portfolio as part of your saving, but this is a case where a valid point of view for one is not a valid point of view for all. It may be completely sensible for you to count your capital gains for the increases in the value of your retirement portfolio when you consider your saving plans, but the economy, as a whole, cannot do that. The economy, as a whole, as we shall see, only has funds for investment if households and other sectors save in the traditional way by spending less than their income. Let's do another example. What would it mean for a business to save? Let's create a business. Frank's Espresso Bar and Café has yearly after-tax profits of $150,000. Frank has decided to use $50,000 of those profits to purchase new kitchen equipment and the remainder to pay off some of the loans he obtained to start the company. Frank's saving is $150,000. It does not matter whether the business is using its saving to buy new capital equipment itself or to lower its debt. Both actions constitute saving. Both actions will lead to investment whether Frank undertakes it or whether someone else does.

Finally, one more example. The City of Why Not, North Carolina—there really is a city called Why Not in North Carolina. We have some great names for cities in the state of North Carolina. The City of Why Not, North Carolina, has revenues from city fees and sales taxes of let's say $1.6 million and expenditures of $1.5 million in its most recent fiscal year. Why Not has decided to add the remaining $100,000 to the town's rainy day fund. Why Not is saving. The town of Why Not is saving and making investment possible.

So with those clarifications and those explanations about what investment is and what savings means, it's now time to think about the connection between saving and investment. One reason that economists try very, very hard to understand the motives that lead various decision makers to save is the simple reason that for the economy as a whole, saving makes investment possible. It would be easy to miss the importance of what I just said. So let me put it a different way. Without saving in an economy, there can be no investment. Without saving, there can be no growth. The amount of investment spending that an economy can undertake in a given period of time equals the sum of saving by firms, households, and governments in that economy plus any borrowing that economy is able to do from other economies in the rest of the world. I've said that several times it's so important but now let me unpack the statement and provide you some intuition.

Every time we produce a dollar's worth of goods in the United States, we generate a dollar's worth of income for someone. For the economy, as a whole, total income in a year is just sufficient to produce all the goods that we produce. If every member of the economy, everyone who received income spent all of the income they received on consumer goods and consumer services, there wouldn't be anything left over. In that kind of a world where no one saved, where everybody spent all of their income on consumer goods, all of GDP would be consumed. Our accounts would change. Our industries would change. We would have nothing but manufacturers of consumer goods.

The only way that our economy can release resources for the production of investment goods is if consumers and firms and government entities spend less than their income on those consumer goods and services. That means that the only way that we can have investment, that we can have plants that focus on the production of investment goods is that if some households, some firms, and some components of government release funds to them, release productive capacity to those plants and firms that produce capital goods.

When households add funds to their 401K accounts, they are saving or, if you like, financially investing but I'm going to say saving. But the act of adding to a 401K account does not in and of itself add productive capital. What it does is release funds for the production of capital. The data show again how this limitation, and by that, I mean how savings limit investment works, and I'm again going to consider data for 2 very different years. Let's think of 2007 first. In 2007, households saved $178.9 billion. Firms saved more, $316 billion. Our federal government, because it was running a deficit even back in 2007, saved –$236.5 billion. So it ate into the total, right? It used up some of the savings by households and firms.

State and local governments ran surpluses and saved but pretty small amounts. The total saving for the United States in that year of 2007, $280.2

billion. What was the investment that year? $990 billion. How did we make that work? In 2007, we borrowed a lot of money from the rest of the world. We borrowed over $725 billion from people outside the United States. 2009, not surprisingly, was a very different year. As I already mentioned, household savings went up. Indeed it more than doubled to $458.6 billion. Not surprising here. Households were feeling that they needed to hedge additional risks, and so they saved. Firms felt the same way and so they increased their saving of $123.4 billion. So you're saying great news, right? We're going to make more investment possible. Maybe that's how we'll get out of this recession. Oops, sorry. The federal government's deficit increased from $236 billion in 2007 to $1 trillion, 226.5 billion in 2009. The federal government more than used up the savings provided by the household and firm sector.

State and local governments, not surprisingly, ran deficits as well but again these were quite small. What was the total amount of saving in the United States? –$363 billion. Whoa, what does that mean? Did we have to eat up our capital to finance that? No. Our investment fell to a very, very small amount, about 1/4 of what it was in 2007 about $278 billion, and we financed the difference by again borrowing from abroad.

In the future, I'm going to talk to you a lot about this borrowing from abroad that we've been doing but today, I'm simply going to set that aside and I'm going to notice here and point out to you for emphasis that investment is limited to the savings we do and funds we can borrow from abroad. I'm going to emphasize that that is true is that investment is the production of something, of capital goods, and we either have to release resources in the United States or borrow those resources from somewhere else in the world in order to build that capital.

These data are from the Federal Reserve funds accounts and if you do the math, if you do the arithmetic, you'll notice that total saving plus foreign powering does not exactly add up to investment. There are statistical discrepancies. These are hard things to measure in a complicated economy like ours. Typically the data are revised so you'd find the discrepancies smaller for 2007 when the data had been revised and larger for 2009 when that revision is not yet complete. Savings rates have varied a lot in the United

States in the last 25 years. Again I'd like to take a look at some data with you. Between 1993 and 2005, the household saving rate in the United States fell until it reached a low point of less than 2%.

While the gross saving rate oscillated, it remained above 14% until 2006 and then it began to fall. It fell more rapidly during the Great Recession until it reached a 20-year low of just over 10%. So when you look at these data, you would say as a nation, we are at our lowest gross savings point in the last 25 years. Investors compete with households and government entities for funds. Federal government deficits use up saving that could be used for investment, thus government deficits curtail growth. That's one of the reasons that we care a lot about them. Government deficits use up our savings, savings that could be used to build capital.

We borrow from foreign nations when we run a trade deficit, different from a fiscal deficit because a trade deficit means that the rest of the world allows us to borrow their productive capacity by sending to us a volume of goods and services of greater value than the goods and services we send back to them. It's like they're lending us goods and services. Foreign borrowing allows investment to be larger than it would've been but foreign nations expect to eventually be paid back in goods and services meaning that some place at some time, we will have to run negative trade deficits in order to pay back these nations that have lent us funds.

How has U.S. investment faired over time? Well the chart shows private gross domestic investment in the United States as a share of GDP from 1947 to 2010. What you see is that if you were to compute an average that average would be about 16%. So on average over this period, we have committed about 16% of our gross domestic product to investment, but it also shows that our investment fell dramatically to the lowest point in the entire graph during the Great Recession. That makes that recession very special. You can see other decreases. You can see other troughs but no trough deeper than the trough associated with the Great Recession depicted in the final years that the graph shows.

Household savings differ across countries. The graph that you're looking at now shows household savings rates for a number of countries in 2010 just to illustrate. Savings rates vary a great deal with households in some nations saving as much as 12% of household income and others saving very little. The nations with the highest saving rates were Belgium 12%, Germany 11.5, Ireland 11, Sweden 10.2, and Switzerland 10.5. The nations with the lowest savings rate were the Czech Republic at 1 and Denmark at −1.

I know that makes you curious. The negative saving rate in Denmark meant that the Danish households consumed more than their income. That was possible because those households borrowed, as all taken together, they borrowed to finance their extra consumption. So they ate into the savings by Danish firms and Danish government. Why would Danish households do negative saving?

Research suggests that Danish households consumed more than their income in response to a large increase in the price of the typical house in Denmark that occurred after financial markets in Denmark were liberalized. Danish households felt richer and spent some of their perceived wealth increase immediately. Again for the individual households, when you feel wealthier, you don't save in traditional ways. You may try to spend part of your wealth. Denmark is not unique. Changes in the prices of assets held by U.S. households are frequently cited as one of the explanations for changes in savings in the United States. Indeed as house prices in the United States fell, it's natural to expect that traditional savings in the U.S. would've increased. The U.S. saving rate for the U.S. in 2010 was 5.7% which was much higher than it had been prior to the Great Recession in part because low value of U.S. households had made individuals look to traditional saving sources in order to meet their retirement goals.

Low household savings rates in the United States that are enforced by large government budget deficits imply that the U.S. faces an unpleasant choice. It can borrow from the rest of the world in order to engage in investment projects. It can allow investment to fall as a fraction GDP implying that growth in the United States will fall and standard of living will eventually fall. No other alternative is possible because as a nation, investment must equal the sum of savings by households, savings by businesses, and borrowing from other nations.

We end this lecture as we began it by considering the silver lining in the cloudy sky of the Great Recession. One legacy the Great Recession may turn out to be that American households rediscover the virtues of saving. American consumers had come to believe that growth in the value of their homes provided a dependable source of wealth for growth in the future and led them to do less of traditional saving. The bursting of the housing bubble in 2007 may have taught American households that to provide for their futures, they must return to traditional forms of saving, setting aside something from every paycheck.

The Real Rate of Interest
Lecture 9

In September 1978, nominal interest rates were high; for example, the one-year Treasury bond rate was 8.6% and on the way up. This rate would continue to increase until it peaked at more than 16% in August 1981. After that, the T-bond rate began to fall and would again hit 8.6% in January 1983. Despite the fact that nominal interest rates were the same in those 2 months, it was much more expensive to borrow in January 1983 than in September 1978. In this lecture, you'll learn the key to resolving this apparent paradox—a concept called the real rate of interest—that will give you a new perspective on the true cost of borrowing.

Figure 9.1

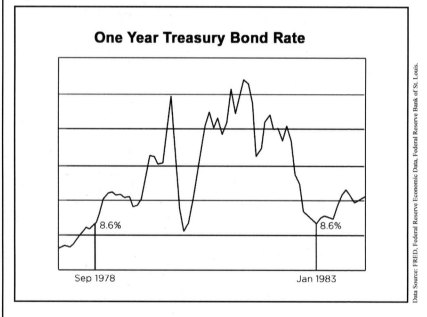

The Nominal Rate of Interest

- The **nominal rate of interest** is what most of us think of when we think of an interest rate. It is typically expressed as a percentage, but in fact, it specifies the number of dollars that a borrower must pay to borrow funds.

- For example, if the nominal rate is 10%, a person who borrows $1000 for one year on January 2 must pay back $1100 on January 2 of the following year. By the same token, a person who lends $1000 at 10% will give up $1000 and receive $1100 one year later.

- Why does the borrower pay interest, and why does the lender receive interest? The simple reason is that the lender gives up something of value to the borrower—in our example, the right to use $1000 one year earlier.

- Consider the case of Joe and Jan. Joe suddenly discovers that his car needs a major repair. He can't function without his car for a year while he saves up the money, so he agrees to pay interest and obtain the right to use in the present funds that he will not earn until a year later. Jan is saving for her daughter's college education. She prefers the future purchase of tuition to purchases she can make in the present. If Jan lends funds to Joe, she will receive a reward for her patience.

- Borrowers typically pay a higher rate of return than the rate received by savers. The difference is compensation received by financial institutions, such as banks, that function as intermediaries between borrowers and lenders. We will return to this issue later in the course.

The Concept of Interest

- Most of us tend to think that the payment and receipt of interest are natural transactions, but some cultures and religious codes frown on the payment of interest. The view that collecting interest on a debt is somehow wrong can be traced to the Greek philosopher Aristotle, who argued that money does not "produce" anything; therefore, borrowing money should not cost anything.

- What Aristotle did not acknowledge, and what is of great importance, is that no one borrows money unless he or she intends to use it. Like someone who rents land to grow a crop, the borrower receives something of value—the right to purchase goods earlier rather than later. This opportunity to use funds sooner is both valuable and productive.

The Real Rate of Interest
- The number of dollars paid (or received) in interest is an inaccurate measure of the cost of borrowing (or the reward from lending). The right way to describe what the lender receives and what the borrower gives up in this transaction is with a concept known as the real rate of interest.

- The real rate of interest measures the size of the "goods bonus" that savers receive by agreeing to defer use of their income. It likewise measures the size of the "goods penalty" that borrowers pay for the right to use that income early.

- Returning to our earlier example, Joe would like to borrow $1000 from Jan at 10% interest to fix his car. Jan would like to lend $1000 to Joe at 10% interest because she is saving for her daughter's college education. What happens if the CPI increases by 6% during the year of the loan?

- When Joe repays the loan, he repays with dollars that have lost 6% of their purchasing power relative to the dollars he borrowed, and Jan receives dollars that can purchase 6% less than the dollars she lent.

- A good estimate of the "goods penalty" that Joe pays by borrowing is 4%—the nominal rate of interest rate minus the inflation rate during the period of the loan. A good estimate of the "goods bonus" that Jan receives by lending is likewise 4%.

- Computation of the real rate of interest involves adjusting the nominal interest rate for the rate of inflation during the period of the loan. Note, however, that at the time of the original loan, Joe and Jan did not know what the rate of inflation would be.

The Connection of Interest Rates and Inflation
- Data show that the nominal rate of interest rises and falls with the inflation rate and varies more than the real rate of interest.

- A graph tracking the one-year Treasury bond rate and the rate of CPI inflation over a period of 50 years shows that the interest rate and the inflation rate tend to rise and fall together, but they do not

Figure 9.2

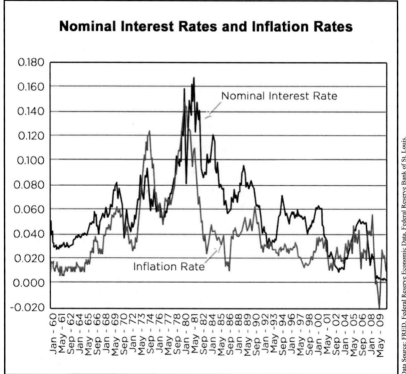

Data Source: FRED, Federal Reserve Economic Data, Federal Reserve Bank of St. Louis.

move in lockstep. The correlation between the nominal interest rate and the rate of inflation is 72%.

- Zooming in on a portion of the graph shows that in September 1978, the inflation rate was almost as high as the interest rate, which makes the real rate of interest small. In contrast, in January 1983, the nominal interest rate was about 5 percentage points higher than the inflation rate, making the real rate of interest higher.

Figure 9.3

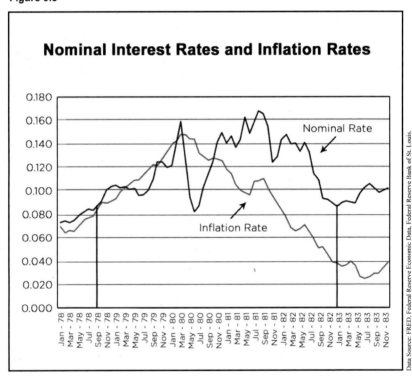

Calculating the True Cost of Borrowing

- The real rate of interest is defined as the nominal interest rate minus the rate of inflation expected (on average) over the life of loan.

- The graph of the Treasury bond rate and the rate of CPI inflation compares nominal interest rates and inflation rates at the same dates, but that comparison is not quite correct. Borrowers and lenders both care about what happens to the purchasing power of the dollars they borrow and lend over the life of the loan.

- The correct inflation rate is not known at the time the loan is consummated. Both borrowers and lenders must guess the future course of inflation in order to estimate the real rate of interest and the true cost of borrowing.

- Consider a graph showing the real rate of interest between 1978 and 1983. Technically speaking, this graph shows, for each month, the one-year nominal interest rate minus the inflation rate that was realized over the year of the loan. That inflation rate is computed as the percentage change in the CPI that occurred between the date the loan was initiated and the date the loan was repaid.

- We can see that the real rate of interest was actually negative between 1978 and 1980 because inflation was higher than individuals expected when they agreed to the terms of their loans.

- Beginning in 1980, nominal interest rates caught up and surpassed the inflation rate; the real rate of interest began to increase until it peaked at just under 12% in 1981.

- Thus, for the two months we are comparing with the same nominal interest rates, the real interest rate was –3.5% (September 1978) and 4.4% (January 1983)—a 7.9% difference!

- Because of its connection to the rate of inflation, the real rate of interest can never be known for sure at the time that borrowing and lending decisions are made.

The Distinction between Nominal and Real Interest Rates

- Why is the distinction between nominal and real rates important? To answer this question, we return again to Jan, who is saving for her daughter's college education.

- Suppose Jan ignores inflation and bases her saving decisions on the nominal rate alone. By doing so, she ignores the likely increases in tuition that will occur between the present and the time that her daughter matriculates.

- By using the real rate of interest in her saving calculations, Jan is using forecasts of CPI inflation as a proxy for changes in tuition. The forecasts may be imperfect, but it is far wiser to assume that tuition will increase along with the CPI than to assume that no increases in tuition will occur.

- Understanding the real rate of interest also helps us better understand why it is important for the Federal Reserve to keep the inflation rate low and steady, making it far easier for borrowers and lenders to estimate the real rate of interest at the point of their credit transaction.

Important Term

nominal rate of interest: Specifies number of dollars borrower must pay to borrow funds.

Suggested Reading

Federal Reserve Bank of New York, "Interest Rates."

Fisher, *The Theory of Interest*.

Kennedy, "Eight Reasons Why"

Mishkin, *The Economics of Money, Banking, and Financial Markets*.

1. The U.S. Treasury sells a bond called TIPS that provides holders with regular interest and maturity payments and, in addition, a payment equal to the rate of inflation that has occurred over the life of the bond. What sort of individual would prefer this bond to a regular Treasury bond?

2. Suppose you are convinced by this lecture that you should use the real rate of interest when calculating how much to save for your retirement. How would you go about estimating the real rate of interest to use in your calculations?

The Real Rate of Interest
Lecture 9—Transcript

In September 1978, nominal interest rates were very high. For example the 1-year Treasury bond rate was 8.6% and it was on the way up. Rates paid by private borrowers were higher but they moved together with the Treasury bond rate. The 1-year Treasury bond rate would continue to rise until it peaked at over 16% in August 1981. Then the T-bond rate and rates generally would begin to fall. On the way back down, the 1-year Treasury bond rate would again hit 8.6% in January of 1983.

So you might ask, what's the point? What is the significance of the simple fact that the 1-year Treasury bond rate was 8.6% in September '78 and then 8.6% again in January 1983. These apparently straightforward numbers embody a fascinating and perplexing puzzle, but why? Why are they puzzling? Because in a very important sense, that is the point of this lecture, it was much more expensive to borrow in January of 1983 than it was to borrow in September of 1978. How can that be? How could this be so? The nominal rates of interest were the same in those 2 months. I can hear you screaming it to me. But the key to resolving this puzzle involves a concept called the "real rate of interest." What the real rate of interest is, how to think about it, and why it is the correct way to measure the cost of borrowing is the subject of this lecture.

By the end of this lecture, you are likely to think in a different way than ever before about the true cost of borrowing. The real rate of interest is one of those economic concepts that has the power to change the way all of us look at the world. Let's begin on familiar ground with what economists call the nominal rate of interest, what we all think of as the rate of interest. The nominal rate of interest is what we think about when we think of an interest rate.

The nominal rate of interest is typically expressed as a percentage, 5%, 6%, 7%, but in fact, it specifies the number of dollars that a borrower must pay to borrow funds. If the nominal rate is 10%, a person who borrows $1000 for one year on January 2 must pay back $1100 on January 2 of the following year, $1000 in principle and 10% of that, $100, in interest.

By the same token, a person who lends $1000 for one year at 10% will give up $1000 on January 2 and receive in return $1100 on January 2 one year later. Why does the borrower pay interest and why does the lender receive interest? The simple reason is that the lender gives up something of value to the borrower, in our example, the right to use $1000 one year earlier.

Suppose Joe is just making ends meet but suddenly discovers that his automobile needs a major repair. Joe could wait and save for the repair but Joe reckons that he cannot function without use of his auto for a whole year. So Joe pays interest and obtains the right to use in the present funds that he will not earn until a year later. Continuing our example, suppose Jan is saving for her daughter's college education. Jan has decided that she prefers purchases that she can make in the future, her daughter's tuition, to purchases that she could make right now. If Jan lends funds to Joe, she will receive a reward for her patience.

All of us know that in reality, borrowers typically pay a higher rate of interest than the rate received by savers. The difference is compensation received by financial institutions such as banks that function as go- betweens, between the borrowers and the lenders, we'll come back to that issue later in the course but for now I'm going to assume that borrowing and lending rates are the same. That will keep our story simple, and it will do absolutely no violence to the points that we're studying today.

You and I may think that the payment of interest when we borrow and the receipt of interest when we save is the most natural thing in the world, but it's interesting that in some cultures, and according to some religious codes, the payment of interest is wrong. The view that collection of interest on a debt is somehow wrong or even immoral can be traced to the Greek philosopher Aristotle, who argued that money does not produce anything and therefore borrowing money should not cost anything. Aristotle thought that someone who used another person's land should pay rent for the land because the person who borrowed the land could use the land to grow a crop, but Aristotle argued that money was not like land and that, ideally, people should not collect interest from one another.

What Aristotle did not acknowledge and what is of great importance is that no one borrows money unless he or she intends to use it. Like the land renter, the borrower does receive something of value, the right to purchase goods earlier rather than later. The opportunity to use funds sooner rather than later is something both valuable and productive. The mutual benefit that borrowers and lenders receive when they transact is a very powerful force, so powerful that it has led practitioners of religions that forbid the collection of interest to find workarounds that allow transactions to go forward but do not technically involve interest payments. Let's think of an example.

An Islamic bank approaches home loans and home loan mortgages in a very different way than Western banks do. They do not loan money to the home buyer and then collect interest. That is forbidden, but yet people who practice Islam wish to buy homes. How does an Islamic bank help them? Well the Islamic bank buys the home itself and then resells it to the buyer at a profit while at the same time allowing the buyer to pay for this home purchase in installments, a workaround that if we thought about it, would implicitly involve interest but does not explicitly involve interest collection. So now we know that a borrower receives something of value, the right to use funds earlier rather than later, but what does the borrower give up for that right? Hmm. What does the lender receive for agreeing to spend later, to be patient and to defer spending until the time that the loan is repaid?

Interest, you would tell me that I have already said that. Ah, yes, but the number of dollars paid or received in interest is an inaccurate measure of the cost of borrowing and an inaccurate measure of the reward from lending. The right way to describe what the lender receives and what the borrower gives up is with that concept called the real rate of interest.

The real rate of interest measures the size of what I'll call a goods bonus that savers receive by agreeing to defer the use of income. It likewise measures the size of a goods penalty that borrowers pay for the right to use their income. Let's return to our example of Joe and Jan. Joe would like to borrow $1000 from Jan at 10% interest to fix his car. Jan would like to lend $1000 to Joe at 10% interest because she is saving for her daughter's college education. Consider the year that starts on the day that Joe borrowed $1000 and ends on the day that he repays the loan.

Suppose during that year, prices rise by 6%. Which prices? Well rather than get bogged down in describing exactly what Joe and Jan consume, let's simply say that they consume the typical bushel basket and at the consumer price index, which rises by 6% is a measure of the inflation that they face. When Joe repays the loan, he repays with dollars that have lost 6% of their purchasing power relative to the dollars that he borrowed. That is, the dollars that he borrowed at the beginning of the year could purchase 6% more than the dollars that he repaid at the end of the year.

Similarly at the time of repayment, Jan receives dollars that can purchase 6% less than the dollars she lent. So a good estimate of the goods penalty that Joe pays by borrowing is 4%, the nominal rate of interest of 10% minus the inflation rate during the period of the loan. A good estimate of the goods bonus that Jan receives is likewise 4%, $10 - 6$. Computation of the real rate of interest then involves adjusting the nominal rate of interest for the rate of inflation during the period of the loan, during the time between borrowing and repayment.

There is a subtle and somewhat difficult issue that we must address however. At the time that Joe and Jan make their arrangement, they do not know what the rate of inflation will turn out to be, and I'm going to return to that point in just a couple of minutes. Data show that the nominal rate of interest rises and falls with the inflation rate and varies more than does the real rate of interest. The chart that you are seeing tracks the 1-year Treasury bond rate and the rate of CPI inflation over 50 years between 1960 and 2010. The nominal rate of interest is in blue and the rate of inflation is in red. What you see here is that the nominal rate of interest largely rises and falls with the rate of inflation. They move together through time. We observe that the blue and red lines rise together and fall together but they are not moving in lock-step. There are times when the inflation rate falls by more than the nominal interest rate or times when it falls by less.

So what does that mean? Let's zoom in to see the data for the years between 1978 and 1973. Why would we want to do that? Well remember our puzzle at the beginning of the lecture. When we zoom in, we see a diagram with 2 black vertical lines. And why? Well those lines mark September 1978 and January 1983. Comparison of the blue interest-rate line and the red-inflation rate line takes us a long way toward resolving the puzzle that the lecture started with. In September 1978, the inflation rate was almost as high as the interest rate. Well, wait a min4ute, that makes the real rate of interest very, very small. But in dramatic contrast, in January of 1983, the nominal rate of interest was about 5 full percentage points higher than the inflation rate, which makes the real rate of interest very high.

The real rate of interest is defined as the nominal interest rate minus the rate of inflation expected on average over the life of the loan. The graph that we just saw compares nominal interest rates and inflation rates at the same date. Another subtle point though, that comparison is not quite right. Borrowers and lenders both care about what happens to the purchasing power of the dollars that they borrow and lend over the life of the loan. The correct inflation rate to use is not known at the time that the loan is consummated. Both borrowers and lenders must guess the future course of inflation in order to estimate the real rate of interest and the true cost of borrowing and the true cost of lending.

The next graph shows the real rate of interest between 1978 and 1983 assuming that borrowers and lenders had guessed the inflation rate correctly. It's sort of a crystal ball exercise. What if they had known in advance exactly what the inflation rate would be?

Technically speaking the graph shows for each month the 1 year nominal interest rate minus the inflation rate that was realized over the year of the loan. That inflation rate is computed as the percentage change in the consumer price index that occurred between the date the loan was initiated and the date the loan was repaid. What we see in this diagram is that the real rate of interest was actually negative between 1978 and 1980 because inflation turned out to be higher than individuals expected when they agreed to the terms of the loan. Beginning in 1980, nominal interest rates caught up and surpassed the inflation rate and the real rate of interest began to rise until it peaked at just under 12% in 1981. We now understand how to resolve the puzzle presented at the beginning of the lecture. It would turn out that the real rate of interest was −3.5% for September 1978 but 4.4% for January 1983. The difference is a large, I would say, a whopping 7.9%.

How can individuals estimate the future inflation rate and thereby estimate the real rate of interest at the point of a decision to borrow and lend? Well, any such estimate is just that. It's an estimate. So the real rate of interest can never be known for sure at the time that borrowing and lending decisions are made. One way to understand why the real rate of interest was negative between January 1978 and September of 1979 is to observe that the inflation rate was rising over this period. Had individuals known that the inflation rate would rise, they would surely have sought and received a higher nominal rate on their loans.

There is a cautionary tale here. We have talked about the importance of a low and stable inflation rate in previous lectures. One reason that low and stable inflation rates are so important is because when the inflation rate is low and stable, it is easier to forecast. When the inflation rate is low and stable, it is harder for borrowers and lenders to make mistakes. When the inflation rate is low and stable, we do not end up by fooling our lenders to actually accept a negative real rate of interest, a negative premium or goods bonus for lending their funds.

Of course if those lenders are people who are lending now in order to save for their retirement, it's very, very crucial to understand why being fooled is very important to those savers and lenders. When the real rate of interest is negative, they are actually receiving a negative return on their funds. That is, they are actually losing the ability to buy goods and services. That's serious business.

We don't have a crystal ball. We cannot forecast the inflation rate perfectly and there are before the fact estimates of future inflation that are available. The Federal Reserve Bank of Philadelphia surveys business persons and asks them for their inflation forecasts. The next chart gives forecasts of CPI inflation since 1981. We can see from the graph that inflation forecasts were falling in the months before January of 1983. As the first graph shows, it turned out that those forecasts were correct. CPI inflation did fall during that period. It's not important for us at this point to ask how accurate those forecasts are. What is important is for us to continue to emphasize the distinction between nominal and real interest rates and to emphasize why that distinction is important.

To understand the importance of real interest rates, it is sufficient to remember Jan's problem. Recall Jan wants to save for her daughter's college education. Suppose Jan ignores inflation and bases her savings decision on the nominal rate alone. By making that mistake, Jan ignores the likely increases in tuition that will occur between the present and the time that her daughter matriculates. Of course, that is a potentially disastrous mistake to make. By using the real rate of interest in her savings calculations, Jan is using forecasts of CPI inflation as a proxy for changes in tuition. The forecasts can turn out to be imperfect but it's far better to assume that tuition costs would rise along with the consumer price index than to assume that no increases in tuition cost would occur.

Understanding the concept of the real rate of interest conveys an additional benefit to us all. It also helps us better understand why it is crucial for the Federal Reserve to keep inflation rates low and steady. If the Federal Reserve keeps inflation low and steady, it is far easier for borrowers and for lenders to estimate the real rate of interest at the point in which they make their credit transactions. That means if I can depend on the Federal Reserve keeping the inflation rate at 2%, I can personally be guaranteed that when I can earn say 4% on very long-term savings vehicles that I will actually receive a goods bonus. That's an extremely valuable piece of information to have and helps me plan so much better for the future.

It also means that we will be unlikely to see again the puzzling situation that we saw at the beginning of today's lecture. Think of how damaging that was. In the late 1970s, individuals were willingly loaning their money, and it would turn out that the rate of inflation was accelerating so rapidly that they actually received, when they were repaid by the Treasury or by private borrowers, dollars that would buy less than the dollars they lent. What kind of a bonus is that? What kind of an incentive is that to save, to actually receive fewer goods and services a year or 2 or 5 later than the goods and services that you gave up when you agreed to let someone else use your funds?

Of course it was a windfall for borrowers, a windfall. They actually paid back dollars that had less value than the dollars they borrowed. That's hardly giving up anything. Now we understand perhaps better why our founding fathers were so worried about inflation. They understood that inflation was a scheme that would transfer wealth from creditors to debtors. We can understand also why, as we will see in coming lectures, most of us and certainly all economists believe that keeping the inflation rate low and steady is an essential goal for monetary policy.

Keeping the inflation rate low and steady is an essential goal for monetary policy for the very, very simple reason that we want borrowers and lenders to understand what the real interest rate will be over not a year, not 2 years, not 5 years but perhaps as long as 10 years. We want individuals to know when they contract what they actually are receiving in interest and what they are actually paying in interest. When people have that knowledge, when they can be confident about that knowledge, they are able to plan better, more efficiently, and the economy, in all of its aspects, is better off as a result.

So I promised you a concept that would change the way that you look at economic issues. Please always remember that the true cost of borrowing and the true benefit from saving is measured properly by the real rate of interest. It's the most important concept that I have offered you today and it's probably one of my top 5 for the entire course. Remember too what the real rate of interest means. It's the actual nominal rate, which tells you what dollars you will receive adjusted for the inflation that you believe you will experience over the course of the loan. Don't forget that very important concept and thank you.

Financial Intermediaries
Lecture 10

Many people believe that it is smart to cut out the middleman. Wouldn't it be great, for example, to swap houses with someone and avoid the fees of real estate agents that eat up 5–10% of property value? But avoiding the middleman isn't always the best course of action. Imagine how much time it would take you to manage your own portfolio of stocks in the absence of mutual funds or how difficult it would be to arrange to borrow funds to purchase a home without the services of a bank or thrift institution. This lecture looks at an important group of middlemen—financial intermediaries—and the role they play in a modern economy.

The Middlemen: Financial Intermediaries
- **Financial intermediaries** are firms, such as banks, that channel funds from savers to investors and other decision makers who have decided to spend more than their current income permits.

- As we saw in the example of Joe and Jan in the last lecture, some financial transactions occur directly, without the intervention of financial firms. But these transactions may carry a degree of uncertainty or risk. How will Joe find someone who is willing to transact with him? What will Jan do if Joe doesn't repay the loan and she doesn't have enough money for her daughter's tuition?

Direct and Indirect Finance
- The essential difference between direct and indirect finance is that with direct finance, the lender holds the IOU of the borrower; with indirect finance, the lender holds the IOU of the financial intermediary.

- In both cases, the lender's cash winds up in the hands of the borrower.

Repackaging IOUs

- A financial intermediary can be viewed as "repackaging" the IOUs of its borrowers. Many lenders prefer exchanging their cash for repackaged IOUs rather than exchanging it for IOUs of specific borrowers. The primary reason that lenders prefer to hold a diversified portfolio of IOUs is to avoid the risk of putting all their eggs in one basket.

- Consider a situation in which 1,000 lenders each wishes to lend $1,000, and 1,000 borrowers each wishes to borrow $1,000. With direct finance and no middleman, the borrowers and lenders pair up, but if 5% of the borrowers cannot repay their loans, then 5% of the lenders lose interest and their entire principal.

Most financial transactions involve a financial intermediary, such as a commercial bank, thrift institution, or investment bank.

- In the same situation with indirect finance, there is no pairing. Each borrower holds an IOU issued by the financial intermediary. That IOU, in turn, is backed by a portfolio of borrower IOUs.

- Because the financial intermediary will charge borrowers a high enough rate of interest to allow for a normal number of defaults, individual lenders will all be paid in full by the intermediary.

- A loan to the intermediary is less risky because, in effect, each lender holds a diversified portfolio of IOUs.

147

Lender and Borrower Time Horizons

- Consider the same situation with 1,000 lenders and 1,000 borrowers. In this case, however, the borrowers want to borrow for two years, but the lenders want to lend for only one. With direct finance, it may not be possible for any borrower-lender pair to negotiate a mutually agreeable transaction.

- Indirect finance can bring borrowers and lenders together. The financial intermediary can lend funds for two years and borrow funds for one provided that, after one year, it replaces old lenders with new lenders.

- In other words, the financial intermediary finds a sequence of one-year lenders who collectively provide the funds desired by the multi-year borrower.

- Some financial firms specialize in maturity intermediation and bear risks when they do. There are not many lenders who want to lend for 30 years.

Liquidity

- Lenders may be more willing to lend if they know that they can quickly and without loss reconvert the IOUs they own to cash.

- A financial asset is said to be "liquid" if it can be rapidly converted to cash with no loss of value.

- Lenders value liquidity because liquid funds are available to the lender if some rainy-day scenario occurs. Jan will be even more willing to lend if she knows that she can trade in her IOU for cash if her own car requires repairs.

- Financial intermediaries create **liquidity**. That is, they offer lenders IOUs that are more liquid than the IOUs that borrowers exchange for the cash they receive. Intermediaries create this liquidity by holding some cash in reserve.

- The intermediary does not know in advance which lender will want to reconvert to cash but can know how much cash will be desired by the lenders as a group. By holding sufficient reserves for the group, each lender can rationally behave as if it can reconvert its IOUs to cash even though few will actually do so.

- It is an amazing cooperative outcome that we can all think of bank deposits as fully liquid.

The Business of Financial Intermediaries

- Financial intermediaries specialize in the evaluation of borrowers and their projects and, therefore, can better assess the riskiness of a borrower than a small lender can.

- A financial intermediary receives many loan applications and develops specialized processes for evaluating and monitoring them.

- Intermediaries also employ specialized legal skills to design and enforce borrowing contracts.

- The government provides oversight of financial intermediaries and, in some cases, special assistance to them that protects individuals who lend them funds.

- Commercial banks are financial intermediaries that also provide their customers with transaction services. Many customers prefer to hold their liquid funds as bank deposits because it is easy to pay them out by writing checks or authorizing electronic transfers.

Specialized Intermediation Services

- Commercial banks accept deposits from household and business depositors, who treat those deposits as transaction balances that they can spend at any time. Commercial banks normally hold about 10% of deposits in the form of cash reserves for depositors who wish to reconvert their deposits to cash. The balance of bank funds is used to make business and consumer loans, thereby earning a profit. Commercial banks create liquidity, provide diversification to their customers, and are specialists in assessing credit worthiness.

- Thrift institutions, such as savings banks and credit unions, accept deposits from depositors who are willing to defer use of their funds for a period of time in order to receive a higher interest rate than they could get on checkable deposits. Thrift institutions use their funds to make consumer loans and issue mortgages. Thrift institutions intermediate maturities, create diversification, and assess credit worthiness of borrowers, especially mortgage borrowers.

- Mutual funds receive funds from those who buy shares. Those shares are sold along with a promise to use the obtained funds to pursue specific financial objectives. The funds are used to construct a portfolio of assets that fund managers believe will achieve the promised objectives. Mutual funds provide diversification and asset management

- Money market funds receive funds from those who buy shares. The shares are sold along with the fund's promise to purchase only assets that are highly liquid and will revert to cash within a short period of time. The funds are used to construct a portfolio of short-term debt instruments. Money market mutual funds create liquidity and provide diversification.

- Insurance companies receive funds from premiums paid by policyholders. They use these funds to pay claims to policyholders and to make long-maturity investments that earn profits to support future claims and cash redemptions. Insurance companies provide policyholders with the opportunity to hedge risk by paying relatively small premiums on a regular schedule in exchange for the right to be repaid if some calamity occurs.

The Benefits of Financial Intermediaries

- Financial intermediaries exist because they provide valuable services to their customers, such as managing stock portfolios, enabling diversification of financial investments, lending funds to purchase homes, or enabling us to provide for our families in the event of disaster. We could not make many of these provisions alone, but we can make them as a group.

- However, financial intermediaries may also create liabilities for an economy—liabilities that are occasionally very costly and require a complex system of regulations.

Important Terms

financial intermediaries: Firms, such as banks, that channel funds from savers to investors and other decision makers who have decided to spend more than their current income permits.

liquidity: A financial asset is said to be "liquid" if it can be rapidly converted to cash with no loss of value.

Suggested Reading

Kolb and Rodriguez, *Financial Institutions*.

Meulendyke, *U. S. Monetary Policy and Financial Markets*.

Mishkin, *The Economics of Money, Banking, and Financial Markets*.

Questions to Consider

1. What are some of the ways in which you take advantage in your domestic or business life in the specialized services provided by financial intermediaries?

2. Have you ever been involved, as either borrower or lender, in a direct loan arrangement with another person? If so, what were some of the problems you faced? How does a bank provide solutions for those problems?

Lecture 10: Financial Intermediaries

Financial Intermediaries
Lecture 10—Transcript

Many people, and perhaps you are one of them, believe that it is very smart to cut out the middle men. They argue, wouldn't it be great to swap houses with someone and avoid those pesky real estate fees, which can eat up between 5 and 10% of a property value? All of us, I know I have, have heard advertising pitches telling us to shop at a warehouse store and cut out the middle men. Many of us believe that middle men such as real estate agents absorb our hard earning money without producing anything.

In this lecture, we will look at the role of financial middle men and think about whether or not they play an important role in a modern economy, but don't be too quick to agree that it's smart to cut out the middle men. Imagine, just for example, how much time it would take you to manage your own portfolio of stocks if there were no mutual funds. You wouldn't be able to buy a little bit of a lot of shares because the minimum purchase is one share. Contemplate the stress you would feel as you, at the early times when your portfolio was small, had to choose the 1 or 2 or 3 different stocks that you could afford to purchase.

Imagine how difficult it would be to arrange to borrow funds to purchase a home without the services of a bank or a thrift institution of savings and loan. Maybe Uncle Joe would lend you the funds. I should have such an Uncle Joe. But sooner or later and maybe sooner than you're ready for, Uncle Joe would want the money he lent you back, certainly when he neared retirement and then what would you do? Imagine how difficult it would be for you to provide for your family in the event of your death if you didn't have access to an insurance company and the insurance policies that they offer. What might you do? Well perhaps you'd make some sort of an agreement with extended family members to care for one another's immediate family in the event of a calamity. That's certainly what happened in my father's time, but if you think about it, that agreement would be essentially the formation of a primitive insurance company.

In today's lecture, we'll take a close look at an important group of middle men, financial intermediaries. Financial intermediaries are firms including banks that channel funds from savers to investors and from savers to other decision makers who have decided to spend more than their current income permits. My talk today is not about the wisdom of spending beyond your means or when it is wise to spend beyond your means and when it is not. I'm going to assume that those decisions to borrow are rational, well-founded, and right for the decision makers who make them. Later on we can talk about when borrowing is wise and when it is not.

So we are talking about people who borrow and other people who lend. Some financial transactions are going to occur directly without the intervention of a financial firm. Remember Joe and Jan from the previous lecture? Joe would like to borrow $1000 to repair his car. He's willing to pay 6% and to repay principle and interest in 1 year. Jan has decided to save for her daughter's college education, and she's willing to lend $1000 for 1 year at 6% interest. Joe and Jan, if they know each other, have the opportunity to make a mutually-beneficial transaction. Joe will be better off. He gets the money to repair his car. Jan will be better off. She will be earning some interest that helps her better pay for her daughter's tuition.

In the transaction between them, Joe will receive $1000 now and he will give his IOU, and that IOU will promise to pay $1060 in 1 year. Jan will give $1000 now, give it to Joe, in cash and she will receive that promissory note from Joe, and both are better off. Ah, but here's the rub. How did Joe and Jan find each other and how comfortable will Jan be trusting Joe? After all, she's taking a risk. For example, Joe's bad luck could continue. His car might require additional repairs or other things might happen, and the result could be that Joe might not be able to repay, and then Jan might not have enough to pay her daughter's tuition.

Most financial transactions involve a financial intermediary such as a commercial bank, thrift institution, investment bank, or some other. Now I want to take a look at a picture that will help us understand what these middle men do. We have a lender and a borrower and their handshake sends cash from the lender to the borrower. What travels in the reverse direction is the borrower's promise to pay, which I call the borrower's IOU.

Contrast that with the flow diagram, which is meant to show what happens when borrower and lender use the services of a financial intermediary. Lender sends cash not to borrower but to the financial intermediary, and we'll see how that works when we become more specific in a minute. It's the financial intermediary who takes the cash they have received and then provides it to the borrower, pretty simple.

What's a little more subtle is the reverse transaction. The borrower, just like Joe, provides his promise to pay his IOU not to Jan but to the financial intermediary, the bank or the thrift institution. The financial intermediary, the middle man, does not simply pass it on to Jan or some other lender. What is passed on is the financial intermediary's own IOU. What the lender gets in exchange is the financial intermediary's promise to repay. It follows then that we can view financial intermediaries as repackaging the IOUs of its borrowers. Many lenders prefer exchanging their cash for repackaged IOUs than exchanging their cash for IOUs of specific borrowers. But why? Lenders prefer to hold a diversified portfolio of IOUs because they dislike risk and do not want to put all of their eggs, or for that matter, all of their dollars, in one basket.

An example will help. So suppose that there are 1000 lenders who each wish to lend $1000, and there are 1000 borrowers who each wish to borrow $1000. I know, those are made up numbers but they help illustrate the point. With direct finance and the use of no middle man, best we could do was to have the borrowers and the lenders pair up. I don't know how they find each other but suppose they do. If say 5% of the borrowers experience bad luck and cannot repay, then 5% of those 1000 lenders lose interest and their entire principle. So there are 5% of those people who are greatly harmed. On the other hand, with indirect finance, there is never any pairing of borrowing and lender. Each borrower holds an IOU issued by the financial intermediary. That IOU is, in turn, backed by the whole portfolio of IOUs.

Why is that important? Because the financial intermediary will charge borrowers a high enough interest rate to allow for the expected number of defaults. Individual lenders will all be paid in full by the intermediary. A loan to the intermediary by someone like Jan is less risky because, in effect, each lender holds a diversified portfolio of IOUs. Evidence of that is the lenders do not even know who is benefiting from the fact that they provided funds. They don't know the name of the person who ultimately got them.

We all know that diversification is valuable. What we may not have realized before is that financial intermediaries provide diversification not only in the case of mutual funds but also in the case of borrowing and lenders. Here's another example of repackaging, which I consider to be very important. In fact, I think you're going to find this one absolutely fascinating.

Borrowers and lenders have different time horizons. Well what do I mean? Well the borrower may want to borrow for a certain number of years and the lender may want to lend for a different number of years. So suppose again that there are 1000 lenders who each want to lend $1000 for 1 year. But to keep things simple suppose there are also 1000 borrowers each of whom wants to borrow $1000 just like before right? Here's the rub.

Suppose that the borrowers want to borrow for 2 years while the lenders while to lend for only 1. Stylized example right? Clearly borrowers might want to borrow for 5 years, 10 years, 30 years and lenders might want to lend for 1 year, 2 years, 3 years but we'll just make it that the lenders want to lend for 1 and the borrowers want to borrow for 2. Direct finance breaks down entirely now. There is just no mutually beneficial transaction that can be made between any borrower, lender, payer. Pick any one of the 1000 borrowers, any one of the 1000 lenders, put them together and say make a deal. They can't make a deal. They do not have a mutually advantageous basis for making a deal. Ah ha, enter the middle man because indirect finance can bring those borrowers and lenders together. It's almost like magic. What would they do? Well the financial intermediary can lend funds for 2 years and borrow funds for 1 provided that after 1 year it just goes out and replaces those old lenders who want their funds back with new lenders.

In short, at the time that they give the funds to the borrower, they don't even know who will provide the funds for the second year. The financial intermediary, in this case, finds a sequence of 1-year lenders who collectively provide the funds desired by the multi-year borrower. Some financial firms specialize in this kind of maturity intermediation, and they bear some risks when they do. There are not many lenders who want to lend for 30 years, a few insurance companies but that's about it. Lenders may be more willing to lend if they know that they can quickly and without loss reconvert the IOUs that they have to cash. Wait a minute, what does that mean? Well I'm talking about a third sort of repackaging here. It involves a new idea called liquidity.

A financial asset is said to be liquid if it can rapidly be converted to cash with no loss of value. Lenders value liquidity because liquid funds are available to the lender if some rainy-day scenario occurs. Jan would be even more willing to lend if she knew that she could trade that IOU in for cash if her own auto requires a repair, for example. So if she thought somehow that the Joe IOU that she held could be converted to cash say in 6 months, she would be more comforted and more willing to lend.

Financial intermediaries create liquidity. That is, they offer lenders IOUs that are more liquid than the IOUs that the borrowers exchange for the cash they receive. Whoa, that's a mindful. Let's think about that for a moment. Financial intermediaries offer the lenders an asset with the promise that it's convertible to cash, but those financial intermediaries don't receive that kind of asset from the people to whom they lend funds.

Now, how do financial intermediaries create liquidity? Well they do so by holding some cash in reserve. The intermediary does not know in advance which lender will want to reconvert to cash, but it probably can make a very shrewd guess about how much cash will be desired by the lenders as a group, and by holding sufficient reserves for the group, each and every lender can rationally behave as if all of them could convert their IOUs to cash even though it will turn out that few will actually do so. This is just an amazing cooperative outcome that we can all think, for example, of our bank deposits as fully liquid.

One more service that financial intermediaries offer their customers is specialization in the evaluation of borrowers and their projects and better assessment of the riskiness of any borrower than could be made by an individual lender. Just imagine for a minute that thousand pairings, those thousand borrowers and lenders put Fred together with Fredo. How will Fred know enough about Fredo to know whether he is likely to be repaid? Banks specialize in assessing the credit worthiness of lenders. A financial intermediary evaluates many loan applications and develops specialized processes for evaluating them and monitoring them. A financial intermediary employs specialized legal skills that it uses to design and enforce borrowing contracts. This is very, very important, and in a later lecture we'll look at those contracts. Government provides oversight of financial intermediaries and, in some cases, special assistance to them, which further protects individuals who lend them funds. That government assistance is not available to people who go it alone, who engage in direct finance.

Commercial banks are financial intermediaries who also provide their customers with transaction services. Your deposits can be used to pay bills and many customers prefer to hold their liquid funds as bank deposits because it's easy to pay them out by writing checks or today by authorizing electronic transfers. Now, we will zero in on that particular intermediary, the commercial bank, in a future lecture. A comparison of different financial intermediaries shows how each specializes in the provision of intermediation services. So I've talked, up until now, about the various repackaging services that intermediaries offer, but I haven't differentiated between the actual types of financial firms.

Now I would like to do so that you can appreciate how each different kind of financial middle man plays its role in the financial world. Let's start with commercial banks. What do they do? Well, commercial banks accept deposits from households and from businesses and treat—and each of those depositors, firms, and the households—treat those deposits as transaction balances that they can spend at any time, liquidity. Banks typically hold about 10% of those deposits in the form of cash and use that cash when depositors wish to reconvert their deposits back to cash, but commercial banks use the balance of their funds to make business in consumer loans and earn a profit. So in terms of those repackaging services that I talked about, commercial banks create liquidity, provide diversification to their customers, and are specialists in assessing credit worthiness.

As I mentioned already, assessing credit worthiness is extremely important. You wouldn't imagine, for a moment, bumping into a stranger and loaning that stranger funds. You would have no idea of the difference between a scam and a good business opportunity. Thrift institutions are slightly different from commercial banks and they include savings banks and credit unions. Savings and loan associations, when I was young, were also thrift institutions that were very different from and very important especially in mortgage lending, but as time and law evolved, savings and loans have become less important and commercial banks also make mortgage loans. But what do these thrift institutions do?

Well they accept depositors' deposits. That is, depositors give them funds and typically those depositors are people who are willing to defer the use of their funds for some period, and what do they get in return? Well, a higher interest rate typically than they can get from their bank if their deposits were checkable, if they were transactions balances. So now we have these thrifts receiving funds from depositors and paying interest for them. How do they use the funds?

Thrifts typically use the funds to make consumer loans and, importantly, mortgage loans. They are the backbone, and have been through history, in the mortgage lending business. With respect to the repackaging services I've been talking about, what do thrift institutions do? Well they are specialists at intermediating maturities. They also create diversification because the people who deposit to them are not linked up or paired with any particular mortgage borrower, and they too assess the credit worthiness of borrowers, especially mortgage borrowers.

We all know about one thrift institution and we learn again about it in most Christmas seasons, the Bailey Building and Loan. The Bailey Building and Loan was George Bailey's family business, and it is the one that's under threat from banker Potter and is likely to experience a run. We ought to think about that run for a minute because it includes an important lesson. Any depository institution that borrows short from its customers and lends long always is fragile if all of the depositors coordinate their activities and ask for their money at the same time.

I can remember the line in the movie when George Bailey says, upon having one of his depositors demand his entire balance at the Bailey Building and Loan, "But Fred your money isn't here. It's out working to build houses. We used it to build George's house and Ralph's house." This is another case where we coordinate our activity by using the services of a thrift institution or a financial intermediary in general. If we suddenly change the nature of this coordination, we cause problems for these institutions.

So what do these thrift institutions do then? As I've already said, their most important repackaging function is to repackage so as to provide intermediation of maturities. They lend long and borrow short. All of us know about mutual funds. That's probably the financial institution that we know the best and value the most. What do mutual funds do? Well they receive funds from those who would like to buy shares, and which shares? Well every mutual fund has to create a prospectus saying what their investment strategy is and saying the kind of shares that the fund will buy.

Those shares, therefore, are sold along with the mutual fund's promise to use the funds obtained by investors, financial investors, to pursue specific financial objectives. The managers of those mutual funds use the funds they receive from their financial investors to construct a portfolio of assets that they believe will achieve the promised objectives.

Clearly mutual funds provide very, very important services to their customers, diversification, and asset management. Remember from the beginning how difficult it would be, especially when you were first starting out to save for retirement, to know what few shares you should purchase? Given the existence of mutual funds, you don't have to make that decision. You can invest a few dollars, maybe as little as $100, and you can, in effect, own a little bit of hundreds and maybe thousands of different corporations. This is a tremendously valuable service that we have long understood and that probably we value the best, but my point today is that other financial intermediaries, other financial middle men, offer very valuable services too.

Let's take a look at one more financial intermediary, the money market mutual fund. What do they do and what sort of services do they offer? Well money market mutual funds receive funds from those who buy shares but unlike a typical mutual fund, this fund, the money market mutual fund, promises to purchase only assets that are themselves highly liquid: Treasury bills, very short-term corporate loan instruments, and the like.

If left untouched, if the money market mutual fund made no additional transactions, all of its assets would naturally reconvert to cash within a short period of time certainly within a year, maybe as little as 90 days. So what that money market mutual fund has done is to use the funds provided them by their customers to construct a portfolio of very short-term debt instrument. Money market mutual funds create liquidity, but they also provide diversification and they allow customers to receive some interest on funds that they consider to be pretty liquid. A very interesting story is how money market mutual funds were first created. They were born out of an attempt to work around a government regulation, but that story will come on a different day.

The last financial intermediary that I'd like to talk to you about is insurance companies. What do they do? Well, they receive funds from policy holders and provide them with promises to pay in certain contingencies. So, for example, if you were to die, a death benefit would be paid to your family. So these firms use funds to pay claims to policyholders, and what do they do with those funds? They make long maturity investments that earn profits to support future claims and cash redemptions. Insurance companies provide policyholders the opportunity to hedge risk by paying a relatively small premium on a regular schedule in exchange for the right to be repaid if some calamity occurs.

Financial intermediaries, banks, thrifts, mutual funds, and insurance companies exist because they provide valuable services to their customers and customers value the service of financial intermediaries. Imagine again how much time it would take you to manage your own portfolio of stocks. Imagine again how better off you are if a deposit at a bank or a thrift institution can be converted to cash, and imagine again how much comfort you feel if you can make small payments, and in a cooperative way with many others like you, receive in return the opportunity to provide for your family in the event of a calamity.

All of those are valuable services and all of those are the reasons that financial firms exist. So as I leave you, please, reconsider, should we cut out the middle man, or are they too valuable?

Thank you.

Commercial Banks
Lecture 11

This lecture takes a dispassionate look at banks and the functions they perform in a modern economy. You will investigate bank balance sheets and learn the role that banks play in channeling funds from savers to investors. You will also see why banks are the only private financial institutions that can create money, and you'll study the process by which that occurs.

The Balance Sheet

- A good place to begin studying the modern bank is with a look at its **balance sheet**. Recall that a balance sheet is a list of the assets, liabilities, and net worth of a firm or individual and that "net worth" is defined to be the value of the firm's assets minus the value of its liabilities. By construction, balance sheets always balance..

Sources of Funds for Banks

- Where do banks get the funds they use to acquire various assets? Part of the answer is that they accept deposits of several types.

- **Transactions deposits** are those against which checks can be written. **Non-transactions deposits** are deposits in savings accounts, from which funds can be withdrawn at any time; banks also accept **time deposits**, which have fixed maturity dates. Large-denomination time deposits are certificates of deposit in amounts at or over $100,000 that are generally purchased by corporations and other banks.

- Banks also borrow funds from other banks, the Federal Reserve, Federal Home Loan Banks, and corporations. In December of 2005, total liabilities of the commercial banks in the United States amounted to slightly more than $8 trillion.

Figure 11.1

Consolidated Balance Sheet of Commercial Banks
December 2005 (Billions of Dollars)

Assets		Liabilities	
Treasury and Agency Securities	1,134	Transaction Deposits	656
Other Securities	907	Large Time Deposits	1,418
Commercial and Industrial Loans	1,045	Other Non-transaction Deposits	3,657
Real Estate Loans	2,904	Borrowing from US Banks	361
Consumer Loans	705	Borrowing from Others	1,360
Security Loans	262	Other Liabilities	568
Other Loans	525		
Interbank Loans	278	Total Liabilities	8,020
Cash Assets	311		
Other Assets	636		
Total Assets	8,707	Net Worth	687

Source: Federal Reserve.

T-account depicting the consolidated balance sheet of commercial banks in the United States at the end of December 2005, when the U.S. and world economies were in the midst of an expansion.

Uses of Funds for Banks

- How do banks use the funds they acquire? They hold Treasury and other government agency securities, as well as other securities, including those of private corporations.

- Banks also lend funds to businesses, for real estate purchases, to consumers in the form of auto loans and other consumer loans, to those who use the borrowed funds to purchase securities, and for some other loan-type activities.

- Banks hold cash assets of two sorts—actual currency and coin in their vaults and deposits at the Federal Reserve.

- In December 2005, total assets held by commercial banks amounted to a bit more than $8.7 trillion. At the same time, U.S. bank net worth (bank capital) equaled $687 billion.

The Relative Importance of Various Sources and Uses of Bank Funds

- Despite the fact that banks actively borrow funds, they are still primarily depository institutions in that 70% of their liabilities are deposits of one sort or another. Note that commercial banks are required to hold reserves only against transactions deposits, and these account for only 8% of liabilities.

- Despite the fact that banks hold various kinds of securities, they are primarily lending institutions in that 62% of their assets are loans of one sort or another.

- In December 2005, banks had net worth or capital equal to 8.6% of their liabilities (and about 8% of their assets). Banks and bank regulators have worked hard, especially in recent years, to determine minimal levels of bank capital needed to ensure bank safety.

- Bank capital drops quickly in bad economic times because the market value of securities falls and, more importantly, because the "true" value of loans falls.

- Banks are always susceptible to **bank runs**, situations in which depositors all try to withdraw deposited funds at the same time.

- In December 2005, commercial bank deposit liabilities totaled $5.7 trillion, of which $656 billion was "demand deposits." Bank cash assets totaled $311 billion—far less than what would be needed to redeem even those deposits that depositors have the right to redeem for cash at any time. It's easy to see that banks are fragile, no matter how well they are managed.

Which Assets Are Money in the United States?

- Keep in mind as we go through the various definitions of money that these definitions share a common intuition: **Money** is an asset that its owners rightly believe they can, quickly and without loss of value, convert to purchasing power. That is, money comprises those assets that can be used to buy the goods, services, and other assets that people wish to buy.

- The narrowest definition of money for the United States and other developed nations is M1, which equals currency held by the public, plus traveler's checks of non-bank issuers, plus demand deposits at commercial banks, plus other checkable deposits.

- A less narrow definition of money and the one favored by economists when they study the relationship between the quantity of money and economic behavior is M2, which equals M1 plus the following: (1) savings deposits, including money market deposit accounts; (2) small-denomination time deposits at depository institutions (except for IRA and Keogh balances); and (3) balances in retail money market deposit accounts (except for IRA and Keogh balances).

Figure 11.2

Money Stock Measures for the U.S.
December 2005 (Billions of Dollars)

Components of M1	
Currency	724
Travelers Checks	7
Demand Deposits	321
Other checkable Deposits	317
M1	1,369
M2	6,676
M3	10,154

Source: Federal Reserve.

Table providing data of the quantity of money in the United States in December 2005.

- The broadest definition of money is M3, which equals M2 plus the following: (1) balances in institutional money market mutual funds; (2) large-denomination time deposits; (3) large repurchase agreements of depository institutions on

U.S. government and federal agency securities; and (4) Eurodollars held by U.S. addressees.

- Notice that bank loans are not counted in any of the definitions of money, but as we shall see, banks create money when they lend to their borrowers.

The Creation of Money
- Commercial banks are the only private financial institutions that create money. The key to understanding this idea is knowing that transactions balances at commercial banks are money.

- Demand deposits at banks (and other depository institutions) are money because economic decision makers regard them as money, using them to buy what they want and to pay what they owe. Sometimes, decision makers have a strong preference for currency, but often, they regard balances in their checking accounts (and, to a lesser extent, their savings accounts) as money. Again, they can easily use savings account and money market balances to buy what they want and pay what they owe.

- To understand how banks create money, let's look at a sequence of stylized balance sheets. The sequence begins with a deposit of $1,000 by a customer who finds it convenient to exchange currency for a bank deposit. The bank faces a legal requirement to hold reserves equal to at least 10% of deposits, but the customer's decision to deposit cash has left the bank with excess reserves; that is, the bank is required to hold only $100 in cash as a reserve against the new deposit but has $1,000.

- The bank now uses its excess reserves to support a new loan of $9,000. It picks one of its loan applicants that it deems to be worthy and lends that individual $9,000, crediting the borrower's deposit account. Thus, the bank has created money.

- Note that the largest increase in deposits that the bank could accommodate with $900 in excess reserves was $900/0.10 = $9,000.

- This scenario assumes that none of the cash "leaks" out of the bank vault when the borrower spends it. If it does leak out, then the leak is captured by another bank, and the "multiplication process" transfers from one bank to another.

- At the end of the day, the deposit of $1,000 in cash increases the money supply by $9,000 because commercial banks use the cash as reserves to support the deposits they create when they write new loans.

- Because banks are required to keep only a fraction of their deposits in the form of reserves (currently, 10%, by law), they create liquidity. That is, they can use $1,000 of currency to support more than $1,000 of deposits.

- The ability to create liquidity is the ability to lend. If banks were required to hold 100% reserves against their deposits, then they would not be able to lend.

Our Image of Bankers

- Our image of bankers as ruthless businessmen may be moderated when we know what bankers really do. They help customers realize plans to purchase homes, cars, and equipment for businesses.

- Of course, our newfound realization of the business of bankers does not completely rehabilitate their image. Banks and bankers came under a tremendous amount of valid criticism for banking practices that contributed to the subprime mortgage crisis. In a later lecture, we will look at that crisis and revisit the role of banks and bankers.

balance sheet: A list of the assets, liabilities, and net worth of a firm or individual and that "net worth" is defined to be the value of the firm's assets minus the value of its liabilities.

bank runs: Situations in which depositors all try to withdraw deposited funds at the same time.

money: An asset that its owners rightly believe they can, quickly and without loss of value, convert to purchasing power.

non-transactions deposits: Deposits in savings accounts, from which funds can be withdrawn at any time.

time deposits: Deposits which have fixed maturity dates.

transactions deposits: Deposits against which checks can be written.

Suggested Reading

Kolb and Rodriguez, *Financial Institutions*.

Meulendyke, *U. S. Monetary Policy and Financial Markets*.

Mishkin, *The Economics of Money, Banking, and Financial Markets*.

Questions to Consider

1. It has sometimes been proposed that banks be required to hold $1.00 of reserves for $1.00 of deposits they accept. In your view, what would be the costs and benefits of such a restriction on commercial bank activity? Would you favor the proposal?

2. Is it a benefit to society that banks are able to create liquidity by holding only a fraction of their deposits in the form of reserves?

3. Commercial loans are inherently illiquid because borrowers use the funds they borrow to undertake business activities that do not immediately produce sufficient cash to pay off the loan. Should banks be allowed to make commercial loans? Why or why not?

Commercial Banks
Lecture 11—Transcript

What do you think of when you hear the word "bank"? If you are like many others, you think of a vault with one of those huge steel vault doors that weighs many tons and requires specially engineered hinges so that it can be swung open. Well there's a reason that the word "bank" evokes such an image. There was a long time ago when the primary function of a bank was to store the wealth of its customers. As we saw in an earlier lecture, a precursor of the modern bank was the European goldsmith who expanded his business from fashioning items out of gold to storing the gold of its customers. Of course Hollywood has helped promote the image of a bank as a vault from Mary Poppins to Bonnie and Clyde. A scene with a bank is almost always a scene with an impressive bank vault.

Another question for you: What do you think when you hear the word "banker"? Again if you are like many, you will think of the famous 20th-century banker J. P. Morgan who had a reputation as a ruthless business man. Or perhaps you will think of Lionel Barrymore, the scion of the famous acting family who played banker Potter, the adversary of Jimmy Stewart's character, George Bailey in the Christmas classic movie *It's a Wonderful Life*. I'm not an expert in psychology, but let me share an opinion.

I think it's likely that the Wall Street versus Main Street metaphor that we encountered earlier was so often used to discuss the subprime financial crisis because it appealed to our society's preconceived notions of banks and of bankers as ruthless business men who have no interest in the common man or his concerns or his needs. In today's lecture we will take a dispassionate look at a bank and the functions it performs in the modern economy. We will learn why banks are the only private financial institutions that can create money. We will investigate bank balance sheets and come to understand the role that banks play in channeling funds from savers to investors. We will study the process by which banks create money. We will also see how the law and, in particular, the Federal Reserve Act, has given an element of control over the process of bank money creation to the Federal Reserve.

The first point that we must have clear is that banks are not repositories. In the very first Harry Potter film, Harry is taken to his vault at Gringotts from which he withdraws a number of coins to buy what he needs for his first year at Hogwarts. In the film, the bank is simply a repository, a place of safekeeping. It's guarded by goblins and, as we later learn, by more ferocious creatures, but it is not a bank in the modern sense. In the United States, the closest thing we have to Gringotts is Fort Knox. Our gold repository, but despite what you may have heard or may have believed, Fort Knox is not a bank.

A good place to begin studying the modern bank is with a look at its balance sheet. Let's think back and recall that a balance sheet is a list of the assets, liabilities, and net worth of a firm or an individual, and in this case it'll be a bank, and that net worth is defined to be the value of a firm's assets minus the value of its liabilities. Therefore, by construction, balance sheets always balance. In this lecture, we are less concerned with any particular bank and more concerned with banks in general and for that reason, we begin our investigation with a look at the consolidated balance sheet of commercial banks. That is, we lump together all the assets, all the liabilities, and look at the banking system as a whole, at the balance sheet of all our commercial banks taken together.

Looking at the T accounts of commercial banks is a lot like paleontology. The numbers we're going to see in the balance sheet are the bones we dig up, and our job is to try to figure out what the ancient animal looked like and how it functioned. The T account depicts the consolidated balance sheet of the commercial banks in the United States at a particular time, the end of December 2005 when the U.S. and world economies were in the midst of an expansion. What do we see? Let's look at the asset side first. The total assets of all the banks taken together was $8 trillion, 707 billion. Well let's break down those assets and see what the bank actually owned.

Treasury securities, so banks own securities that were issued by the Treasury, and that was $1 trillion, 134 billion, or about 13% of all the assets. Banks also owned other securities including securities of some private firms to the tune of $907 billion, or about 10% of its total assets. Banks made commercial and industrial loans of $1 trillion, $45 billion, about 12% of its assets; real estate loans, $2 trillion 904 billion, or about 33% of its total assets; consumer loans, $705 billion or about 8% of total assets; loans to those who were borrowing to buy securities, to buy stocks and bonds, $262 billion, about 3% of assets; and other sorts of loans, $525 billion, 6% of total assets.

Banks also made loans to other banks to the tune of $278 billion, about 3% of total assets. And then we come to an interesting item: cash assets, $311 billion, only 4% of the $8 trillion, 707 billion, that collectively the banks owned. We have a rounding out item, other assets to the tune of $636 billion or 7%. So that's what banks owned.

Collectively, what were their liabilities? This is also a very interesting list but it's somewhat shorter. Collectively, commercial banks had accepted transactions deposits from customers. Customers had deposited funds into the banks, $656 billion, or 8% of the asset total. We'll use the asset total for computing percentages here. They also had large time deposits. Now what are those? Well some customers of a bank will deposit funds that they agree not to reclaim for a period of time. For that reason, those deposits are called "time deposits" and they typically provide the customer with a higher rate of interest. There were $1 trillion, 418 billion of time deposits held at commercial banks, or about 16% of assets. There are other kinds of deposits, $3 trillion, 657 billion, or about 42% of total assets.

As I said before, banks borrow from other banks and the borrowings from other U.S. banks were $361 billion, or 4% of total assets, and borrowings from all other entities about $1 trillion, 360 billion. So banks go out and attempt to borrow funds to do their business and that amounted to 16% of total assets, and other liabilities about $568 billion, or 7%. Net worth: The difference between assets and liabilities: $687 billion, or about 8%.

That's a lot of numbers, but we would like to understand these numbers using the language of sources of funds and uses of funds. A bank's sources of funds are the places from which it gets the funds it uses to prosecute its business. Where does the bank get the funds that it uses to acquire all these assets? Well, banks accept deposits of several types. Transactions deposits are those against which checks can be written. Nontransaction deposits are deposits in savings accounts from which funds can be withdrawn at any time, and time deposits, which have as I've already explained, fixed maturity dates. Large denomination time deposits are certificates of deposits in amounts at or over $100,000 that are generally purchased by corporations and other banks. As I've said, banks borrow funds from other banks, from the Federal Reserve, from the Federal Home Loan Bank, and from corporations. In December of 2005, total liabilities of the commercial banks in the United States amounted to slightly more than $8 trillion.

How did the banks use the funds that they acquired by accepting those deposits and doing those borrowings? As we've seen, banks hold, to some extent, Treasury securities and other government agency securities. So they hold a bond portfolio. Banks hold, to some extent, bonds and other securities of private corporations. But primarily banks lend funds to businesses for real estate purchases, to consumers in the form of auto loans and other types of consumer loans, and to those who use the borrowed funds to purchase securities and for some other types of loan activities. Banks hold cash assets of 2 sorts, actual physical currency in their vaults and deposits at the Federal Reserve. Both are considered cash assets. In December 2005, total assets held by commercial banks amounted to a bit more than $8.7 trillion. In 2005 also bank net worth equaled $687 billion.

What is the relative importance of various sources and uses of bank funds? Despite the fact that banks actively go out and borrow funds, they are still primarily depository institutions in that 70% of their liabilities are deposits of one sort or another. By the way, it's important to keep track of the fact that it's only transactions deposits against which commercial banks are required to hold reserves, and transactions deposits account for only about 8% of all liabilities. Despite the fact that banks hold various kinds of securities, they are primarily lending institutions, and 62% of their assets are loans of one sort or another. In 2005, banks had net worth or capital equal to 8.6% of their liabilities and about 8% of their assets. Banks and bank regulators have worked hard especially in recent years to determine minimal levels of bank capital needed to assure bank safety.

Bank capital is a tricky business. The value of bank capital can drop very quickly in bad economic times because the market value of the securities that the bank owns can fall and, more importantly, because the true value of bank loans fall. We'll talk in later lectures about the true value of loans and how it changes in that value affect the stability of the banking system, but for now, keep in mind that what is important is to understand that bank capital isn't something physical that's locked in a vault. Bank capital changes when the value of assets changes and falls when the value of assets fall. A related point and very important one is to realize that banks are always susceptible to bank runs. Remember, again, *It's a Wonderful Life*. Those are events where depositors all try to withdrawal their deposited funds at the same time. Why? In December 2005, commercial bank deposit liabilities totaled $5.7 trillion and of that, $656 billion were demand deposits but bank cash assets totaled only $311 billion, less by far than would be needed to redeem even those deposits that depositors had the right to redeem for cash at any time. In this sense, banks are fragile no matter how well they are managed.

Now that we have a more precise understanding of the assets and liabilities of commercial banks, we are in a position for the first time in this course to define money in a formal way. We've used the term "money" often. I've talked about how the government quote/unquote prints money to finance deficits. Now we're actually going to define what is considered to be money in the United States. In particular, we're going to ask and answer the question, which assets in the United States are considered part of the money supply in the United States. I'm going to assure you that the definitions that we use in the United States are pretty much the same as the definitions used by all economies in the world. Our reference point will again be December of 2005. If you have, at some time in your life, taken a principles of economics course some of the following points may be familiar, but don't worry I'm not going to dwell on arcane facts. Keep in mind though that as we go through the various definitions of money, these various definitions share a common intuition. I like to dwell on that intuition.

Money is some asset that its owners rightly believe they can quickly and without loss of value convert to purchasing power. What? Well let's say it a different way. Money comprises those assets that can be used to buy the goods, services, and other assets that people wish to buy. That's what I meant by purchasing power, but the point is so important that I want to say a few more words in clarification. I wished I owned a painting by Van Gogh. If I owned a painting by Van Gogh, I'd be happy, and I'd be wealthy. However, I would never think of a Van Gogh painting as money. It's not a liquid asset. It would be exceedingly difficult to convert it to cash. Think about how difficult. I'd have to determine what its potential value was. I'd have to arrange some way to sell it. I'd have to allow for bids. Oh, it might be a great asset but it would never be money. It could take me years to convert a Van Gogh to cash.

The narrowest definition of money that we use in the United States and other developed nations use as well is what's called M1, capital M, number 1, which equals currency held by the public plus traveler's checks by nonbank issuers plus demand deposits at commercial banks and any other checkable deposits.

Well that's very, very intuitive. Clearly we can pay with cash. We can pay with our checking accounts, and we can pay with traveler's checks. So all of that belongs in M1. But that's probably not a broad enough definition of money to really capture the notion of money as purchasing power. So a less narrow definition of money and the one favored by economists when they studied the relationship between the quantity of money and economic behavior is called M2, capital M, number 2. That definition of money, M2, equals everything in M1 plus savings deposits, including money market deposit accounts and small denomination time deposits at depository institutions, leaving out IRA and Keogh balances, and balances in retail money market deposit accounts, again excepting IRA and Keogh balances.

Let's pause for a minute and understand that. Why ought those items be part of our definition of money? Very simply if you've got funds in a money market mutual fund or something like it, you realize that you can quickly deposit those in your checking account or receive a cashier's check for them and use them to purchase goods. That's why they're part of our money supply. By the way, when I showed you a graph earlier in which I showed you the connection between money growth and inflation, it was M2 that I used.

Our broadest definition of money is M3, which includes everything in M2 plus balances in institutional money markets and large denomination time deposits and large so-called repurchase agreements of depository institutions, and also euro dollars. These are dollars held by U.S. citizens at foreign locations. I'm not even going to talk about that. Most economists acknowledge that M3 includes additional highly liquid assets but typically revert to M2 when they're interested in talking about the money supply.

Take a look at a table that provides data on the quantity of money in the United States in December 2005. Let's first take a look at the components of M1 so we can answer the question, how large was the money supply back then. Currency, $724 billion on that December time; traveler's checks, $7 billion; demand deposits, $321 billion; and other checkable deposits, $317 billion. So M1, the narrowest definition of money was $1 trillion, 369 billion; M2, which added all those other assets that were liquid like money market mutual fund balances, much larger, $6 trillion, 676 billion; and M3 larger still, $10 trillion, 154 billion. Now notice before we go on that bank loans are not counted in any of our money definitions but, and somewhat ironically, as we shall now see banks create money when they lend to borrowers.

Commercial banks of all our financial intermediaries are special firms in that they are the only private financial institutions that can and do create money, but how do they do that? The key is that transactions balances at commercial banks are counted as money. They're part of even the narrowest definition of the money supply. So the first thing we must realize is that demand deposits at banks are money. They are money because economic decision makers regard them to be money, and they use those balances, those decision makers, in much the same way they use currency, to buy what they want and pay what they owe.

Sometimes decision makers do have a strong preference for currency. Every time I go to New York, I carry more cash than I normally would when I go to other places or stay at home because New York is a place where sometimes only cash can be used to buy things, but generally and most of the time, decision makers regard balances in their checking account to be money. Why? Because they can easily use those balances to buy what they want and pay what they owe.

So exactly how do banks create money? I'm going to illustrate this story with a sequence of stylized balances sheets, T accounts. The story begins with a deposit of $1000 in cash by some bank customers who finds it convenient to exchange currency for a bank deposit. The bank, I assume, faces a legal requirement to hold reserves equal to at least 10% of deposits, but the customer's decision to deposit cash has now left the bank with extra reserves or excess reserves. For that $1000 deposit, the bank is only required to hold $100 in cash as a reserve against the new deposit but has a whole $1000 in cash after the deposit is made. So the bank now uses its excess reserves to support a new loan of $9000. It picks one of its loan applicants that it deems worthy and lends that individual $9000. It credits the deposit account of the borrower with $9000. It adds $9000 to that depositor account, and at that moment, the bank has created money.

How did I choose $9000? Well I chose it as the largest increase in deposits that the bank could accommodate with $900 in excess reserves given that the reserve requirement is 10%, and simply 900 divided by 10.1 is $9000. Now, I'm making a simplifying assumption. None of the cash leaks out of the bank vault or out of the bank's balance sheet when the borrowers spend it, but don't worry about that. If bank customers spend those new loan funds with customers at other banks, that simply means that this expansion of money process transfers from one bank to another. It's not really important, and I won't really dwell on it.

At the end of the day, the deposit of $1000 in cash increases the money supply by $9000 because commercial banks use the cash as reserves, super dollars, to support the deposits they create when they write new loans. Because banks are required, by law, to only keep a fraction of their deposits in the form of reserves, banks create liquidity. That is, they could use $1000 of currency to support more than $1000 of deposits. We saw $10,000. The ability to create liquidity is the ability to lend. If banks were required to hold 100% of their reserves against their deposits, they would not be able to lend, and they would be simple repositories.

As we shall see in a later lecture, bank loans are a crucial source of funds for investors. Without loans, many potential investors would not be able to grow their businesses if the reserve requirement had been 20%, it's not, the deposit of $1000 would've allowed the banks to create only $4000 in deposits in money. On the other hand, if it had been lower, 5%, the deposit would've allowed banks to create ultimately $20,000 in deposits in money.

As we come to the end of this lecture, it's fair to ask now how people should think of bankers once they really know what bankers do. A banker is someone who helps a customer realize plans, plans to purchase equipment for their businesses, purchase a home, purchase a car, or purchase something else. Of course our new found realization of the business of bankers does not completely rehabilitate their image. Banks and bankers came under a tremendous amount of valid criticism for banking practices that contributed to the subprime mortgage crisis. In a later lecture, we'll look at that crisis and think about the role of banks and bankers again, but for now, let me ask you, how do you think about banks and how do you think about bankers?

Central Banks

Lecture 12

This lecture looks at the most important financial institution in the United States, the institution that is entrusted to maintain and protect the wealth of our nation, guard the value of the U.S. dollar, and exercise regulatory control over commercial banks and other financial firms: The Federal Reserve. This powerful bank—and other central banks around the world—does not offer banking services to private citizens; instead, it provides banking services to commercial banks. It also enforces some of that laws that regulate financial firms, but the real source of its power is that it is entrusted with the ability to control our economy's interest rates and the responsibility to fight inflation and recessions.

Central Banks around the World

- Although the U.S. Federal Reserve is widely considered to be the most powerful of central banks (in part because people around the world hold dollars as part of their financial strategies), other central banks are also important.

- The Bank of England was founded in 1694 to act as the government's banker and debt manager. It is the oldest central bank that we will consider in this lecture series.

- Also of great importance is the European Central Bank (ECB), which was created by the Treaty of Amsterdam in 1998 to oversee monetary policy in the euro area. The ECB is located in Frankfurt, Germany.

- A central bank that is increasingly important in the 21st century is the People's Bank of China in Beijing.

A Brief History of the U.S. Federal Reserve

- President Woodrow Wilson signed the Federal Reserve Act in December of 1913. Its stated intent was "to provide for the establishment of the Federal reserve banks, to furnish an elastic currency, to afford means of rediscounting commercial paper, to establish a more effective supervision of banking in the United States, and for other purposes."

- As you recall, the United States had tried earlier to create a federal bank entity. It chartered the First Bank of the United States in 1791 and the Second Bank of the United States in 1816. Both banks were given initial charters of 20 years, but neither saw its charter renewed.

- The Federal Reserve Act has been amended many times. In the 1930s, for example, it was amended to create the Federal Open Market Committee (FOMC), which is empowered to conduct monetary policy. This committee oversees purchases and sales of government bonds by the Federal Reserve in the open market; it also decides on interest rate targets.

- An announcement by the FOMC of an increase in the federal funds rate quickly tightens credit markets and raises interest rates. A decrease in the federal funds rate is a harbinger of lower interest rates and looser credit markets.

- In 1978, President Carter signed the Humphrey-Hawkins Act into law. This act requires the Federal Reserve chairman to report twice annually to Congress on the Fed's monetary policy goals and objectives. It also explicitly instructs the nation to strive toward four ultimate goals: full employment, growth in production, price stability, and balance of trade and budget.

- In 1999, President Clinton signed the Financial Services Modernization Act, which effectively repealed some of the restrictions placed on banks in the 1930s after the Great Depression.

What Does a Central Bank Do?

- One way to explore the role and responsibilities of a central bank is to take a look at its balance sheet.

- The balance sheet of the Federal Reserve as of December 28, 2005, shows that it holds gold certificates, a holdover from the period of the gold standard.

- The Fed's most important asset item is Treasury securities.

- The Fed also holds special drawing rights. These are assets created by the International Monetary Fund in 1969 in an attempt to support the gold standard. They functioned like paper gold and were used by central banks as a substitute for gold holdings.

Figure 12.1

Balance Sheet of the Federal Reserve
December 28, 2005 (Billions of Dollars)

Assets		Liabilities	
Gold Certificates	11.0	Federal Reserve Notes	759.2
Special Drawing Rights	2.2	Reverse Repurchase Agreements	30.4
Coin	0.7	Depository Institution Deposits	17.1
US Treasury Securities	744.2	US Treasury Deposits	4.2
Federal Agency Securities	0.0	Foreign Official Deposits	0.09
Repurchase Agreements	45.3	Other Deposits	0.3
Loans	0.1	Deferred Availability of Cash Items	6.7
Items in the Process of Collection	7.8	Other Liabilities	4.4
Bank Premises	1.8	**Total Liabilities**	822.4
Other Assets	37.3		
Total Assets	850.4	Net Worth	28.0

Source: Federal Reserve.

- The Fed often conducts monetary policy using a derivative called a repurchase agreement.

- A look at the other side of the balance sheet shows that the Fed's most important liability is Federal Reserve Notes. This is the paper currency of the United States, which is issued by and is the liability of the Federal Reserve.

- Note, too, that the Federal Reserve is the bankers' bank. Banks hold deposits at the Fed that totaled $17.1 billion on December 28, 2005. Commercial banks sometimes borrow funds from the Fed, and when they do, the Fed credits their deposit accounts.

- The Fed balance sheet helps us understand what economists mean when they say that governments sometimes print money to finance their deficits. The Treasury issues bonds and bills to finance its deficits, but the Fed sometimes buys those bonds and bills. When it buys them, it finances those purchases by creating new deposits.

- In the previous lecture, we learned that commercial banks create money. When a commercial bank makes a new loan to a customer, it adds funds to the customer's deposit account. Because the money supply of the United States includes checkable deposits, the commercial bank increases the supply of money when it makes a new loan.

- When the Federal Reserve buys a Treasury security, it pays for the security by adding funds to the deposit account of a commercial bank. That, in turn, makes it possible for the bank to make new loans and create new deposits.

- The Fed also helps commercial banks clear checks: The entries in the balance sheet labeled "Items in Process of Collection" and "Deferred Availability of Cash Items" result when the Fed receives a check from a commercial bank and holds it for a time until it can be presented to the commercial bank of the individual that wrote the check in the first place.

- Finally, the Fed functions as the paymaster of the Treasury. The Treasury actually has a "checking account" at the Fed.

The Balance Sheet of the Bank of England
- The balance sheet of the Bank of England tells a similar story, with a few differences.

- Assets equal liabilities for the Bank of England because, under British law, the Bank of England's net worth is the property of the British Treasury.

- The largest asset and liability items on this balance sheet are securities owned by the bank and currency issued by the bank.

- Both commercial banks and private citizens may have deposits at the Bank of England. The Bank of England also makes loans to commercial banks.

- The Bank of England maintains separate accounts for deposits that commercial banks hold as reserves and other deposits.

Figure 12.2

Balance Sheet of the Bank of England
December 28, 2005 (Billions of Pounds Sterling)

Assets		Liabilities	
Government Securities	15.5	Pound Streling Notes in Circulation	40.3
Other Securities	26.9	Public Deposits	0.8
Advances	15.7	Deposits of Banks	3.3
Bank Premises and Equipment	7.7	Deposits in Reserve Accounts	21.4
Total Assets	65.8	Total Liabilities	65.8

Source: Bank of England.

The Most Powerful Financial Institutions in the World

- Central banks are considered the most powerful financial institutions in the world because they are responsible for the growth in their nations' supplies of money.

- When the Fed creates additional money and, thus, increases the money supply at an appropriate rate, it helps the economy grow by providing the new dollars necessary to support the transactions associated with growth.

- When the Fed increases the money supply too rapidly, the rate of inflation increases and the value of the dollar, in terms of other currencies, falls. In later lectures, we will look in more detail at how central banks stimulate and de-stimulate economies.

Figure 12.3

Excessive Money Growth Results in Inflation
Ten Year Growth Rates in Annual Terms

Period	Money Base Growth	Real GDP Growth	Inflation
1955 - 65	3.0	3.9	1.8

Data Source: FRED, Federal Reserve Economic Data, Federal Reserve Bank of St. Louis.

Suggested Reading

Kolb and Rodriguez, *Financial Institutions*.

Mishkin, *The Economics of Money, Banking, and Financial Markets*.

———, "What Should Central Banks Do?"

1. How would you characterize the evidence that supports the conclusion that central banks are responsible when excess inflation occurs in an economy? What is the nature of the evidence? Is the evidence strong or weak?

2. Why is it reasonable to describe a central bank as a "banker's bank"?

3. How does the Federal Reserve differ from the U.S. Treasury?

Central Banks
Lecture 12—Transcript

In today's lecture, we are going to talk about the most important financial institution in the United States. This institution is entrusted to maintain and protect the wealth of the United States. This institution is in charge of guarding the value of the U.S. dollar. This institution has strong regulatory control over commercial banks and other financial firms. Every developed nation in the world has one of these institutions. So what is this powerful institution?

The first answer that will come to mind to many when we talk about the wealth of the United States is Fort Knox, the U.S. gold repository; but Fort Knox, while formidable in appearance, is nowhere near as important as the institution about which I will speak today. In fact, the role of Fort Knox today is like the role of our strategic petroleum reserve. I think I've mentioned that before. It's a secure storehouse of a valuable resource. It's nothing more.

The institution I have in mind appears far less formidable than Fort Knox, but it is far more important to our national wealth. It is far more important to our national welfare. It is far more powerful, and it is far more essential to our financial system. The institution I have in mind is the Federal Reserve. The building that might be considered the home of the Federal Reserve, although the Fed, as we call it, has many branches in many building, is the Martin Building in Washington DC, which houses the offices of the board of governors of the Federal Reserve. The board of governors comprises the individuals who control the United States Federal Reserve, the Central Bank of the United States.

In today's lecture, I will look at central banks and explain why they are the most important financial institutions in the world. Ironically, central banks do not offer banking services to private citizens like you or like me or like the business where you work. Instead, they provide banking services to commercial banks, and that's why the Federal Reserve is sometimes referred to as the bankers' bank; and as I mentioned, they also enforce some of the laws that regulate commercial banks and other financial firms. But the real source of the power of the U.S. Federal Reserve and of central banks throughout the world is that they are entrusted with the ability to control an economy's interest rates, and they are entrusted with the responsibility to fight inflation and recessions.

While the U.S. Federal Reserve is widely considered to be the most powerful among the central banks, in part because people all over the world hold dollars as part of their financial strategies, other central banks are also very important. The Bank of England was founded in 1694 to act as the government's banker and debt manager. It is the oldest central bank that we will consider in this lecture series. The Central Bank of Sweden, founded in 1668, is generally considered to be the oldest. Also of great importance is a very young central bank, the European Central Bank. The European Central Bank was created by the Treaty of Amsterdam to oversee monetary policy in the euro area. Leaders of the European Economic Community reached agreement on a currency union in which union member nations would adopt a common currency, and they reached that agreement with the Maastricht Treaty in February of 1992.

The euro, as you may remember, was launched in 1999, and euro paper currency and coins began to circulate in 2002. The European Central Bank is located in Frankfurt, Germany, and the sculpture pictured in front of the European Central Bank is the actual logo of the euro. Finally, let's take a brief look at a central bank that is increasingly important in the 21st century and will be even more important as time passes. The picture is of the People's Bank of China, and the building that houses that bank in Beijing, about which we will learn much more in future lectures.

Let me offer you a brief history of the United States Federal Reserve. It was front-page news when President Woodrow Wilson signed the Federal Reserve Act in December of 1913. The Act stated that its intent was, and I quote, "to provide for the establishment of the Federal Reserve Banks, to furnish an elastic currency, to afford means of rediscounting commercial paper, to establish a more effective supervision of banking in the United States, and for other purposes."

Let me unpack that statement for you for a moment. What the enactors of the Federal Reserve meant by an elastic currency was that the Federal Reserve would have the tools necessary to expand the money supply and contract it, to make the currency stretch, if you like, and snap back. That was considered to be very, very important as part of the strategy of allowing the Federal Reserve Bank to not only facilitate growth in the United States but also to be a bull work against banking panics. What the Act meant when it said the rediscounting of commercial paper, it simply meant that the Federal Reserve Act allowed the Federal Reserve to accept from banks loans that they had made to private companies in exchange for currency. This would be very, very important when a rush would occur on commercial banks, and they did not have sufficient cash to be able to meet the demand for their depositors. Enter the Fed, which could exchange some of their loans for cash.

As we certainly recall from the first and second lectures, the United States had tried before to create a Federal Reserve Bank. It chartered the first bank of the United States in 1791 and the second bank of the United States in 1860, but we also know that both banks were given initial charters only of 20 years, and that neither bank saw its charter renewed. The Federal Reserve Act has been amended many times since its initial enactment in December of 1913. I'm only going to hit a few highlights.

In the 1930s, the Federal Reserve Act was amended to create the Federal Open Market Committee, which was empowered to conduct monetary policy. That committee is called the Open Market Committee because it oversees purchases by the Fed and sales by the Fed of government bonds in the open market. So in point of fact, it is the Federal Open Market Committee that decides on purchases of Treasury bonds and sale of Treasury bonds. It follows that it is the Federal Open Market Committee that decides on interest rate targets for the Federal Reserve and decides on strategies to hit those targets. Announcements by the Federal Reserve Open Market Committee are closely watched by financial analysts. It's big news when FOMC announces an increase in the so-called Federal funds rate. We'll learn about the Federal funds rate in the future.

Analysts know that an increase in the Federal funds rate will shortly tighten credit markets and raise interest rates across the board. As a result, investment projects will be harder to finance, mortgage rates and rates on auto loans will rise as well. Of course it's also big news when the FOMC announces a decrease in the Federal funds rate because that decrease is a harbinger of lower rates and looser credit markets. We'll see how this works later in the course when we talk specifically about monetary policy.

Another amendment of the Federal Reserve Act was put in place when President Carter signed the Humphrey Hawkins Act into law in 1978. The Humphrey is Hubert Humphrey. The Act required the Federal Reserve chairman to report twice annually to Congress. We've pictures of Bernanke going up the Hill, in part, because of that Act. That Act, the Humphrey Hawkins Act, also spoke to the monetary policy goals and objectives of the Federal Reserve. The Act explicitly instructs the nation to strive toward 4 ultimate goals: full employment of resources, growth in production, price stability, and balance of trade and budget. Although in modern times in the current year, we normally think of the Fed's mandate as having 2 parts: Stable prices and low inflation rates is the first part of the mandate and full employment of resources is the second.

In 1999, President Clinton signed into law the Financial Services Modernization Act which effectively repealed some of the restrictions placed on banks in the 1930s after the Great Depression. That turns out to be very important, so important that we'll study the what and why of that particular Act in a later lecture.

What does a central bank do? One way to answer the question is to take a look at the balance sheet of a central bank. We will see that investigating the balance sheet is as close as economists come to archaeology, if you like. The balance sheet contains current evidence about the Fed's behavior and evidence that reveals its history. So let's dig.

What we see as one of the most important assets of the Federal Reserve are gold certificates, $11 billion worth on December 28, 2005. Why that date? Let me explain. I chose that date in particular because the United States was near full employment, and we could imagine that the balance sheet of the Federal Reserve was, shall we say, in a condition that was normal for a time when the economy was at full employment, where times were good economically speaking. We're going to see a little later on that the Fed's balance sheet looks very, very different in the depths of a recession, but I digress.

We see that the Federal Reserve owns something called gold certificates, $11 billion worth, and it also owns something called special drawing rights, $2.2 billion worth. These are vestiges from the gold standard. The Federal Reserve acquired those gold certificates as a result of an earlier time when it was required to back the U.S. dollar with gold, and it acquired the special drawing rights as part of an IMF attempt to keep the gold standard alive by issuing paper gold.

The Federal Reserve also has coin among its assets and importantly, far more important than the coin, $744 billion worth of U.S. Treasury securities. Those Treasury securities are a very important part of history. We've talked many times already in this course, and we will continue to talk about governments that print money in order to pay their bills and finance their deficits. This is a time when we do a check here and realize that's not literally true. What happens is that treasuries borrow to finance deficits, but central banks and the U.S. Federal Reserve sometimes buy some of those bonds, essentially printing or creating money to do that acquisition. That's how our Federal Reserve has ended up with $744 billion in government bonds at least at the end of 2005.

We also have something on the asset side of the balance sheet called a repurchase agreement. This is an interesting asset as well. A repurchase agreement is a particular kind of reversible agreement, and the Federal Reserve uses these when it attempts to, say, buy government bonds and also hold them for only a particular amount of time and then resell them. The actual asset it ends up acquiring is called a repurchase agreement.

There are some other asset items relatively small. We see loans, those are to banks. Items in the process of collection; those are important because the Federal Reserve has, through time, helped clear checks; and of course, there's bank premises and other assets. Total assets? $850 billion. The liability side of the Federal Reserve balance sheet is also interesting. Here we see something extremely important right at the top. The number 1 liability of the Federal Reserve are Federal Reserve notes, are paper currency, $759 billion worth.

We also have an item called reverse repurchase agreements. They're the counterpart of repurchase agreements but in the opposite direction. We have deposits by depository institutions. So $17.1 billion, and what are these? These are the deposits of commercial banks at the Federal Reserve. Likewise, our own Treasury has deposits of $4.2 billion at our Federal Reserve. So the Federal Reserve is not only the bankers' bank. It's also our government's bank. Our Treasury pays its bills by drawing on its deposit account at the Federal Reserve. The deferred availability of cash items is the counterpart, an accounting entry that again refers to the fact that the Federal Reserve plays a role in clearing checks. The net worth of the Federal Reserve is $28 billion.

So in summary, what is it that we learn when we do this archaeology activity from the balance sheet of the Fed? The most important things we learn are that the Fed balance sheet helps us to understand what economists mean when they say that governments sometimes print money to finance their deficits. The Treasury issues bonds and bills to finance its deficits but the Fed sometimes buys those bonds and bills. When it buys them, it finances those purchases by creating new deposits. So when we say that governments sometimes print money to finance their deficits, what we mean is that governments issue bonds and that central banks create new deposits in favor of commercial banks and use those balances to buy the bonds from the Treasury.

In the previous lecture, I explained that commercial banks create money. Let me clarify. When a commercial bank makes a new loan to a customer, it adds funds to a customer's deposit account because the money supply the United States includes checkable deposits, the commercial bank increases the supply of money when it makes a new loan. When the Federal Reserve buys a Treasury security, it pays for the security by adding funds to the deposit account of a commercial bank. Remember it's the bankers' bank. That in turn makes it possible for the bank to make new loans and create new deposits. We'll look at this process in detail a bit later.

We also learned that the Fed helps commercial banks clear checks. The items in process of collection and the deferred availability of cash item entries in the balance sheet result when the Fed receives a check from a commercial bank, holds it for a time until it can be presented to another commercial bank for payment. The check may actually pass from coast to coast from the Federal Reserve Bank of New York to the Federal Reserve Bank of San Francisco.

We also understand from our study of the balance sheet of the Fed that the Fed functions as the pay master of the Treasury. The Treasury actually has a checking account at the Fed. It would be interesting even if the Federal Reserve Bank of the United States had a balance sheet that was somewhat unique, but let's check for a minute and verify that the balance sheet of the Bank of England tells a very similar story with only a couple of differences.

Looking at the balance sheet of the Bank of England, we see that it too owns government securities, about $15.5 billion pounds. It owns some other securities, $26.9 billion. It makes loans, which in their balance sheet are called advances, and it owns bank premises. On the liability side, we see that it too has as a liability pound sterling notes, $40.3 billion of them. However unusually there are some public deposits at the Bank of England, which are of historical interest but not of interest to us, and we also note that it too, the Bank of England, also is the bankers' bank. Banks have about $3.3 billion pounds of deposits at the Bank of England.

At the end of the day, we realize that the Bank of England functions a lot like the Federal Reserve Bank. The largest assets and liabilities are securities owned by the bank and currency issued by the bank. Both commercial banks and private citizens may have deposits at the Bank of England. The Bank of England makes loans to commercial banks and the Bank of England maintains separate accounts for deposits that commercial banks hold as reserves and other deposits.

One interesting difference is that the Bank of England does not list any net worth. Its assets equal its liabilities. The reason for that is that the Treasury of England owns, by law, the net worth of the Bank of England. That's a matter of law and of no particular importance for us. What is very important is a better understanding of why central banks are the most powerful financial institutions in the world. Well, central banks are responsible for growth in the nation's supply of money.

When the Fed creates additional money and thus increases in the money supply at an appropriate rate, it helps the economy grow by providing the new dollars that are necessary to support the transactions associated with growth. We saw, in a previous lecture, that in a period of time when the money supply grew not rapidly enough in the last quarter of the 19th century, there was actual price deflation. There were 2 recessions and there was a banking panic. So it's very, very important for the Federal Reserve to allow the money supply to grow at a rate that keeps pace with the productive growth in an economy.

When we looked at across country comparison of inflation and money growth rates, remember please that we defined excess money growth as the money growth that created inflation. We defined excess money growth as money growth beyond the rate necessary to just keep pace with real economic growth, which we measured in that case as the growth in income.

When the Federal Reserve increases money supply too rapidly however, the rate of inflation does increase and the value of the dollar in terms of other currency falls. Looking over some decades of data provides examples of when the Fed has gotten it right and when the Fed has gotten it wrong. If we look between 1955 and 1965, at that decade, the growth in the base money supply, the supply that the Federal Reserve controls, was 3%, real GDP growth was 3.9% and inflation was very, very small, 1.8%. It was a very different story about the decade from '65 to '75. Money growth, 6.8%, real growth in gross domestic product only 2.9%, and not surprisingly the inflation rate rose to 5.5% on average in the decade. I know that you know that certain years in that decade had higher inflation rates, but we've got an even worse decade just ahead. In the decade between 1975 and 1985, the Fed allowed the money growth rate to rise to 8.1%. Yes, real GDP growth was slightly higher, 3.4%, but the major impact was an inflation rate, on average for that decade, of 6.1%.

In the next decade, '85 to '95, the Fed allowed the money growth rate to be 8% again. The GDP growth rate was 2.8%, and surprisingly the inflation rate was only 2.8% but I attribute that to the belief on the part of individuals that under first the Volker regime at the Federal Reserve and then the Greenspan regime at the Federal Reserve that the Fed was beginning to decrease the rate of money growth. Indeed between 1995 and 2005, the money growth rate fell to 6%. The growth rate of the United States, the real growth rate, rose to 3.3% and inflation came under control to 2.1%.

We will look in more detail at how central banks stimulate and de-stimulate the economy in later lectures. For now we're going to end by reconsidering how crucial it is for central banks to get it right. We have learned today that central banks are the most powerful institutions in the world because they have the power to increase or decrease the money supplies of their respective economies. When they get it right, economies grow and inflation stays in check. When they get it wrong, they either stifle growth by keeping money growth too low, or they create inflation by allowing money growth to be too high. When they get it very wrong, as in the case of Germany in the 1920s, or Zimbabwe today, hyperinflation can be the result.

The bottom line is that the Federal Reserve, because of its power and awesome responsibility, is the most powerful financial institution in the world. Thank you very much.

Present Value

Lecture 13

All of us need to move money through time at some point in our lives. We may, for example, need to move money from the future into the present to buy a house. That's what we do when we sign a note and take out a mortgage. Business managers move money through time when they borrow against expected future profits to obtain funds to build and install equipment in a new plant. Deciding on how to move money through time requires us to be able to compare the value of a dollar at two different dates, and in this lecture, you'll learn about the tool that allows us to make that comparison: present value.

The Puzzle of Pat and Jean

- We begin with a puzzle we can solve using the idea of present value: Pat and Jean are twins who just celebrated their 21st birthday. As a birthday gift, their grandmother gave them a U.S. savings bond that will pay $10,000 on their 31st birthday and nothing before then. Put another way, a fair division of the birthday gift will provide Pat and Jean each with $5000 in 10 years.

- Pat has worked for several years, currently has $15,000 in a bank account, and is content to wait to receive his share of the gift. Jean has started a business into which she has poured all of her funds; she would like to have her share of the gift now.

- Jean suggests that Pat give her $5000 now from his bank account in exchange for her share of the gift. She reasons that Pat will get the money back in 10 years when he receives both halves of the gift. But if Pat left the money in his bank account, he would receive interest on the $5000. He thinks it would be fair to pay Jean a lesser amount for her share of the gift.

- The key to solving Pat and Jean's problem is the concept of present value.

The Concept of Present Value

- The concept of present value is central to understanding the relationship between bond prices and interest rates. It is also the key to determining what a share of stock should be worth and, by extension, when stock is overvalued. This concept guides business managers in deciding whether or not to invest and household decision makers as they decide on savings plans to fund future college expenses or retirement.

- With rare exceptions, a dollar that will be received (or paid) in the future (a future dollar) is worth less than a dollar in hand today (dollar today).

- A dollar today provides its owner with a larger set of opportunities than a future dollar provides. One of these opportunities is to hold the dollar until the future arrives. A dollar today is more valuable because the extra opportunities it affords are valuable.

- Usually, you can earn interest on a dollar today and, at a future date, have both the dollar plus the earned interest.

- The Treasury bill market provides an example. A Treasury bill is the U.S. Treasury's promise to pay an amount (say, $1000) at a date in the future. The current market price of a Treasury bill is always less than the face value of the bill; that is, the bill sells at a discount. As the date of payment grows closer, the market price of the bill converges to its face value.

Computing Present Value

- To compute the present value of a future payment is to discount the future payment.

- A **discount rate** is a positive number that defines the rate at which a future payment loses value as the date of the payment moves further into the future. It is expressed as a decimal.

Figure 13.1

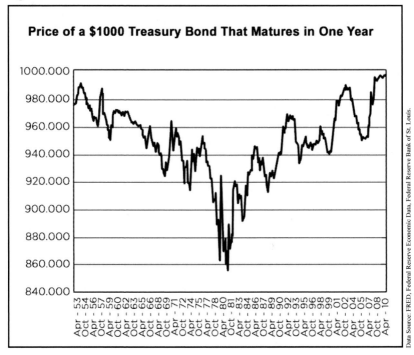

Price of a $1000 Treasury Bond That Matures in One Year

Data Source: FRED, Federal Reserve Economic Data, Federal Reserve Bank of St. Louis.

- As an example, suppose the time is measured in years and the discount rate is $d = 0.07$ (or 7%). Then, a dollar to be received after one year is worth 7% less than a dollar in hand today.

- To discount a future payment is to divide it by a number greater than 1.0 $(1 + d)$.

Present-Value Formula
- The present value of a payment to be made at a future date is an amount just large enough so that it will grow to the size of the future payment by the future date.

- For example, the present value (PV) of $1.00 to be received in one year is as follows:

$$PV = \$1.00/(1 + d)$$

$$PV = \$1.00/1.07$$

$$PV = \$0.935$$

- We can rewrite the formula to illustrate that the present value grows into the future value (FV), as follows:

$$FV = \$1.00$$

$$FV = (1 + d) \times PV$$

$$\$1.00 = (1.07) \times \$0.935$$

- The present-value formula shows how to compute the present value of a stream of payments. Suppose, again, that time is measured in years. Let t be the present date, $t + 1$ is a date one year into the future, $t + 2$ is a date two years into the future, and so on. The stream of payments is represented as: S_{t+1} dollars at time $t + 1$, S_{t+2} dollars at $t + 2$, and so forth. The present-value formula is as follows:

$$PV = S(t + 1) / (1 + d) + S(t + 2) / (1 + d)^2 + \ldots + S(t + m) / (1 + d)^m$$

- Suppose the stream of payments is $100 at $t + 1$, $100 at $t + 2$, and $1100 at $t + 3$ so that $m = 3$. This is the stream of payments promised by a bond with a face value of $1,000 and a coupon rate of 10%. The formula would read as follows:

$$PV = \$100 / (1.07) + \$100 / ((1.07)^2 + \$1,100 / (1.07)^3$$

$$PV = \$93.458 + \$87.344 + \$897.928 = \$1,078.73$$

- Thus, $1078.73 is the present value of the stream of payments ($100, $100, $1100) when the discount rate is 7%.

- The present value of a stream of payments is the exact amount that is sufficient to replicate the stream of payments provided that one can borrow and lend at the discount rate used in the present-value calculation.

- If we start with an amount equal to the present value of the stream of payments, deposit that amount in an account paying 7% (the discount rate assumed), and make withdrawals just sufficient to make the payments in the stream, then we will exhaust the available funds on the date of the last payment.

- This example shows the sense in which the present value of a stream of payments is equivalent to the stream and a fair price for purchasing the stream.

Present Value and Savings
- The concept of present value is crucial in figuring out a savings plan to provide sufficient funds for planned future payments.

- Suppose you decide to save for your child's education by depositing an amount each year into a special fund. Your goal is to have $100,000 in the fund on the child's 18th birthday. The key to determining how much you must save each year is to use the present-value formula.

- The present value of the fund is: P Val Fund = $100,000 / $(1 + d)^{18}$.

- The present value of your saving plan is: P Val Plan = $x + x / (1 + d)$ $= x / (1 + d)^2 + \ldots + x / (1 + d)^{18}$.

- In these formulas, d is the discount; it would be appropriate to use the rate of interest you can earn on your saving plan funds for d.

- In the second formula, x is the unknown amount you must save. To calculate the saving plan is to find the value of x such that the present value of the fund equals the present value of the plan.

- If $d = 0.02$—that is, if you can earn 2% on your funds—then $x = \$4378.18$.

What about Pat and Jean?

- Armed with our knowledge of present value, we return to the question of how much Pat should pay Jean today to fairly compensate Pat for giving up the claim to $5,000 to be paid 10 years from today.

- The present-value formula tells us that Pat should pay Jean: Present Value $= \$5000 / (1 + d)^{10}$. Pat can earn 3% in a savings account at his credit union; thus, the twins agree that $d = 0.03$ is fair.

- Pat should pay Jean:

  P Val $= \$5000 / (1.03)^{10}$

  P Val $= \$5000 / 1.344$

  P Val $= \$3720.47$

- In addition to solving Pat and Jean's problem, present value is an important tool used by economists and financial analysts to compute bond yields and fundamental values for stocks.

Important Term

discount rate: A positive number that defines the rate at which a future payment loses value as the date of the payment moves further into the future.

Suggested Reading

Eichberger and Harper, *Financial Economics*.

Federal Reserve Bank of New York Public, "Interest Rates."

Mishkin, *The Economics of Money, Banking, and Financial Markets*.

Questions to Consider

1. Identify some other problems in your home or professional life that could be solved using the concept of present value.

2. Explain why present value and compound interest are closely related concepts.

3. How would you use present value to decide how much to save for your retirement? What discount rate would you use in your calculations? Why?

Present Value
Lecture 13—Transcript

Every one of us needs to move money through time at some point in his or her life. In the household, we may need to move money from our future into our present in order to buy a house. After all, that is what we do when we sign a note and take out a mortgage. At another time, generally later in our lives, we may wish to move money from our present into our future in order to provide ourselves with a retirement income. One way of doing this is by contributing to a retirement fund.

Business managers also move money through time when they borrow against the expected future profits from a new plant or retail store in order to obtain the funds that they need to build and install equipment, to build, outfit, and provide inventory for their store. All of us need to move money through time. But, and it's a big but, deciding on how to move money through time requires us to be able to compare the value of a dollar at 2 different dates. I can hear you saying hold on, a dollar is a dollar is a dollar whenever we get it and whenever we give it, but that is simply not true. A dollar today is worth more than a dollar tomorrow. What we need is a measuring stick or a set of scales that allow us to properly compare the value of a dollar at different times.

Today's lecture will provide what is needed, the tool that is universally regarded as the right one for the job is called present value. Let's begin with an example, a puzzle really, to make matters concrete and to give us a particular problem that we can solve using present value. Pat and Jean are twins who just celebrated their 21st birthday. As a birthday gift, their grandmother has given them a U.S. savings bond that will pay $10,000 on their 31st birthday and nothing before then or after then. Put another way, a fair division of the birthday gift will provide Pat and Jean each with $5000 but not until 10 years from now. Of course, there's a problem. There often is with siblings.

Although they are twins, Pat and Jean are quite different in some ways. Pat has worked for several years, currently has a bank account of $15,000 and is happy to wait to receive his share of the gift. Jean is different. Jean has started a business into which she has poured all of her funds. She would like to have her share of the gift right now so that she can make further improvements to her business.

Jean suggests to Pat that Pat give her $5000 now in exchange for her share of the gift. That is, and let's be clear, Jean wants Pat to use some of the money in his bank account to pay her $5000 now. Jean reasons that Pat will get the money back in 10 years' time when Pat can lay claim to both halves of the grandmother's gift. Pat is not so sure. Pat believes that it's not fair to pay $5000 for Jean's share of the gift that won't pay anything for 10 more years. After all, he reckons, I could earn interest on the money in my bank account, interest I won't receive if I pay Jean $5000 for her share of the gift but, and here is the rub, Pat does not know what would be fair.

Let's put that a slightly different way. Pat does not know a fair amount of money to pay Jean for her share of the gift and, and maybe more importantly, Pat does not know how to explain to Jean what fair means in the situation and how to explain to Jean that the fair amount is actually fair. The key to solving the problem is to use the concept of present value as we will see in this lecture. So by the end, we'll solve Pat and Jean's problem.

Present value is one of the most important concepts that we will encounter in this course. Understanding present value is central to an understanding of the relationship between bond prices and interest rates. Present value is the key when asking what a share of stocks should be worth and, by extension, when asking when a share of stock is overvalued. Many economists believe that the Federal Reserve should take countermeasures when either the stock market becomes overvalued or the bond market becomes undervalued, but doing so only makes sense if one can say what the right value for stock prices is and what the right value for bond prices is. Again present value is essential to such a determination.

Finally, present value is a concept that can usefully guide business managers as they decide whether or not to invest and present value can usefully guide householders like you and me as they decide on saving plans for funding retirement or for future college expenses.

With rare exceptions, and this is the beginning of an understanding of present value, we must understand that a dollar that will be received or paid in the future is worth less than a dollar in our hands today. That's why Wimpy always said I'll gladly pay you Tuesday for a hamburger today. A dollar in hand today provides its owner with a larger set of opportunities than a future dollar provides. One of these opportunities is to hold the dollar until the future arrives. So a dollar today is more valuable because the extra opportunities that it affords are valuable, and of course, that includes the receipt of interest because normally one can earn interest on a dollar today and have available in the future not only the dollar but the interest you could earn and that would be paid at a future date.

Our own Treasury bill market provides evidence of what I'm saying. What's a Treasury bill? Well, a Treasury bill is the U.S. Treasury's promise to pay an amount, let's say $1000, at a date in the future, let's say 52 weeks from now. The current price of a Treasury bill is always less than that $1000, the so-called face value of the bill. That is to say the bill sells at a discount. As the date of the payment grows closer, that is as we get nearer to the end of the 52-week period, the market price of that bill converges to its face value.

I show you in the graph the price of a $1000 Treasury bill maturing in 1 year for many, many, many months between 1953 and 2010. So every point in the line you're seeing now is the price of $1000 to be received in 1 year at different points in our history. The price you should observe is different in different months. Sometimes it's almost $1000. Other times it could be as low as $850, but it is never as high as $1000. When we look at the data for the '70s, we see that the price is about $960. When we look at more recent data, we learn that the price is just slightly lower than $1000, and we'll come to understand the precise relationship between bond prices and current interest rate conditions in a future lecture.

Why is the price of that bond always less than its face value of $1000? That is so because the discount rates set by the market varies with economic conditions, but is always bigger than 1, but the thing one should notice is that the price of that $1000 Treasury bill that will provide the owner with 1001 years in time is always less than $1000—always less than $1000. Therefore a dollar in hand today is worth more than a dollar tomorrow. We know that because markets say it's true. There is a rare exception. Economists always deal with these arcane cases in order to check our thinking. Imagine for a moment that a horrific natural disaster, a hurricane or a flood, was several days away but pretty sure to happen, it would then be normal for market prices to be such that you would trade a loaf of bread today for less than a loaf of bread to be paid after the disaster occurred, but that's easy to understand. In that rare situation, bread tomorrow would be worth more than bread today simply because bread tomorrow would be very, very scarce. Ovens would be shut down by the natural disaster. After all, you just can't store bread especially when the electricity is out. So for that reason, we can imagine that bread tomorrow might actually be more valuable than bread today, but that's an unusual situation. It's a nitpicky point of the sort, as I said before, that economists make in order to check their understanding of why the values of things change.

What does it mean to compute the present value of a future payment? It means to discount that future payment. A discount rate is a positive number that defines the rate at which a future payment loses value as the date of the payment moves further into the future. The discount rate is expressed as a decimal. Right away we want to do an example. So I'm going to use the symbol D for the discount rate. I'm going to assume that time is measured in years, and I'm going to assume a discount rate of 7% so that my D is equal to 0.07. It's typical in these examples to use decimal expressions for percentages. Then a dollar to be received after 1 year is worth 7% less than a dollar in hand today. To discount a future payment of a dollar is to divide it by a number bigger than 1.

So when we think of discounting, we can say that a synonym for discounting is shrinking. To discount is to divide by $1 + D$. To divide—shrink—by $1 + D$. The present value of a payment to be made at a future date turns out to be an amount of money just large enough so that that amount of money will grow to the size of the future payment by the future date when the growth rate is D. Again an example, the present value of a dollar to be received in 1 year is one dollar divided by $1 + D$. Again, I'm using my 7% as my discount rate and therefore $1 + D$ is 1.07 so the present value of a dollar to be received in 1 year is \$1 divided by $1 + D$. Again I'm using my 7% as my discount rate and therefore, $1 + D$ is 1.07. So the present value of a dollar to be received in 1 year is $1 divided or shrunk by 1.07. That's 93 1/2 cents.

It's important for us to understand the relationship between present and future value. To do that, we can rewrite the formula to illustrate that present value grows into the future value of $1. So remember, the future value is $1. If present value is a dollar divided by 1.07 or $1 + D$ then by simply multiplying through, we understand that future value is equal to $1 + D$ times present value. So $1 is 1.07 × 93 1/2 cents. No other number beside 93 1/2 cents makes that true. So when we write the equation in that way, that simple equation, we see that the discount rate is the rate at which present value grows through time.

Now we're going to take on a bit of a challenge. We're going to take a look at something called the present value formula. The present value formula shows how to compute the present value of a stream of future payments. I have to explain what I mean by a stream of future payments.

Suppose that time is measured in years, and I'm going to use the letter lower case t to be the present date and therefore $t + 1$ will be a date 1 year in the future, $t + 2$, a date 2 years in the future, and so forth. So suppose a stream of payments, s at time $t + 1$ are the dollars we'll receive in 1 year at time $t + 1$. S, with an indicator of $t + 2$, are the dollars we'll receive 2 years from now at time $t + 2$, and so forth. What is that present value equation? The present value equation is a sum of discounted values of each component of the stream of payments. The first component is the dollars we'll get at $t + 1$, $s(t + 1)$. That's 1 year in the future, so we shrink it by dividing by $1 + D$. Suppose we're also going to get some payments 2 years from now designated $s(t + 2)$. Well, wait a minute, we've got to discount those payments all the way back to the present so we have to shrink them twice by dividing by $1 + D$ and then $1 + D$ again, so dividing by $(1 + D)^2$.

The payments we would receive in 3 years, $s(t + 3)$ would be divided by $(1 + D)^3$, a triple shrinking and so forth and so on. So payments in general that we would receive at some time M years in the future would be shrunk M times, that is divided by $(1 + D)^M$, but you know I want to do an example to make sure this is clear.

Now we're going to have a simple stream of payments. You're going to get $100 at the end of 1 year, a second payment of $100 at the end of 2 years, and $1100 at the end of 3 years. So I have chosen a stream of payments that is a lot like the payments promised by a coupon bond, which has a face value of $1000 and a coupon rate of 10%.

You might be asking about that coupon rate of 10%. Well that tells us how big our coupon payments are and of course, 10% of $1000 is $100. So that's why we're receiving $100 after year 1, $100 after year 2, and $1000 + $100 after year 3. What I really would like to do is use the formula to find the present value of the stream of payments. I would like to point out to you that that present value has 3 parts. The first is the present value of the first payment we'll receive, $100 in 1 year. That payment adds $100 divided by our discount rate of 1.07. That turns out to be $93.46.

The second payment we're going to receive if we own that bond is $100 in 2 years, but that $100 has to be shrunk twice because we're not going to get it for 2 years. So we divide by 1.07 and then again by 1.07. When we do that we get, not surprisingly, a number smaller than $93.46. We get in particular $87.34.

Finally after 3 years, we're going to get $1000 + $100. That has to be shrunk 3 times or divided by 1.07^3 and that is $897.93. When we add those 3 numbers up, we learn that the present value of those payments is $1078.73. That's an interesting number because the coupon rate is 10% and the discount rate is only 7 we actually have a present value greater than $1000. So we have learned that $1078.73 is the present value of the stream of payments, $100 after 1 year, $100 after 2 years, and $1100 after 3 when the discount rate is 7%; and now you're asking me so what? Is there some way to understand why that dollar amount, $1078.73, is a fair amount to exchange for the stream of payments itself because, after all, that's where we are going.

Remember our problem at the beginning, and yes there is a way to understand why present value is a fair amount to exchange for a stream of payments. What is that way? That way is to understand that the present value of a stream of payments is the exact, to the penny amount that is just enough to actually replicate the stream of payments. If you can borrow and lend at the discount rate you have used in the present value calculation. There's an equivalence there, and it's so important that I'm going to do another example to show you how it works.

So let's imagine that you started out with a present value, $1,078.73 and you put it in an interest earning account at 7%. After 1 year, you'd earn some interest. How much? You can double check with a calculator but it's $75.51. Hey, but after 1 year, you're obligated to make a $100 payment because we're replicating the stream. After you do that, you are left with $1,054.24, but you're not done. That $1,054.24 stays in the bank and earns interest for another year at 7% with an interest payment of $73.80 but at the end of year 2, you have to pay out a second $100 because that's the name of the game. At the end of the second year you have then $1,028.04 but you're still not finished. You're going to leave that $1,028.04 for a third year.

You're going to earn a third year's interest at 7% of $71.96. At the end of the year, you're going to pay $1100 making the last payment in the stream of payments, and guess what you're left with? Zero. You have exactly replicated the stream.

If one starts with an amount equal to the present value of the stream of payments, deposits that amount in an account paying 7% and makes withdrawals just sufficient to make payments in the streams, then that individual will exactly exhaust the available funds on the date of the last payment. This example shows us the sense in which present value of a stream of payments is equivalent to the stream of payments, and it's a fair price for purchasing the stream of payments.

The concept of present value is crucial in figuring out a savings plan designed to provide sufficient funds for planned future payments such as those associated with college tuition, house down payments, or retirement. Suppose that you decide at the birth of your child to save an amount each year, on the child's birthday, say, to create a fund to pay for that child's college education. Suppose further that your goal is to have $100,000 in the fund on your child's 18th birthday. How much must you save each year? The key to finding the answer is proper use of the present value formula. For example, the present value of the fund (that is, the present value of what you want in 18 years) is $100,000 discounted by dividing by 1 plus the discount rate to the 18th power because you need the money in 18 years.

Now, the present value of your savings plan is much more complicated in equation terms but it's pretty easy to understand. Every year, you're going to save an amount you're trying to calculate. We'll call it x, we're trying to find x. So in the first year, you put x aside. In the second year, you again put x aside. In the third year, you again put x aside. You do that for every year but the present value of those x dollar savings amounts is not the same. The first one we'll say is worth x on the child's birth date. After 1 year, his first anniversary or her first anniversary, the present value is $x / (1 + D)$ and so forth and so on. The present value of the last payment is x divided by $(1 + D)^{18}$. In the above formulas, D is the discount rate and would it be appropriate for you to use for D the rate of interest you could earn on your savings plan. So you ask yourself, "What will I be paid from my savings account?"

In the above formula, x is unknown. It's the unknown amount you must save. How are we going to calculate x? That's what we want to do. We want to get x. To calculate the savings plan is to find the value of x so that the present value of the fund equals the present value of the plan. I'm going to use a different D now, 2%. So suppose you can earn 2% on your funds. Then, and you can verify this, x is equal to $4378.18. How could you verify that? With a spreadsheet or a financial calculator. Armed with the knowledge of present value, we are going to return to the question of how much Pat should pay Jean today, which would be fair compensation to Pat for giving up the claim to $5000 paid 10 years from today.

Now, the present value formula tells us that Pat should pay Jean the present value of $5000 to be received in 10 years or $5000 divided by $(1 + D)^{10}$. What value should Pat and Jean agree on for D? Well Jean would like D to be as small as possible, probably prefer $D = 0$. In that case Jean would get $5000 today, but Pat would like D to be somewhat higher. The larger D gets, the smaller the current payment to Jean will be. Pat explains to Jean that he could earn 3% in a savings account or his credit union and they thus agree that D equal to 0.03 is fair. So Pat should pay Jean the present value of $5000 to be received in 10 years, which is $5000 divided by 1.03^{10}, which is $5000 divided by 1.344, which is $3720.47.

In this lecture, we have learned about an important tool: present value. Economists and financial analysts use present value to compute current dollar equivalents for payments that will be received or made in the future. This tool plays a crucial role in our course. Bonds promise future payments and economists compute bond yields by assuming that market forces drive the price of the bond to equal the present value of the bond's payments.

Stocks promise future dividends and economists compute fundamental values, a term that we'll learn more about later, for those stocks by assuming that fundamental value is equal to the present value of future dividends.

As I said at the outset, present value is a powerful tool. It's a tool we will use often in this course, and it's a tool that you can use in your own life.

Probability, Expected Value, and Uncertainty
Lecture 14

T his lecture begins an investigation of decision making in the face of uncertainty. You will encounter the concepts of probability and expected value and learn how they can be used to guide decision making. These concepts help us think through many kinds of decisions we face in our lives and better understand the importance of financial markets in our society. These concepts also provide a background for investigating financial institutions, which routinely make decisions in the face of uncertainty when they decide whether to lend funds or underwrite an initial public offering of stock.

A Random-Outcome Generator

- To introduce decision making in the face of uncertain outcomes, we will use a "random-outcome generator"—the roll of one fair die. Begin by considering random events with only 6 outcomes; if the die is fair, the probability of each outcome is 1/6.

- Suppose you have the opportunity to play the game depicted in the following table:

Probabilities and Payouts

Outcome	1	2	3	4	5	6
Probability	1/6	1/6	1/6	1/6	1/6	1/6
Payout	–$5.00	–$1.00	0	0	$1.00	$5.00

- The **expected value** (EV) of the game is the probability weighted average of the game's payouts: EV = (–\$5.00)(1/6) + (–\$1.00)(1/6) + (\$0)(1/3) + (\$1.00)(1/6) + (\$5.00)(1/6) = \$0.00.

- The probability weighted average is different than a simple average. The 0 outcome has a weight of 1/3 because that outcome is twice as likely as the others.

- When the expected payout of a game is 0, the game is said to be "fair." If the expected value were positive, we would call the game "better than fair," or a **player-advantage game**. If the expected value were negative, we would call the game "worse than fair," or a **house-advantage game**.

- The expected value of the game may be interpreted as the average prize you would receive if you played the game many times. Clearly, you should not expect to make a profit by playing this game.

More Complicated Decisions

- The owner of a toy store must decide in July on the kind and quantity of toys to order for the holiday shopping season. This July, the decision is particularly difficult because there is great uncertainty about consumer confidence. When consumers fear that a recession may come and unemployment may rise, they often spend less during the holiday season in order to build up their cash reserves.

- The toy shop owner has two available strategies. In the aggressive strategy, the owner purchases a large quantity of toys, including a good supply of the newest and most expensive ones. In the conservative strategy, the owner purchases a much smaller inventory and sticks with tried-and-true toys rather than new, expensive ones.

- Both strategies entail risks. If consumer confidence is low and the owner pursues the aggressive strategy, he or she will be stuck with inventory that can only be sold at a loss. If consumer confidence is high and the owner pursues the conservative strategy, he or she will miss out on the opportunity to make many profitable sales.

- The table below shows the owner's assessment of the costs and benefits of each strategy as a function of consumer confidence.

Toy Store Profits (Thousands of Dollars)

Consumer Confidence	High					Low
	6	5	4	3	2	1
Probability	1/6	1/6	1/6	1/6	1/6	1/6
Aggressive	100	75	50	0	−25	−50
Conservative	20	20	20	10	−5	−10

- The conservative strategy loses only in the worst two states, and when it loses, it loses relatively little. But the conservative strategy tops out at a $20,000 profit and does not benefit from the high levels of spending associated with a truly good holiday shopping season.

- The aggressive strategy is profitable in only half of the states, and in the worst two states, losses are high. But in the best three states, profits are large relative to the other strategy.

- The expected profit of the aggressive strategy is $25,000. The expected profit of the conservative strategy is $9,167. What decision should the toy store owner make?

- Some decision makers believe that they should always choose the strategy with the higher expected return. In this case, the aggressive strategy clearly dominates. However, by any reasonable measure, the aggressive strategy is riskier.

Not a Game of Chance

- It's important to note that the toy store decision is not like a game of chance in at least two very important respects. First, it is generally not possible to play the game multiple times.

- To appreciate the importance of this point, consider a modification of the first game, as presented in the following table:

Better-than-Fair Game

Outcome	1	2	3	4	5	6
Probability	1/6	1/6	1/6	1/6	1/6	1/6
Payout	*–$5.00*	*–$1.00*	*0*	*0*	*$1.00*	*$6.00*

- Only one feature of the game has changed: The payout associated with outcome 6 is now $6.00, rather than $5.00. This means that the expected payout of the game is now $0.16. If you can play this game without limit, you should, because your wealth will grow without bound.

- As the game is played multiple times, the law of large numbers tells us that the average return becomes a certain return. This, by the way, is the business model of a casino. Casino games are invariably house games; that is, they are less-than-fair games with negative expected payouts for the player and positive expected payouts for the house.

- Our toy store scenario is not one that an entrepreneur can repeat without limit.

- An entrepreneur who believed that he or she had a strategy with a positive expected profit might try to replicate it in a number of different markets. However, in our example, the law of large numbers would not work to the entrepreneur's advantage because the source of risk—consumer confidence—would not be determined by independent, random events. Consumer confidence is an economy-wide phenomenon based on the overall prospects for the economy.

- Thus, it is not obvious that one of the two strategies is better. The aggressive strategy has a higher expected profit, but it is also riskier by any reasonable definition of risk.

Sources of Information about Relevant Probabilities
- There is a second important difference between the toy store decision and the decision to play a casino game. That difference centers on the source of information about the relevant probabilities of events.

- For the first game, randomness is generated by a random-number generator (a die) with specific, well-understood properties. No such random-number generator exists for generating different consumer confidence outcomes that define the random states of the world in the toy store scenario.

- In real-world decision scenarios, decision makers must often define the relevant states and estimate the relevant probabilities themselves (or hire experts to do so). Frequently, this is done by analyzing data on similar past events with the assumption that the frequencies of events in the past are good estimates of the probabilities of similar events in the future.

- A new example will help us understand the difference between decision scenarios where probabilities are estimated and decision scenarios where they are known on a priori grounds.

- The following table contains a frequency distribution of annual real returns on all the stocks traded on the New York Stock Exchange (NYSE) between 1945 and 2007.

- **Real returns** are defined as the sum of percentage capital gains and dividends earned on the NYSE market portfolio minus the rate of inflation.

- A positive return means an individual holding the NYSE portfolio experienced a gain in purchasing power. A negative return means that individual experienced a loss in purchasing power.

- For each sextile, the table reports the average of returns with the sextile. The probabilities are the frequencies observed in historical data.

Real-Return Sextiles for the NYSE, 1945–2007

Sextiles	1	2	3	4	5	6
Probability	1/6	1/6	1/6	1/6	1/6	1/6
Payout	−0.18	−0.02	0.07	0.13	0.19	0.28

- The stock market, as characterized by this table, is a better-than-fair game. The average real return between 1945 and 2007 is 0.08. But that does not necessarily mean that an investor should expect an 8% return in the future. In 2008, the real return on the NYSE was −0.44, lower than any other return experience over the historical period.

- Real-world decision making is different from decision making in the casino because we may only be able to estimate the probabilities of various outcomes.

Initial Rules of Thumb

- If a game or an investment opportunity has a positive expected return, a rational agent should play rather than pass.

- If a rational agent has to choose among games or investments, the agent should choose the one with the largest expected return.

Important Terms

expected value (EV): The probability-weighted average of the game's payouts.

house-advantage game: When the expected value is negative.

player-advantage game: When the expected value is positive.

real returns: The sum of percentage capital gains and dividends earned on the NYSE market portfolio minus the rate of inflation.

Suggested Reading

Eichberger and Harper, *Financial Economics*.

Stat Trek, "Statistics Tutorial."

Questions to Consider

1. Is it reasonable to liken a business decision that must be made without knowing all the facts that will determine profitability to a game of chance? Why or why not?

2. Why is it reasonable to characterize the U.S. stock market as a "better-than-fair" game?

3. Should all rational individuals be willing to play a better-than-fair game? Why or why not?

Probability, Expected Value, and Uncertainty
Lecture 14—Transcript

Our lives, as household and business decision makers, are filled with situations that require us to make decisions without knowing for sure the consequences of our actions. For example, should a restaurant owner open the restaurant for lunch? What sort of collision insurance should an auto owner buy? Is it better to invest, financially invest, retirement funds in stocks, bonds, or money market mutual fund shares? Should an apartment renter purchase insurance to protect her furnishings? Should we allow our children to drive as soon as the law says they can?

In each of these cases, decision making would be easy if we could see the future and know how the relevant uncertainties resolve themselves. If we could know how many diners would choose our restaurant at lunchtime, we would know whether it made sense to open it. If we knew in advance whether or not we would have an auto accident, who would be at fault and how expensive the auto repairs would be, we would know exactly the right kind of collision insurance to buy.

If we knew in advance the price of stocks and bonds on the day we wish to convert our retirement funds to annuities and if we knew the consumer price index on that day, we would know whether stocks, bonds, or something else was the best strategy for our retirement saving. If we knew in advance whether we would experience a fire or a burglary, we would know whether or not to buy renter's insurance, and if we knew whether our children would be involved in an accident and whether or not they would drive responsibly, we would know whether or not to let them drive early. Of course we know none of these things but still in each and every case, we make a decision.

Keep in mind that we make a decision either actively or passively. Ignoring the decision to purchase renter's insurance is a decision, a decision not to buy the insurance. And this is very important: Please remember that it never, never makes sense to judge the wisdom of a decision that involves uncertainty after the uncertainty is resolved. For an auto owner to say after 5 years of accident-free driving that buying collision insurance was a mistake is illogical; it's just downright silly. One can only assess the wisdom of a choice before the fact, that is, before one knows what is going to happen.

In this lecture we will begin an investigation of decision making in the face of uncertainty. We're going to meet concepts of probability and expected value, and we will come to understand how they can be used to guide decision making when outcomes are uncertain. At the beginning of the lecture, we'll stick with simple examples of uncertainty that allow us to easily introduce the concepts of probability and expected value, but as the lecture proceeds, we will consider far more realistic examples.

The concepts we encounter in this lecture are important for several reasons. First, they help us think through many kinds of decisions that we face in our lives. Second, they help us better understand the importance of financial markets in our society. Third, they provide a background for investigating financial institutions, which after all, routinely make decisions in the face of uncertainty, when they decide whether to lend funds or, for example, to underwrite an initial public offering of stock.

We can better understand several concepts used to introduce decision making in the face of uncertainty with the help of a random outcome generator, with the roll of a simple fair die. We all know what a die is. It's a cube with 6 sides, each of which is embossed with 1 number between 1 and 6. If the die is fair, it is manufactured in a way that makes each side of the die equally likely to come out on top when the die is tossed onto a horizontal surface. In some parlor and casino games, the die or dice, if there's more than one, are placed in a cup and the cup is spilled onto the playing surface in order to ensure that the roll of the die or dice is fair.

To keep things simple, we will begin by considering random events with only 6 outcomes, the numbers 1–6. If the die is fair then the probability of each outcome is 1/6. Now let's consider a decision involving uncertainty created by the roll of this fair die. Suppose you have the opportunity to play the game depicted in the following table. If the roll of the die comes up 1, you'll lose $5. If the roll of the die comes up 2, you'll lose only $1. If the roll of the die comes up 3 or if it comes up 4, you'll lose nothing. Uh-huh, here comes the good news. If the roll of the die comes up 5, you will win $1 and if the roll of the die comes up 6, you're a big winner. You will win $5.

Should you play the game? Some of you may think that it is immoral to gamble and make the decision on those grounds, but keep in mind that the game I present is only a metaphor, a metaphor for the uncertainty we face in life and the decisions that we must make before the uncertainty is resolved.

Before we answer the question, it is useful to introduce a statistical tool and use that tool to characterize the game. The expected value of the game is the probability weighted average of the game's payouts. So what is this expected value? Well, we're going to multiply the $5 loss by 1/6 and add it to the $1 loss multiplied by 1/6 and add it to the zero loss multiplied by 1/3 because 2 of the 6 sides of the die imply no loss at all, and then we're going to add that total to $1 multiplied by 1/6, and finally we're going to add in $5 multiplied by 1/6.

So what've we done here? We've taken each of the possible prizes and losses associated with each of the faces of the die and we've multiplied each of those possibilities by its probability of 1/6, multiplied and added them all together. What do we get when we do that? We get that the expected value of the game is 0. Now, please keep in mind that the probability weighted average is different than a simple average. In fact the example is good for pointing that out. The 0 outcome got a weight of 1/3 because that outcome happened with 2 faces of the die and is thus twice as likely. So we simply would not get the right answer if we just average the various prizes.

When the expected payout of a game is 0, the game is said to be a fair game. Please be alert to the fact that I'm using the word fair in a second way now where we describe the game rather than the die. There can be fair games, and there could be fair die, and not every game involving a fair die is a fair game. If the expected value were positive, we would call the game better than fair or a player advantage game. If the expected value were negative, we would call the game a worse than fair game or, in the common parlance, a house advantage game.

The expected value of the game may be interpreted as the average prize you could receive if you played the game many, many times. Well should we play the game? Whether or not we play, whether or not we decide to play, it should be clear to us that we should not expect to make a profit by playing because the expected value is 0, but it might be rational to play the game if you found playing it enjoyable. Indeed many friendly wagers are undertaken by friends every day. For example, 2 friends might lunch together every week and agree to flip a coin at the end of the meal to decide who will play. Over time, if the coin is fair, each friend can expect to pay the same amount and the same number of times.

Now let's consider a more complicated decision. We will again use the role of a die as a metaphor for the uncertainty faced by the decision maker. Here's the set up. Imagine that you are the owner of a toy store, and you have to decide in July on the kind and the quantity of toys to order for the holiday shopping season. This particular July the decision is very difficult because there's a great amount of uncertainty about consumer confidence. When consumers fear that a recession may come and unemployment may rise, they often spend less during the holiday season in order to build up their cash reserves. Our toy shop owner, let's suppose, has 2 available strategies. I'm keeping it simple now, only 2 strategies. Strategy 1 is called an aggressive strategy.

On the aggressive strategy, the owner purchases a large quantity of toys including a good supply of the newest and most expensive toys. Strategy number 2 is conservative. On the conservative strategy, the owner purchases a much smaller inventory of toys and sticks with tried and true toys rather than the new expensive ones. Note that both strategies entail risk. If consumer confidence turns out to be low and the owner pursues the aggressive strategy, the owner will be stuck with inventory that can only be sold at a loss. If consumer confidence turns out to be higher, however, but the owner pursued the conservative strategy, the owner will miss the opportunity to make many profitable sales. The table you are seeing provides the owner's assessment, imagine your assessment, of the costs and the benefits of each strategy as it varies with consumer confidence. So let's take a look.

We see in this table consumer confidence ranging from 6 when it's very high down to 1 when it's very low, so there are 6 possibilities. I'm assuming again that each of these outcomes, 6, 5, 4, 3, 2, and 1 is equally likely. So the probability of each outcome is 1/6. Notice that I have 2 rows, the implications of the aggressive strategy and the implications of the conservative strategy. When consumer confidence is high, the aggressive strategy works very well. Indeed the numbers that you see in the table are toy store profits in thousands of dollars. So an aggressive strategy, when consumer confidence is at its highest, is worth $100,000 in profit. All the way on the other end of the table, an aggressive strategy when consumer confidence is at its lowest is a loss of $50,000. You get the picture.

Similarly think about the conservative strategy. Using the conservative strategy when consumer confidence is very high gives the shop owner a profit of $20,000. Indeed half of the outcomes, 6, 5, and 4 all give the shop owner $20,000; but when consumer confidence is low, the conservative strategy implies a loss but a much smaller loss than the aggressive strategy. So you get to see now the feeling of the difference between the implication of the conservative and aggressive strategy.

The conservative strategy only loses in the worse 2 states in the world, the worse 2 rolls of the die. When it loses, it loses relatively little, but the conservative strategy tops out at a $20,000 profit and does not benefit from the high levels of spending associated with a really good holiday shopping season. The aggressive strategy is only profitable in half the states of the world. In the worse 2 states, losses are very, very high, but in the best 3 states, the profits are very large relative to the other strategy.

The expected profit of the 2 strategies differs. The expected profit of the aggressive strategy turns out to be $25,000. The expected profit of the conservative strategy is $9167. You can verify that for yourself by applying the expected value formula that we have seen already, probability weighted averages. What you want to know is what decision the toy store owner should make. Now, some decision makers believe that the right thing to do is to always choose the strategy with the higher expected return. In that case, the shop owner, yourself, would choose the aggressive strategy. It clearly dominates because its expected value is higher, but as we shall see by any reasonable measure, the aggressive strategy is riskier.

It's important to realize that the toy store decision, even though I've modeled it with the roll of a die, is not like a game of chance that one could play with your friends or at a casino, and it's not like that game of chance in 2 very important respects that we really should understand.

First, and this is quite important, it is generally not possible to play the toy store game, if I may call it that, multiple times like you can a casino game. To appreciate the importance of this point, we consider a modification of the first game presented in the following table. So remember that we were rolling a die and if the outcome was 1, we would lose $5. If the outcome was 2, we would lose $1. If the outcome was 3 or 4, we would break even losing nothing but winning nothing. If the outcome was 5, we would win $1. If the outcome was 6, we would earn, we said $5 before but now I want to change that $5 to $6. I have changed only one feature of the game, the payout associated with the 6. It's now $6 rather than $5. The expected payout of the game is now $0.16.

If one can play the game without limit, one should do so because one's wealth will grow without bound. As the game is played multiple times, the law of large numbers tells us that the average return becomes a virtually certain return. What does that mean? That means as we play many, many, many, many, many times, our average return converges to our expected return. Playing that game thousands of times virtually guarantees that on average, every time we play we will get $0.16. That's why I say our wealth could grow without bounds.

By the way, I have just explained the business model of a casino. Casino games are invariably house games. So from the point of view of the house, they're better than fair games. From the point of view of players like you and me, they are less than fair games. For that reason, the number 1 rule in a casino is keep the players playing.

In contrast, however, our toy store scenario is not one that an entrepreneur can repeat without limit. An entrepreneur who believed that he or she had a strategy with positive expected profit might try to replicate the strategy in lots of different markets with lots of different stores, but that won't work. In our example, the law of large numbers would not work to the entrepreneur's advantage because the source of risk, variation in consumer confidence, would not be determined by events that were different at different locales of his stores. Consumer confidence is an economy-wide phenomenon based on the overall prospects for the economy, and it would be the same for him in every store. So he would bear risk.

Thus it's simply not obvious that one of the 2 strategies is better. The aggressive strategy has a higher expected profit, but as I will now point out and as we will see in future lectures, it's also riskier by any reasonable definition of risk.

There is a second very important difference between the toy store decision and the decision to play a casino game. That difference centers on the source of our information of the relevant probabilities of events. Remember that for simplicity, I generated the uncertainty of all the games we have seen so far with a random number generator with well understood properties, the roll of a die. But no such random number generator exists for generating different levels of consumer confidence. Those define the relative states of the world for the toy store scenario.

In real world decisions, decision makers must often define the relative states of the world not assume they're 1, 2, 3, 4, 5, 6 like the faces of a die, and they themselves must estimate the probabilities of each of those relevant states of the world, each of those relevant possible outcomes. Frequently this is done by analyzing data on similar past events with the assumption that the future will be like the past in the sense that the frequencies of events in the past are good estimates of the probabilities of similar events in the future.

I know that's a lot to understand and I think a new example will help us understand the difference between decision scenarios where probabilities are estimated and decision scenarios where the probabilities are known on our priority grounds like the fact that a die is fair.

I'm going to show you one more table. It's a table containing the frequency distribution of annual real returns on all of the stocks traded on the New York Stock Exchange between 1945 and 2007. You'll see what I mean. I'll take this slowly. Real returns are defined as the sum of percentage capital gains and dividends earned on the New York Stock Exchange market portfolio minus the rate of inflation. Hold on a second, what does that mean?

If you hold all of the stocks on the New York Stock Exchange, if you simply bought a mutual fund that had every single New York Exchange stock in it, you would receive every year dividends and capital gains. That would define the percentage return in a nominal sense but we understand that real values matter and so from that, we would subtract the CPI rate of inflation for that same year.

A positive return would mean that the person holding the whole New York Stock Exchange portfolio would experience a gain purchasing power. A negative return would mean that the person holding the entire portfolio of stocks traded on the New York Stock Exchange would experience a loss in purchasing power.

Now, intentionally, I have constructed the table to be similar to the payout tables we've seen earlier in today's lecture by computing real return sextiles. What does that mean? That means I rate the returns, and I grouped the lowest 1/6 together, the next 1/6 together, the next 1/6 together, and so forth. For each of these sextiles, the table reports the average of returns within the sextiles. So let's turn to the table.

The worst case, the lowest sextile, and again by definition, that's probability 1/6, had a payout of −18% in real terms. That's bad news losing 18% of your wealth. The next sextile was also a loser but a lesser loser, only −2%. The third sextile was a winner, happily, 7%. The fourth, a bigger winner, by construction, 13%. The real good news comes in outcomes 5 and 6, the top 2 sextiles. The fifth sextile is associated returns of 19% and the sixth of returns of 28%. That's where we would hope to be right? We'd love to be in that last sextile. The stock market, as characterized by this table, is a better than fair game. Do the math. The average real return between 1945 and 2007 is 8%, but does this mean that an investor should expect an 8% return in the future?

Well if the future is like the past, that assumption is reasonable. However a cautionary note, in 2008 the real return on a portfolio of New York Stock Exchange stocks was, hold on to your horses, −44%, lower than any other return experienced over the historical period. That's a source of risk that the table doesn't capture. Real world decision making is different from the decision making in the casino because we may only be able to estimate the probabilities of the various outcomes.

As scholars began to grapple with the question of how a rational decision maker should make a decision in the face of uncertainty, they came to the conclusion in the 18th century that expected value was the key. A rule of thumb about if a game or investment opportunity had a positive expected return, a rational agent should play rather than pass. If that rational agent had to choose among games or investments, the agent should choose the one with the largest expected return. In the next lecture, we will learn why and how this rule of thumb changed.

Thank you.

Risk and Risk Aversion
Lecture 15

In this lecture, you return to the question of how economists think about risk and decision making in the face of uncertainty. Such issues are the cornerstones of our understanding of equity markets, insurance, and derivative securities. They help us understand why we decide to insure ourselves against some hazards but not others, and they help us determine when bank regulations are likely to make banks safer and when they may have the unintended consequence of making them riskier.

A Review of Fair Games and Expected Value

- A fair coin toss means that the probability of landing on either heads or tails is 50% and that the outcome is in no way controlled by the person who flips the coin. With that in mind, consider a game in which, if the outcome is heads, you are paid $1.00; if the outcome is tails, you must pay $1.00.

- The game is fair because the expected payout is 0: Exp Pay = $-(1/2) \times \$1.00 + (1/2) \times \$1.00 = \$0.00$

- In a better-than-fair version of this game, you would receive $1.10 when the outcome is heads, and you would pay $1.00 when the outcome is tails.

- For a long time, it was believed that rational decision makers would always choose to play a better-than-fair game and, faced with the choice of several games, would always choose the game with the highest expected value. Thus, a rational individual would always be willing to play the second version of the coin-toss game.

The St. Petersburg Paradox

- This traditional thinking changed when scholars confronted a puzzle called the St. Petersburg Paradox.

- In the St. Petersburg game, players flip a fair coin until the first tails appears. If it appears on the first toss, the game pays $1.00; on the second toss, the prize doubles to $2.00; on the third toss, $4.00; and so on.

- What would you pay to play the St. Petersburg game? Of course, everyone will pay at least $1.00 because $1.00 is the minimum payout of the game. In fact, when given the opportunity to purchase a play of the St. Petersburg game, most experimental subjects are willing to pay between $2.00 and $3.00.

- However, the expected payout of the game is infinite, as the following computation confirms: Exp Pay = $(1/2)$ $1.00 + $(1/4)$ $2.00 + $(1/8)$ $4.00 + ... = $0.50 + $0.50 + ...

- The paradox is as follows: If rational decision making means playing a game any time its expected outcome is greater than 0, then rational decision makers should be willing to pay any amount to play the St. Petersburg game. But clearly, there is a limit to what people are willing to pay to play.

- The resolution of the paradox is that most rational agents are risk averse. They will not play some better-than-fair games because those games are risky, and they are willing to pay to have risk eliminated from their lives.

Definition of "Risk"

- To define "risk," we will use three similar but different coin-toss games. In each game, there will be only one toss of the coin, and you will win if the coin shows heads and lose if the coin shows tails. What makes the games different is the size of the wager.

Game	Heads	Tails	Exp Pay
A	$1.10	−$1.00	$0.05
B	$2.10	−$2.00	$0.05
C	−$3.10	−$3.00	$0.05

- All three games have the same expected payout, $0.05, which means that all three games are better than fair. Clearly, however, game C is riskier than game B, which is riskier than game A.

- The standard measure of risk is a measure of the dispersion of the payouts. A graph of the probability weighted payouts of games A, B, and C shows that the possible payouts of game C (−$3.00, $3.10) are more widely dispersed (separated) than the payouts of game B (−$2.00, $2.10), which are more widely dispersed than the payouts of game A (−$1.00, $1.10).

- Another way to understand why game C is the riskiest is to note that probability weighted loss is greater for game C (.5 × $3.00 = $1.50) than for game B (.5 × $2.00 = $1.00) and for game A (.5 × $1.00 = $0.50).

- For those who are familiar with statistics, a standard measure of dispersion is the standard deviation of payouts.

Resolution of the Paradox
- The resolution of the St. Petersburg Paradox is generally attributed to the mathematician Daniel Bernoulli. It has two essential components.

- The first component is the idea that the value to an individual of additional wealth falls as wealth increases. It follows that the satisfaction derived from gaining an additional dollar is less than the satisfaction lost from losing a dollar.

- Bernoulli's first idea is embodied in the hypothesis that the utility an individual derives from wealth is a concave function of wealth. The concavity of the function implies that the utility gained from the gain of an additional dollar of wealth is smaller than the utility lost from the loss of a dollar of wealth. Put another way, the marginal value of wealth falls as our wealth increases.

- Bernoulli's utility-of-wealth function has a solid intuition behind it. When an individual has little wealth, it is used to acquire the things he or she values most. As wealth increase, an individual can acquire new things that add to his or her utility but add less than the important things acquired when the individual had less wealth.

- The second component of the resolution is the hypothesis that a rational decision maker maximizes expected utility rather than expected value. Expected utility is the probability weighted average of the utility of the wealth that would result from each possible random outcome.

Daniel Bernoulli (1700–1782), a mathematician who is attributed with the resolution to the St. Petersburg Paradox.

Images from the History of Medicine (NLM).

- By way of example, let's ask whether a person who maximizes expected utility and whose preferences are described by the concave utility function would play a fair coin toss game for $10.00.

- The answer is no because by not playing the game, the risk-averse individual can keep his or her utility at 0—the normalized starting point for our utility measure. By playing the game, the individual would have a 50% chance of winning $10.00 and a 50% chance of losing $10.00. But the gain in utility associated with winning $10.00 is smaller than the loss in utility associated with losing $10.00.

- Why does the expected utility hypothesis resolve the St. Petersburg Paradox? A person with little wealth places a great deal of utility weight on each dollar he or she must spend for a "ticket" to play the St. Petersburg game. The person places less utility weight on each dollar he or she would win if it took many coin tosses for the first heads to appear.

Lessons from Bernoulli

- Most individuals do not make decisions in the face of uncertainty by considering only the expected value associated with the random event.

- Bernoulli's resolution of the St. Petersburg Paradox suggests that individuals are risk averse because they value the dollars they might lose more highly at the margin than they value the dollars they might win.

- The expected utility hypothesis is not the last word on decision making in the face of uncertainty. For example, it's a puzzle for researchers to explain why individuals buy property insurance or lottery tickets. Milton Friedman and Leonard Savage hypothesized that the typical household has a utility-of-wealth function that is concave in the vicinity of "normal wealth" but turns convex at much higher levels.

- In sum, the resolution of the St. Petersburg Paradox tells us that most decision makers are risk averse. They dislike dispersion of payouts and the prospect of losing. Bernoulli's expected utility hypothesis is a simple but powerful idea: We place greater value on a dollar we lose than on a dollar we gain.

Questions to Consider

1. Does the utility-of-wealth diagram presented in this lecture provide a good description of the way your personal utility varies with wealth? Why or why not?

2. Would you describe yourself as "risk averse" in the sense of this lecture?

3. Consider an individual whose utility-of-wealth function was convex rather than concave. How would that person behave when faced with an opportunity to gamble?

Risk and Risk Aversion
Lecture 15—Transcript

It's a fact, a fact that we ignore at our own peril. Risk and uncertainty are part of our lives. Sometimes we choose them but sometimes they choose us. In this lecture I will return to the question of how economists think about risk and how economists think about decision making in the face of uncertainty.

These issues are interesting and these issues are important. They are the cornerstone of our understanding of equity markets, stock markets, and insurance and derivative securities, all of which we will think about. They help us to understand why we decide to insure ourselves against some hazards but not against other hazards. They help us to understand when bank regulations are likely to make banks safer and when they may have unintended consequences and actually make banks riskier.

At the beginning of the lecture, we will return to our simple model of uncertainty, uncertainty generated by a simple, random number generator, the physical properties of which are well known. Today we will use the simplest of the simple, the flip of a fair coin. As we proceed, I will again extend the lecture to consider sources of risk in more realistic settings.

It's useful to quickly review several ideas from the previous lecture. Suppose a fair coin toss, recall that when describing a coin toss, fair means that the probability of a heads and the probability of a tails are each 50%, and that that outcome is in no way controlled by the person who flips the coin. Let's consider a simple game. If the outcome is heads, I pay you $1. If the outcome is tails, you pay me $1. That game is what we call a fair game.

Remember that when describing a game, fair means having an expected payout of 0. This game is fair because the expected payout is 0. To confirm that is simple. The expected payout is simply $-\$1 \times 0.5 + \$1 \times 0.5$. Of course that total is 0. Suppose we modify the game slightly so that you receive $1.10 when the outcome is heads and still pay $1 when the outcome is tails. Now according to our language, the game is better than fair. For a long time, it was believed that any rational decision maker would always choose to pay a better than fair game.

It was also believed that faced with a choice of several games, a rational decision maker would always choose the game with the highest expected value. So traditional thinking would include the belief that a rational individual would always be willing to play the coin toss game I just described.

Standard thinking changed when scholars confronted a famous puzzle called the St. Petersburg Paradox. Gambling was very important in the courts of Europe in the 17th and 18th centuries. Some nobles studied the mathematics of gambling, and they even hired experts to analyze games of chance and gambling strategies. From this connection came the St. Petersburg Paradox. The resolution of the paradox gave rise to a way of thinking that is still widely in use today. The paradox begins with the St. Petersburg game. Let me explain that game.

The game involves flipping a fair coin until the first tails appears. If the first tails appears on the first toss, the game pays the player a prize of $1. If the first tails appears on the second toss, the prize doubles to $2. If the first tails appeared on the third toss, the prize would double again to $4 and so forth. The prize continued to double.

What would you play? What would you pay to play the St. Petersburg game? Of course everyone will pay at least $1 because $1 is the minimum payout for the game, but how much more than $1 would you pay? When faced with the opportunity to purchase a play of the St. Petersburg game, most experimental subjects are willing to pay between $2 and $3 and no more but, and this is stunning, the expected payout of the game is infinite as the following computation quickly confirms.

Remember expected payout is the probability of weighted average of the payouts. So with probability 1/2, you get $1. Add to that to the fact that with probability 1/4, you get $2. Add to that the payout of $4 that you get with probability 1/8 and so forth and so on. The prize is doubling but the probability of each prize is being multiplied each time by half but when you do that half, you see that the expected payout, $0.50, the value associated with tails on the first toss, $0.50 associated with the second toss, an entire stream of $0.50 without limit. Add those altogether and you get an infinite number. That's the paradox. If rational decision making means playing a game any time it's expected outcome is greater than 0, rational decision makers should be willing to pay any amount to play the St. Petersburg game. Clearly there appears to be a limit to what people are willing to pay to play the St. Petersburg game. I imagine yourself were thinking about what that limit was for you.

Now, are we to conclude that those folks, including me and probably you, are irrational, or should we use this evidence to rethink our theory of how people make decisions in the face of uncertainty? The resolution of the paradox is that most rational agents are also risk averse. They dislike risk. They will not play some better than fair games because those games are risky, and they're willing to pay to have risk eliminated from their lives. But to appreciate what this means, we first have to have a working definition of risk. As an example, we will use 3 similar but different coin toss games. In each game, there will be one and only one toss of the coin. In each game, you will win if the coin shows heads and lose if the coin shows tails. What makes the 3 games different is the size of the wager. We'll call these games A, B, and C.

In game A, if heads comes up, you receive $1.10. If tails comes up, you lose $1. That's an expected payout of that game of $0.05. In game B, if heads comes up, you win $2.10. If tails comes up, you lose $2, again, an expected payout of $0.05 and—you got the pattern now. In game 3, if heads comes up, you receive $3.10 and if tails comes up, you lose $3, once more the expected payout is $0.05. So let's be clear as to how to compare the games. All 3 games have the same expected payout, $0.05, which means that all 5 games are better than fair games but clearly your intuition tells you that game C is riskier than game B and game B is riskier than game A. The standard measure of risk used by economists and financial analysts is some measure of the dispersion of payouts. To see what dispersion means, let's look at a graph of the probability weighted payouts of games A, B, and C.

In the graph, we see that game A has its 2 payouts depicted in yellow, minus $1 and $1.10. They're both relatively close to the expected value of $0.05. Game B has both of its payouts further away from the expected value. Game B is pictured in orange and minus $2 and $2.10 are further away from the expected value and finally, in red, we see that the dispersion is greatest because game Cs payouts are furthest away from the expected value, –$3 and

$3.10. The red lines are outside of the orange lines are outside of the yellow lines. That is a pictorial representation of the fact that game C has a bigger dispersion than game B, and game Bs payouts has a bigger dispersion than game As payouts, or put another way, game C is riskier than game B is riskier than game A. Another way to understand why game C is the riskiest is to note that the probability weighted loss is greater for game C. That's 1/2 times $3, or 1 1/2. It's greater than the probability weighted loss for game B, which is $1/2 \times 2$ or $1.00 and, in turn, that is greater than the probability weighted loss for game A, 0.5 times $1 or $0.50. Some economists prefer to think of risk that way. By that measure also, C is riskier than B is riskier than A.

For those who are familiar with statistics, a standard measure of dispersion is the standard deviation of payouts, but you know, don't worry about that. The picture captures the idea that a game or any endeavor involving random payouts or random events is riskier if the dispersion of the payouts is greater. We're now prepared to understand the resolution of the St. Petersburg Paradox. The paradox's resolution is generally attributed to Daniel Bernoulli, a Dutch-Swiss mathematician who was, for a time, a professor of mathematics at the University in St. Petersburg. There are 2 essential components to the resolution.

The first component is the idea that the value to an individual of additional wealth falls as wealth increases. It follows that the satisfaction derived from an individual from gaining an additional dollar is smaller than the satisfaction lost from losing $1. Let's take that a slightly different way. We are happier when we win $1 than when we don't but the happiness we gain, according to Bernoulli, is a smaller increment than the happiness we lose when we lose $1. Bernoulli's first idea is embodied in the hypothesis that the utility that an individual derives from his or her wealth is a concave function of wealth. You can always recognize a concave function because it makes a little cave. There's a mind check for you. An example of a concave function is given in the graph that you are looking at now. The graph is shown for an individual who would start with $100 of wealth arbitrarily and it's drawn so that the utility of $100 is 0, just to normalize it. The concavity of the function implies that the utility gained from the additional gain of $1 is smaller than the utility lost from the loss of $1, as I've already said. Put another way, the marginal value of wealth falls to the person whose utility is pictured. Bernoulli thought our utility was a lot like that pictured in the diagram.

Now, Bernoulli's utility of wealth function has a solid intuition behind it. When an individual has little wealth, she uses it to acquire the things that she values most. As her wealth increases, she can acquire new things that add to her utility, but it's likely that they add less to her utility than the really important things that she's already purchased. The second component of the resolution of the paradox is a hypothesis that a rational decision maker maximizes expected utility rather than expected payout. Expected utility is the probability weighted average of the utility of the wealth that would result from each possible random outcome. By way of example, let's ask whether a person who maximizes expected utility and whose preferences are described by the pictured concave utility function would play a fair coin toss game for $10. The answer is no. By not playing the game, the risk averse individual can keep his or her utility at 0, the normalized starting point. By playing the game, the individual would have a 1/2 chance, a 1/2 chance of winning $10 and a 1/2 chance of losing $10 but the gain in utility associated with winning $10 is smaller in size than the loss in utility associated with losing $10.

One can read the utility from the graph, and I have done so in a numerical example because this idea is so important. So let's go ahead and compute expected utility. The decision to not play leaves us exactly with our $100 probability one. The decision to play leaves us with negative expected utility. I've already explained why. Let me explain why a second time. Expected utility is $0.5 \times -0.105 + 0.5$ times a smaller number, 0.095. Where did I get this -0.105 and $+0.095$? From the utility function, -1.05 is your utility if you lose that $10. You started at 0. You would fall to -0.105. Where did I get the 0.095? That's the utility you would get if you won the $10, and your wealth became not $100 but $110. So what happens is, as I have explained in words, that the utility of your gains is smaller in size than the utility of your loss. Therefore your expected utility from that fair game of 50/50 coin toss involving a prize of $10 is actually negative. You will not play.

Let's be clear, why does the expected utility hypothesis resolve the St. Petersburg Paradox? A person with little wealth places a lot of utility weight on each $1 they must spend for a ticket to play the St. Petersburg game. The person places less utility weight on each $1 they would win if they were very lucky, and it took many coin tosses for the heads to appear. As a footnote, it's interesting that behavioral economists have a slightly different take on the resolution of the St. Petersburg Paradox. They believe that most individuals act as if they will never experience a very, very, very rare event. In the context of the St. Petersburg game, that means that most individuals think that the probability that it will take more than say 9 tosses for a heads to show up is 0. Now in fact it's a very small number but they round it down to 0. They don't think they'll ever see that in their lifetime. As a result, experiential economists tend to resolve the paradox by saying that individuals do not use actual probabilities. They instead use a perceived probability, and they underweight very, very rare events believing that they will never see them.

What do we learn from our friend Daniel Bernoulli many, many decades later? We learn several very important things. Most individuals do not make decisions in the face of uncertainty by considering only the expected value associated with random events. Bernoulli's resolution of the St. Petersburg Paradox suggest that individuals are risk averse because they value the dollars they might lose more highly at the margin than they value the dollars they might win. In a later lecture, we will see that expected utility maximizers with concave utility functions will willingly buy insurance to avoid risk. They want to stay at the utility of 0 and will pay money to get to stay there. If they own a flip of the coin, if they've been endowed with the flip of a coin, they will pay money to get someone to take the outcome away from them. They'll happily pay for that service.

The expected utility hypothesis is not the last word on decision making in the face of uncertainty. It is a puzzle for researchers to explain why individuals often both buy property insurance and buy lottery tickets. Think about that for a minute. Buying property insurance only makes sense if the agent is risk averse with a concave utility function. Buying lottery tickets only makes sense if the decision maker is not risk averse, since lottery tickets are a less than fair game. We know they're profit-making schemes. So how do we square those 2 possibilities? Well in a very, very famous paper, Milton Friedman and Leonard Savage hypothesized that the typical household has a utility of wealth function that is concave in the vicinity of, call it their normal wealth, but it would turn convex at much higher levels of wealth.

What's that mean? Well the idea is that people would pay something for the chance to win a prize so large that it would substantially change the way that they could live. It would take them to a whole new place on their utility of wealth function.

Another challenge, and another puzzle, involves offering an individual a choice between 2 lotteries, each of which is equivalent to a coin toss game. In lottery 1, the individual will receive $1000 a year for every year of their life if heads comes up and nothing if tails comes up. Let's be clear, one coin toss, if you win, $1000 a year for every year until you die. Lottery 2 is very different. In lottery 2, the individual will repeat the coin toss every year. In any year, if heads comes up, the individual will win $1000 for that year and if tails come up, they receive nothing that year but the game goes on. Future coin tosses are still available to them. It's not hard to verify that the expected payout of both lotteries is the same. It's not hard to verify that the expected utility of both lotteries is the same, but ask yourself which game would you prefer to play? If you had a choice of buying either game at the same price, which game would you pay more for? If you are like most experimental subjects, and if you are like me, you would very much prefer lottery 2 and would pay more in order to get it.

At the end of the day, what do we learn from the St. Petersburg Paradox and from Daniel Bernoulli? We learn that most decision makers are risk averse. They dislike dispersion of payouts. They like situations where the payouts are close to the mean, better than situations when the payouts are further away. They dislike, in other words, the prospect of losing. Daniel Bernoulli changed thinking about decision making in risky situations forever when he put forward the expected utility hypothesis. It is such a simple but such a powerful idea. We place a greater value on a $1 we lose than on a $1 we gain, but research into human behavior goes on precisely because newer paradoxes have replaced older ones. This research is of great value to us. It helps us to understand, not casino gambling, that's only interesting if it leads to greater insights. It is important because it helps us understand the nature and value of insurance. It helps us to predict what individuals will pay in order to buy insurance and have someone take the risk away from them.

Thank you.

An Introduction to Bond Markets
Lecture 16

T his lecture introduces the bond market and explains the various types of government and non-government debt obligations. You also look at the connection between debt securities and the federal deficit and revisit the summer of 2011, when the United States faced the possibility of defaulting on bonds for the first time in its history.

U.S. Treasury Bills, Notes, and Bonds

- U.S. Treasury bills are short-term debt instruments. A **T-bill** is the promise of the Treasury to pay the face value of the bill at maturity. The market price of a T-bill is less than its face value; in other words, T-bills always sell at a discount.

- U.S. Treasury notes are medium-term debt instruments. A Treasury note is the promise of the Treasury to pay the face value of the note at maturity and to pay coupon payments every six months. The note is thus defined by its face value, the size of the coupon payments, and the date of its maturity.

- When the Treasury issues new notes, it typically sets the coupon rate (which will be locked for the life of the note) close to the current interest rate. As time passes, the coupon rate may turn out to be greater or less than the prevailing market rate of interest. The market price of a Treasury note can be either larger or smaller than its face value.

- U.S. Treasury bonds are long-term debt instruments. **Bonds** are like Treasury notes in all respects except one: Treasury notes mature in 2–10 years, while bonds offer a maturity of 30 years.

- Government bills, **notes**, and bonds are all considered to be less risky than stocks, primarily because they specify in advance the payments they will make.

STRIPS and TIPS

- The Treasury sells additional securities, including those known as **STRIPS** (Separate Trading of Registered Interest and Principal Securities).

- STRIPS are the result of "stripping" the coupon payments from a Treasury bond or note and using the payments to create another government debt obligation that makes a single payment on its maturity date. Thus, STRIPS are "zero-coupon" securities.

- STRIPS are popular with investors who want to receive a known payment on a specific future date. For example, a financial institution that has a future obligation to pay a known amount of funds might purchase STRIPS with a maturity date equal or close to the date at which its obligation must be paid.

U.S. Treasury Department, Washington DC.

© iStockphoto/Thinkstock.

- STRIPS are not issued or sold directly to investors. They can be purchased and held only through financial institutions and government securities brokers and dealers.

- The U.S. Treasury also sells **TIPS** (Treasury Inflation Protected Securities); the principal of a TIPS increases with inflation and decreases with deflation, as measured by the CPI. When a TIPS bond matures, the owner is paid the adjusted principal or original principal, whichever is greater.

- Since 2004, a non-protected bond had an average yield about 2% greater than the yield on a TIPS bond, indicating that the market values the inflation protection that TIPS provide.

- As of June 2009, TIPS represented 8% of the $6.6 trillion public Treasury debt.

The Federal Deficit and the National Debt
- The U.S. government supplies debt securities to the marketplace when it operates at a **deficit**, which occurs when government revenues are less than expenditures. The deficit is a flow—its units are dollars per year or per quarter.

- The **national debt** is the accumulation of deficits; it is a stock rather than a flow. If the government deficit is likened to the amount of water spilling over a dam, then the debt is the amount of water collected in the pool under the dam. The units of the national debt are dollars.

- When the federal government runs a deficit, the national debt increases. When the government runs a **surplus** (tax revenues greater than expenditures), the national debt decreases.

- Every year, the government must pay interest on the national debt; this interest is a current expenditure. In that sense, a higher debt means higher interest expenses, which means a higher deficit (or a lower surplus) if other factors remain unchanged.

- If a government ever had a debt so large that the interest on the debt exceeded its total tax revenues, the government would certainly fail. In fact, many economists believe that governments would fail at lower levels of the debt. Whether the levels of the debt and deficit are too large or not is a question that should be answered in the context of the size of the economy.

- A graph of the federal deficit as a share of GDP shows that the largest fraction of GDP (13%) occurred during World War II. The federal deficit exceeded 8% of GDP during the Great Recession of 2007–2009. Large deficits imply large new Treasury security issues.

- A graph of the national debt as a share of GDP shows that the largest fraction of GDP (110%) was reached at the end of the World War II. The figure hit a low of 25% in 1975, increased to a peak of 50% in 1995, fell to 32% in 2001 (after the Clinton tax increases),

Figure 16.1

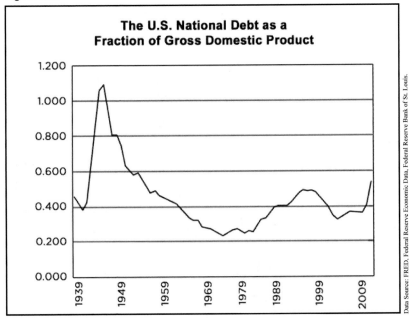

and began to increase again with the Bush tax cuts and the large deficits associated with the Great Recession.

- The national debt held by the public is the supply of government securities that must be willingly held by private citizens here and abroad.

Other Bond Markets
- Other important bond markets are those through which corporations and state and local governments borrow funds. An overview of market activity in the corporate bond market shows three categories of bonds: (1) investment-grade bonds (highly rated), (2) high-yield bonds (low ratings; sometimes called "junk bonds"), and (3) convertible bonds (can be converted to stock under certain conditions).

- On November 19, 2010, 5500 different bond issues were traded with a total value of more than $14 billion. On that day, about half the traded issues saw their prices increase, while half saw their prices decrease.

- Typically, the yields of the best investment-grade corporate bonds are higher than the yields of government bonds of the same maturity because market participants believe that there is greater risk that a corporation will not be able to keep its promises than there is that the U.S. government will be able to keep its promises.

- Other government entities also borrow funds in the bond markets. For example, state and local governments and various government entities, such as toll road authorities and government water and sewer systems, issue bonds in order to finance construction of public facilities.

- Many savers, especially those with high incomes, prefer to hold municipal bonds because of the preferred tax treatment they receive for the interest payments made by those bonds.

The Importance of Bond Markets

- Bond markets are where corporations, the federal government, state and local governments, and other public entities compete with one another for scarce funds provided by savers.

- Savers lend funds to these borrowers in anticipation of receiving interest payments that come in the form of coupons or capital gains or some combination of the two.

- Bond markets determine several key issues: a nation's interest rates, whether borrowing is expensive or inexpensive, which investment projects are funded and which are not, and how much you will pay to borrow funds to buy a house or car.

The Debt Ceiling

- During the Great Recession and the fragile recovery that followed, both the federal deficit and the national debt increased as a share of GDP. In the summer of 2011, the national debt approached its previously authorized ceiling of $14.294 trillion.

- A national debate raged about whether or not to raise the debt ceiling. Republicans were willing to raise the ceiling only if Congress agreed to large permanent cuts in federal spending. Democrats would agree to spending cuts, but only if they were accompanied by policy changes that would raise new revenues.

- As the date when the national debt would exceed its authorized maximum approached, the nation wondered whether Congress would authorize an increase or whether, for the first time in its history, the United States would default on its promises to pay.

Important Terms

bond: A certificate promising to repay money at a fixed rate of interest at a specified time.

deficit: When government revenues are less than expenditures. The deficit is a flow—its units are dollars per year or per quarter.

national debt: The accumulation of deficits; it is a stock rather than a flow.

notes: Medium-turn debt instruments of the Treasury; the promise of the Treasury to pay the face value of the note at maturity and also to pay coupon payments every six months.

STRIPS (Separate Trading of Registered Interest and Principal Securities): The result of stripping the coupon payments from a Treasury bond or note and using those coupon payments to create another government debt obligation that makes a single payment on its maturity date.

surplus: When tax revenues are greater than expenditures.

T-bill: Short-turn debt instruments of the Treasury; the promise of the Treasury to pay the face value of the bill at maturity.

TIPS (Treasury Inflation Protected Securities): The principal of a TIPS increases with inflation and decreases with deflation, as measured by the CPI. When a TIPS bond matures, the owner is paid the adjusted principal or original principal, whichever is greater.

Suggested Reading

Federal Reserve Bank of New York, "Interest Rates."

Mishkin, *The Economics of Money, Banking, and Financial Markets*.

1. Why does it make sense for U.S. Treasury securities to sell at prices that imply lower yields to maturity than are implied by the prices of bonds of reputable U.S. corporations?

2. How would you explain to someone who has not studied financial markets why owning bonds is less risky than owning shares of stock? How would you explain to them why owning bonds is not riskless?

3. What is the implication for bond markets when the U.S. federal deficit grows as a share of GDP?

An Introduction to Bond Markets
Lecture 16—Transcript

What do a wedding ring and a U.S. Treasury bond have in common? The Oxford English dictionary tells us that the word "bond" means an agreement with legal force. In the context of finance, a bond is a certificate issued by a government or a public company promising to repay borrowed money at a fixed rate of interest at a specified time. But the Oxford English dictionary also tells us that the root of the word "bond" is the middle English word "band," one meaning of which is a plain ring for the finger, such as a gold wedding ring. So a wedding ring and a Treasury bond are both promises. In its entire history, the United States has never broken its Treasury bond promises. It has never defaulted on a bond. It has always kept its promises to pay. The same cannot be said for the promises made by those who exchange rings, but during the summer of 2011, bond markets held their breath waiting to see if Congress would pass legislation that raise the debt ceiling in the United States. If the legislation were not passed, there was a serious danger that for the first time in its history, the U.S. would fail to keep a promise to pay someone to whom it owed funds.

Why are bond markets important? Bond markets are important because they provide an efficient way for savers to channel funds to corporations and government entities that choose to implement projects that require funding beyond the levels permitted by current revenues. Larger corporations issue bonds to finance the building of new physical facilities, the development of new product lines, and the implementation of new technologies. Governments borrow for many reasons. They borrow when they wish to build new roads and to spread the cost of those roads over many years. They borrow in recessions when tax revenues have fallen in order not to lower expenditures and thereby deepen the recession. They borrow to finance wars and not all government borrowing is bad. Sometimes it simply makes sense for a government to use future tax revenues to undertake projects or provide services in advance. It makes sense to not make people wait for those goods or for those services. Whether it's a good idea for a government to borrow or not depends on the value of the projects that they execute with the funds that they have received through borrowing, and the value of having those goods and services now rather than waiting for them after they have the appropriate tax revenues.

In this lecture, I will introduce the bond market. I will explain the various types of government and nongovernment debt obligations that we typically lump together under the term bonds. I will also investigate how the government has supplied bonds to the market place over its history. We begin with an introduction to the market for U.S. Treasury securities and, in particular, with the market for Treasury bills, notes, and bonds, 3 technical terms. So right off the bat, we want to know what bonds, bills, and notes are. If we look at the market report pages of the *Wall Street Journal*, we will see a bond market overview that reports the prices and yields on Treasury bills, notes, and bonds.

The example that you're looking at was taken from the electronic version of the *Wall Street Journal* on November 18, 2010. What we see there is a whole host of so-called Treasuries, 1-month bills, 3-month bills, 6-month bills, 1-year notes, 2-year notes, and so forth, to 7-year notes, and finally 10-year notes and 30-year bonds and also in that report, we see information about price changes, which are measured in 30 seconds and yields. I'm not going to dive too deeply into the meaning of the price changes and the yields. That comes at a later lecture. But for now, I want to explain all these different Treasury securities to you.

I'm motivated by what the vendors at Wrigley Field cry out, you can't tell the players without a score card. The first step to understanding the bond market that was pictured is to define bills, notes, and bonds. U.S. Treasury bills are short-term debt instruments of the U.S. Treasury. A U.S. Treasury bill, which is informally called a T-bill, is the promise of the United States Treasury to pay the face value of the bill at maturity. Why would the Treasury ever borrow on short-term? For the very simple reason that it borrows in anticipation of income and other tax revenues. While the U.S. Treasury will sell Treasury bills in any multiple of $100, we will typically assume that the face value of a Treasury bill is $1000 and that's for simplicity. A Treasury bill makes only one promised payment. It pays its face value at the maturity date and thus, as we've seen earlier from the lecture on present value, it makes sense to understand that the Treasury bills that we see always sell at a discount. That is, the market price of a Treasury bill is always less than its $1000 face value.

The return to the purchaser, to the person who is lending money to the federal government, is thus the difference between what the purchaser pays to buy the Treasury bill and the face value of the Treasury bill that they will receive later. The U.S. Treasury currently offers T-bills with maturities of 4 weeks, 13 weeks, 26 weeks, and 52 weeks, although as we will see later, those Treasury bills are sold from Peter to Paul many times before they're finally mature and are finally paid off.

What about U.S. Treasury notes? These are medium-term debt instruments of the U.S. Treasury. A Treasury note is the promise of the U.S. Treasury to pay the bearer the face value of the note at maturity and also to pay coupon payments every 6 months. The note is thus defined by its face value. The size of the coupon payments that occur intermediate to the final payment at the time of maturity and of course, by the date of the maturity itself. Again, the U.S. Treasury will sell notes in any multiple of $100 but we will assume a standard face value of $1000 to keep ideas simple.

When the Treasury issues new notes, it typically sets the coupon rate to be close to the current interest rate but upon issuance of the note, the Treasury locks in the coupon rate for the life of the note. So the coupons are always of the same dollar size and as time passes, the coupon rate can turn out to be bigger than or less than the market prevailing market rate of interest. For reasons I will shortly explain, the market price of a Treasury note can be either larger than or smaller than its face value. In common parlance, the note can sell at a premium when its price is higher than its face value or at a discount when its price is lower than its face value. The Treasury currently offers notes with maturities of 2, 3, 5, 7, or 10 years.

Now we go to U.S. Treasury bonds. These are the long-term debt instruments of the U.S. Treasury. Treasury bonds are like Treasury notes in all respects except one. They make coupon payments every 6 months. They can sell at a premium or a discount. They can be purchased from the U.S. Treasury in multiples of $100, but the U.S. Treasury currently offers bonds with a maturity of 30 years. Government bills, notes, and bonds are all considered to be less risky than stocks and from the last lecture, we understand that most individuals dislike risk, but why do we think the Treasury's bills, notes, and bonds are less risky than stocks? There are several reasons, but the most important reason is that bills, notes, and bonds specify, in advance, the payments that the bearer is entitled to receive, the payments that the government will make.

A stock does not promise to pay a particular dividend in advance. A stock does not guarantee a value on the date that you wish to sell it. The Treasury sells additional securities and they're quite interesting and we're going to focus on 2 of them. The first is called STRIPS, and I'll talk about STRIPS on at least 2 occasions in this course. Well of course, as you might've guessed, STRIPS is an acronym for Separate Trading of Registered Interest and Principle of Securities. What a mouth full. The reason the acronym makes sense is that STRIPS are the result of stripping the coupon payments from a Treasury bond or note and using those coupon payments to create another government debt obligation that makes a single payment on its maturity date. Thus STRIPS are zero-coupon securities. The only time an investor receives a payment if he owns a STRIPS is at the time of maturity. So here's an example, and it explains what's going on.

Suppose a 2-year Treasury note, the note promises 4 coupon payments plus a final payment. The payments will occur in 6, 12, 18, and 24 months. STRIPS separate these 4 payments into 4 zero-coupon securities. The first security is payable in 6 months. The second security is payable in 12 months, the third in 18 months, and the fourth in 24 months. STRIPS are popular with investors who want to receive a known payment on one specific future date. So what STRIPS do, in effect, is replicate the payment stream of a Treasury bill but for longer horizons. Who likes STRIPS? Here's an example. A financial institution that has a future obligation to pay a known amount of funds might purchase and hold STRIPS with a maturity equal to or close to the date at which that obligation must be paid. Think about how good that is. At the point that financial institution purchased the STRIP, they would know that its value will grow to the size of the future payment they have to make. STRIPS are not issued or sold directly to investors. STRIPS can be purchased and held only through financial institutions and government securities brokers and dealers.

As we'll see later, STRIPS are an early and fairly simple example of something we call a financial derivative. While many of you think these days a derivative is a dirty economic word, we'll talk about them later in which we cover STRIPS again and think about why they aren't such a dirty word. Here's one more example of another kind of security offered by the U.S. Treasury to individuals and to corporations. It's called TIPs. It rhymes with STRIPS but it's very, very different. TIPS are Treasury Inflation-Protected Securities. You want to know about these. The principle of a TIPS increases with inflation and decreases with deflation as measured by the consumer price index. When a TIPS bond matures, the owner is paid an adjusted principle or the original principle, whichever is greater. Since 2004, a non-protected bond had an average yield of about 2% greater than the yield on TIPS. What do I mean by that? Since 2004, if we have TIPS and a bond that does not include inflation protection and those are of the same maturity, the yield, the percentage that the government has to pay to get people to buy the non-protected bond has been, on average, 2% higher than the yield on the TIPS bond which does give inflation protection, and that indicates very, very clearly that those who buy government Treasury securities value the inflation protection that TIPS provide.

TIPS have been offered by the U.S. Treasury since 1997. As of June 2009, TIPS securities represented 8% of the $6.6 trillion public Treasury debt. The U.S. government supplies debt securities to the market place when the federal government operates at a deficit. By that I mean when the federal government spends more than its tax revenues. The government operates at a deficit when its revenues are less than its expenditures and think about this, the deficit is a flow. Its units are dollars per year or per quarter, depending upon how you wish to measure them. The national debt is the accumulation of deficits. It is a stock rather than a flow. If we liken the government deficit to the amount of water spilling over a dam then the debt is the amount of water that is collected in the pool under the dam. The deficit always has time associated with its measure. The deficit is a trillion dollars a year or $500 billion a year. The debt never has a unit of time. It may have a date associated with it but we would say the national debt is so many trillions of dollars on a date.

When the federal government runs a deficit, the national debt does increase. When the federal government runs a surplus, that is tax revenues are greater than expenditure, the national debt decreases. Every year and this is very,

very important, the government must pay interest on the national debt. The interest it pays on the national debt is a current expenditure of government. That means in a very, very real sense that higher debt means higher interest expenses, which means, other things equal, higher deficits unless taxes are raised. So deficits kind of feed on themselves because they imply higher interest payments. If a government ever had a debt so large that the interest on the debt exceeded its total tax revenues, bet your bottom dollar that that government would certainly fail. In fact, many economists believe that governments would fail at even lower levels of debt than that, but we won't get into that today.

Whether the levels of the debt and the deficit are too large or not is a question that has to be answered in the context of the size of the economy. So as we often do, let's look at some data. The chart that you are looking at now is the U.S. Federal deficit as a fraction of gross domestic product. What do we see? Well the dramatic thing is that the Federal deficits were largest. That is the red ink was the greatest during the time of World War II, but frighteningly, we also see that our deficits in 2009 were uncomfortably close to that level. We also see that if we divide this period of 1939 to 2009 into 2 halves, aside from World War II, the deficit kind of averaged 0 in the first half of the period but averaged something negative in the second half. That is what bothers those individuals who are very concerned about changing the laws of the land and government commitment to spending to lower the deficits currently. On average, we've had deficits in the second half of this long period. Notice the one exception here. That exception where, in 1999 to about 2001, that we had surpluses, those were due to Clinton's tax increases.

Now, large deficits imply large new Treasury security issues and the next chart that you'll see shows the water in the pool, if you like, the Federal debt, but it shows it as a fraction of gross domestic product in order to control for the size of the economy. When we looked at that graph, we see that the national debt as a share of gross domestic product has never been higher than it was in World War II, when it was greater than our gross domestic product. Now in recent years, it's varied between 40 and 50% of our gross domestic product although many people think that is too large.

In summary, the U.S. debt reached its larger fraction of GDP, 110%, at the end of World War II. It fell continually until it reached a low of about 25% of GDP in 1975. It then began to increase because deficits were persistently negative until it hit a peak of about 50% in 1995. It then fell after the Clinton tax increase until it reached a low—relative low, local low—of 32% in about 2001. Finally, it began to increase again with the Bush tax cuts and to increase rapidly with the large deficits associated with the Great Recession. The national debt, held by the public, is the supply of government securities, which must be willingly held by private citizens not only in the United States but in the rest of the world.

Now there are other important bond markets and these are bond markets where other entities than the fiscal authorities of the United States are able to borrow. For example, corporations and state and local governments also use bond markets to borrow funds. We can see from the *Wall Street Journal* online edition, a table entitled market depth and it describes the corporate bond market. Along the top, we see the kinds of issues on a particular day, November 19, 2010, 5518 different bonds traded. Of those, 3964 were considered investment grade, very high quality with the borrowers very likely to repay; 1346 of those bonds were considered high yield bonds. They used to be called junk bonds but now they're called high yield bonds, and some of those bonds were of a particular kind that can be converted to stocks at the option of the borrower, and those are called convertibles. We see some statistics about those, and I really don't care about those statistics today, but the dollar volume is huge, $14 billion for all issues.

So economists would say the market is very deep, 5500 different bond issues traded on that day with a total value of over $14 billion. The market was mixed on November 19, 2010, in the sense that about half the traded issues saw their prices increase while half saw their prices decrease. The yields on the best investment grade corporate bonds are higher than the yields of government bonds of the same maturity. Why? Well because market participants believe that there's a greater risk that a corporation will not be able to keep its promises than there is that the U.S. government will not be able to keep its promises. Other government entities also borrow funds in the bond market, state and local governments, and various government entities such as the toll road authorities and water and sewer systems issue bonds in order to finance construction of public facilities. Of course this makes sense. You don't want people to wait for clean water, until the tax revenues increase. It makes sense to borrow the funds, build the water facilities, and then pay down the bonds through fees from the users of the water system.

Many savers, especially those with high incomes, like very much to hold municipal bonds, that is, city bonds, because of the preferred tax treatment they receive for interest payments made by those bonds. Bond markets are important markets where corporations, the federal government, state and local governments, and other public entities compete with one another for scarce funds provided by savers. Savers lend funds to these borrowers in anticipation of receiving interest payments that come in the form of either coupons or capital gains or some combination of the 2. Bond markets determine the nation's interest rates. They determine whether borrowing is expensive or inexpensive. Because they determine the nation's interest rates, bond markets determine which investment projects are going to be funded, are going to be viable, and which investment projects will stay on the shelf because they're not viable. Bond markets determine how much you will pay to borrow funds to buy a house or a car.

As we end this lecture, let me refocus for a moment on events that unfolded during the summer of 2011. As we observed from the timelines, both the Federal deficit and the national debt had been rising as a share of gross domestic product during the Great Recession and the fragile recovery, which followed. Of course they did. The fact that there was a recession meant that tax revenues had fallen and Congress and the executive branch were not willing to cut expenditures proportionately. It is a matter of law that the U.S. Congress must authorize any increase in the so-called debt ceiling, the maximum legal size of the national debt.

During the summer of 2011, the national debt ceiling approached its previously authorized ceiling of $14 trillion, 294 billion, authorized by Congress on February 12, 2010. A national debate raged on whether or not to raise the debt ceiling. Republicans were willing to raise the debt ceiling only if Congress agreed to large, permanent cuts in Federal spending. Democrats would agree to spending cuts but only if they were accompanied by policy changes that would raise new revenues. As the date when the national debt would exceed its authorized maximum approached, the entire nation wondered whether Congress would authorize an increase or whether, for the first time in its history, the United States would default on its promises to pay. In the next lecture, we will zero in and see exactly how bond markets determine interest rates, and we will think about what a U.S. government default would imply for interest rates.

Thank you.

Bond Prices and Yields
Lecture 17

B ond markets are where interest rates paid by borrowers and earned by lenders are determined. But exactly how does this happen? The short answer is that by setting the price of bonds, bond markets determine the yields to maturity of those bonds, and bond yields are interest rates; thus, bond markets determine interest rates. It's important to understand the relationship between bond prices and yields to maturity for a number of reasons, including the fact that yields to maturity determined in the bond market are market standards to which other interest rates, such as those paid by home buyers, adjust.

Secondary Markets

- Although the U.S. Treasury is the original seller of Treasury securities, such as bills, bonds, and notes, private individuals and businesses buy and sell these securities in the secondary market. The existence of a secondary market means that it is easy to convert a Treasury security into cash on any business day.

- The existence of a secondary market also means that individuals who wish to move money from the present to the future have a larger menu of maturity dates than that offered for new issues by the Treasury.

- Suppose that in 2000, the Treasury issued 30-year bonds with a coupon rate of 4%. The maturity date of those bonds is 2030, but they will continue to trade in secondary markets until they mature. In 2005, those bonds provided an opportunity equivalent to a 25-year bond; in 2010, they provided an opportunity equivalent to a 20-year bond; and so on.

Figure 17.1

Treasury Statistics

Security Name US Treasury	Curr	Trade prices: 11/17/2010				Average Daily Volumes: 09/2010	Average Closing Quotes	
		High	Low	Median	No. of Trades	Volume	Bid	Offer
2.0 30/11/2013 S	USD	103.62	103.62	103.62	<1	57809		
2.375 31/07/2017 S	USD	102.16	102.16	102.16	<1	375428	101.70	101.74
2.5 30/04/2015 S	USD	105.23	105.23	105.23	<1	118095	104.95	104.98
2.625 15/08/2020 S	USD	100.39	97.63	98.64	161	144231971	97.76	97.80
2.625 15/11/2020 S	USD	98.50	97.11	98.06			97.71	97.72
2.625 31/07/2014 S	USD	105.84	105.84	105.84	<1	2857	105.61	105.65
2.75 15/02/2019 S	USD	102.47	102.47	102.47	1	552247	101.88	101.93

Source: Bondmarketprices.com.

- Let's consider a Treasury bond that will mature on February 15, 2019, with a coupon rate of 2.75%. On November 17, 2010, its median trade price was 102.47% of its face value, or $1024.70 for a $1000 bond. The reason the bond sold at a premium was that its coupon rate was higher than market interest rates on November 17, 2010.

- The fact that Treasury securities trade on secondary markets means that their prices and yields change with every change in price.

Yield to Maturity

- The yield to maturity of a Treasury security is the internal rate of return on the stream of payments promised by the security.

- Recall from an earlier lecture the formula for present value, as shown below. According to the formula, the present value of a set of payments to be made on different future dates is the sum of the appropriately discounted value of each of those payments, where d is the discount rate: $PV = S(t + 1)/(1+ d) + S(t + 2)/(1 + d)^2 + \ldots + S(t + m)/(1 + d)^m$.

- Let's look at the stream of payments promised by a 52-week Treasury bill. On November 1, 2010, such a bill with a face value of $1000 had a secondary market price of $997.90.

- The yield to maturity (YTM) of this Treasury bill is the value of the discount rate that sets the present value of the payments the bill will make equal to its market price. The formula for this is:

Market Price = (Payment in 1 Year) / (1 + YTM)

$997.90 = $1000 / (1 + YTM)

- The value of YTM in this case is 0.0021.

- Let's now move to November 15, 2010, and compute the yield to maturity of a Treasury note with a coupon rate of 0.5%, a face value of $1000, a maturity date of November 15, 2013, and a market price of $991.50.

Stream of Payments Promised by the Exemplar Treasury Note

Date	May 15, 2011	Nov 15, 2011	May 15, 2012	Nov 15, 2012	May 15, 2013	Nov 15, 2013
Payment	$2.50	$2.50	$2.50	$2.50	$2.50	$1002.50

- The YTM of this Treasury note is the value of x that sets the present value of the stream of payments equal to its price, as shown below:

$991.50 = 2.50/(1 + x) + 2.50/(1 + x)^2 + 2.50/ (1 + x)^3 + 2.50/ (1 + x)^4 + 2.50/(1 + x)^5 + 1002.50/(1 + x)^6$

- The value of x is 0.00285, or a semiannual yield of 0.285%, or an annual yield of 0.57%.

- Why do the prices and yields of Treasury securities move in opposite directions? To answer that question, let's return to the earlier Treasury bill example. Recall the formula we used:

Market Price = (Payment in 1 Year) / (1 + YTM)

- When the market price rises, YTM must fall. Conversely, when the market price falls, YTM must rise. The same is true for a bond that pays coupons. A decrease in the market price of a bond always implies an increase in its YTM.

Holding Period Yield

- The holding period yield of a Treasury security is not generally the same as the yield to maturity.

- The **yield to maturity** is the ex ante yield that a bill, note, or bond purchaser will earn if the bond is held from the date of purchase to maturity. Put another way, the yield to maturity is the rate at which the purchaser's initial investment will grow between the date of purchase and the date on which the security matures.

- The purchaser may, however, decide to sell the security before it matures. The holding period yield on the bond is the rate of return earned on the initial financial investment between the date the bond is purchased and the date it is sold.

- If the yield to maturity of a bond increases between the time of purchase and the time of sale, then the holding period yield will be smaller than the yield to maturity calculated when the bond was purchased. The price of the bond will be lower when it is sold than originally expected.

- If the yield to maturity of the bond falls between the time of purchase and the time of sale, then the holding period yield will be higher than the yield to maturity calculated when the bond was purchased. The price of the bond will be higher when it is sold than originally expected.

Capital Loss or Gain?

- Suppose you purchase a 10-year U.S. Treasury bond that you expect to sell after 5 years. What sort of economic news would likely create a capital loss or gain for your bond holdings? The answer to this question depends on what has happened to the yield to maturity in the time between the purchase and sale of the bond.

- If the yield to maturity has risen, you will experience a capital loss because the market price of the bond you sell will be lower in order to make the bond competitive with newer bonds that are promising higher yields to maturity.

- If the yield to maturity has fallen, you can expect a capital gain because the market price of the bond you sell will be higher given that it offers a higher yield to maturity than newer bonds.

- What sort of economic events would make yields to maturity rise or fall? If economic growth increases beyond the expectations that were in place when you bought the bond, then yields to maturity will rise and you will sell your bond at a lower price than you expected.

- Harkening back to our discussion of the debt ceiling, if anything happens to make it more likely that the U.S. government will default on its bonds, then the yield to maturity on newly issued bonds will rise as market participants demand higher yields as compensation for the higher risks they face in lending to the government. Again, you will realize a capital loss because a lower price for the bond you are selling is required to make it attractive to prospective buyers.

Takeaway Points
- The present-value equation provides the crucial link between bond prices and yields to maturity.

- The yield to maturity for a discount security (a Treasury bill or STRIPS) is the rate at which the current market price for the security must grow so that the security is worth its face value on the day of maturity.

- A bond or note that has coupons provides two sources of payment: the coupon payment and the capital gain (or loss) associated with paying the market price and receiving the face value at maturity.

- The yield to maturity is computed using the present-value formula to account for the amount and timing of all payments. In fact, the yield to maturity is the discount rate that makes the present value of the payments offered by the bond equal to its market price.

- Someone who purchases a bond and sells it prior to maturity can receive a holding period yield different from the yield to maturity computed at the time of purchase.

Important Term

yield to maturity: The ex ante yield that a bill, note, or bond purchaser will earn if the bond is held from the date of purchase to maturity.

Suggested Reading

Eichberger and Harper, *Financial Economics*.

Federal Reserve Bank of New York, "Interest Rates: An Introduction."

Mishkin, *The Economics of Money, Banking, and Financial Markets*.

1. What is the difference between the yield to maturity of a bond and the holding period yield of a bond? When will those two yields be different? Will they ever be the same?

2. Suppose you have purchased 10-year U.S. Treasury bonds that you expect to hold for 5 years and then sell. What sort of economic news would likely create a capital loss for your bond holdings? What sort of news would likely create a capital gain?

Bond Prices and Yields
Lecture 17—Transcript

Bond markets determine interest rates paid by borrowers and earned by lenders. It is bond markets where these very important prices and rates are determined. These are prices and rates that allocate funds and determine which projects go forward and which do not. But exactly how does this happen? The short answer is that by setting the price of bonds, bond markets determine the yields to maturity of those bonds. Yields are interest rates. So bond markets determine interest rates. How bond prices determine yields to maturity is not obvious, but it will be clear at the end of this lecture. To make it clear, we will use our old friend present value.

Why is it important to understand the relationship between bond prices and the yields to maturity of those bonds? The yield to maturity is the rate that a corporation which issues the bonds should compare to the loan rate quoted to it by a bank well before deciding which funding strategy to employ. The yield of maturity is the rate that a corporation, which issues bonds, should compare to the productivity of its investment project to determine if that project is worth doing. The yield to maturity is also the rate that a lender should compare to the interest rate she can earn on say a certificate of deposit at her bank before she decides on her own financial strategy. Yields to maturity determined in the bond market are market standards to which other interest rates adjust including rates paid by consumers and home buyers.

The first step is to understand that after they are issued, the great majority of bonds and other debt instruments trade on secondary markets. Treasury bills, Treasury notes, and Treasury bonds trade on secondary markets, and we will focus on these debt instruments in our examples. So Treasury bills, bonds, and notes are sold and resold in secondary markets every business day. What does that mean? Well, while the U.S. Treasury is the original seller of each of those securities—each bill, note, and bond—private individuals and businesses buy and sell those Treasury securities from one another in the secondary market. These are second and third sales. That's why the term secondary market makes sense. The financial media regularly report data on secondary market purchases and sales of Treasury bills, bonds, and notes.

Let's, as we often do, look at some data. This data describes trades in the secondary market for Treasury securities. What we see in the left column is a description of the Treasury security itself, and this is only one page of a multi-page report. In the next column, we see that the currency, so this particular web site, is prepared to talk about dollar and non-dollar securities. More interesting is the data on price. We see a high price, the low price, and the median or middle price for November 17, 2010, for each of the securities. Not all the securities were traded that day and so in the next column, we see the number of trades and we see evidence about the volume of trades. Finally as that market closed, we see the final bid and the final ask, and we know that that is the offer price and the demand price, and we see that they're quite close together.

The existence of a secondary market means that it is easy to convert a Treasury security into cash on any business day. Put another way, Treasury securities are highly liquid but not liquid enough to be considered part of the money supply. The existence of a secondary market also means that individuals who wish to move money from the present to the future have a large menu of maturity date and opportunities than the menu offered by the Treasury for the newly issued securities. Suppose, for example, that the U.S. Treasury issued a 4%, 30-year bond in the year 2000, and by 4% I meant that its coupon was 4%. The maturity date of that bond is thus 2030. Those bonds will continue to trade in secondary markets until they mature. So in 2005, those bonds will provide an opportunity equivalent to the opportunity provided by a newly issued 25-year bond. In 2010, those bonds, although they were issued in 2000, will provide an opportunity to a purchaser equivalent to the opportunity provided by a newly issued 20-year bond, and so forth.

The table presents a set of Treasury securities and their market prices for November 17, 2010. We can zero in on one entry in order to understand better how the secondary market works. The last line of the table describes a Treasury bond that will mature on February 15, 2019, and has a coupon rate of 2.75%. Remember that the coupon rate determines the periodic payments that one receives typically every 6 months. That bond was actively traded on November 17, 2010, with a median trade price of 102.47% of the bond's face value. What's that mean? It simply means that if the face value of the bond is $1000 that bond traded for $1024.70 on November 17. The reason that the bond sold at a premium for more than its face value was that its coupon rate was higher than market interest rates on November 17, 2010.

Now it makes sense that a bond sold at a premium because the bond offered coupons that were larger dollar amounts than the interest payments someone could have received by financially investing $1000 at the rates that prevailed on November 17. In effect, the price made the bonds yield close to prevailing interest rates as we shall see. The fact that Treasury securities trade on secondary markets means that their prices and yields change with every change in price. Put another way, the yields on Treasury securities change constantly, every trading day and many times within the trading day. The Treasury bond market overview for November 18, 2010, the next day, reported the prices of most Treasury securities were slightly lower than they had been the day before. Shortly we will confirm that the overview also reported that Treasury yields had risen.

The yield to maturity of a Treasury security is what is called the internal rate of return on the stream of payments promised by the security. Now recall from an earlier lecture the formula for present value. The present value of a stream of payments is the value of the stream of payments divided by the appropriate discount rate. So the payment that will be received 1 period in the future is divided by 1 plus the discount rate. The payment that will be received 2 periods in the future is divided by 1 plus the discount rate squared because it has to be shrunk twice and so forth and so on. The value of a payment to be received M periods in the future is shrunk M times by dividing by $1 + D^M$. Add all those various payments' present value together and you get the present value of the stream of payments. The formula says that the present value of a set of payments to be made on different future dates is the sum of the appropriately discount value of each of those payments. Remember that D is the discount rate.

So let's begin with a relatively simple example, the stream of payments promised by a 52-week Treasury bill, no coupons. On November 1, 2010, a 52-week Treasury bill with the face value of $1000 had a secondary market price of $997.90. T-bills always trade at a discount. The yield to maturity of this Treasury bill is the value of the discount rate that makes the present values of the payments the bill will make just equal to its market price. Let's call that value of the discount rate, that special value, that the value that we're trying to find, YTM for yield to maturity, a good memory peg. The formula is that market price, that's one pan of the scale, must equal present value of the payment the bond will make, which is the payment itself that will be received in 1 year divided by one plus the yield to maturity. In our example, that's $997.90 in the left pan of the scale and in the right pan of the scale, $1000 divided by one plus the yield to maturity.

The value of YTM implied by that equation, in other words, if we solve the equation for YTM, we will get 0.0021 or slightly more than 0.2%. Clearly the yield to maturity of Treasury bills was very, very small, less than 0.5% in annual terms in November 2010. In a later lecture, I'll take a look at this period of time, and I'll ask carefully why interest rates yields to maturity were so low back then. For now, we simply use these data as an example for computing the Treasury bill yield. Let's now make things slightly more difficult and consider a bond, which promises some coupon payments. Now suppose the data's November 15, 2010, and we want to compute the yield to maturity of the Treasury note listed in the third line of the table that you are seeing. The coupon has a rate of 0.5%. That's going to define the size of the coupons, a face value of $1000, a maturity date of November 15, 2013, and a market price of $990.50.

Now for the sake of simplicity, I will assume the time is measured exactly in 1/2-year periods, and I will also assume that the very first payment is going to occur in exactly 1/2 year. It does no violence to my point, allows me to keep things simple. The stream of payments promised by the note is given in the table. On May 15, 2011, 1/2 year after the note is issued, the bearer will receive $2.50 in a coupon. On November 15, 2011, a year later, another $2.50, on May 15, 2012, yet another $2.50, on November 15, 2012, $2.50 and on May 15, 2013, $2.50, and finally the last of the 1, 2, 3, 4, 5, 6 payments will be the final coupon plus the face value paid on November 15, 2013, and that amount will be $1002.50. So what? Well, remember we are going to assume that the market price is equal to the present value of that stream of payments and figure out what discount rate makes that true.

The yield of maturity of this Treasury note is the value of x, C is the unknown, that sets the present value to the stream equal to its price. So again, in one pan of the scale, $991.50. In the other pan of the scale, the present value of the 6 different payments, $2.50, which we'll get in 6 months divided by 1 + x. $2.50 which we'll get in 2 6-month periods, that is $2.50 divided by (1 + x)^2 and so forth until we get to the final payment, $1002.50 divided by (1 + x)^6. Now notice I have used a unit of time of 6 months. So x is going to be 1/2 year rather than a full year rate. The value of x is 0.00285. So what? Well that's a semi-annual yield of 0.285%, again very, very low but that's equivalent to an annual yield of about 0.5%, in fact, 0.57%. Again very, very low and we'll come back to why the yields were so low in that period of time.

Now before you run out and get a paper and pencil and try this on your own, you cannot find the value of x that solves that equation. That is, you can't easily find with paper and pencil the value of x that makes market price equal the present value. You're going to need a financial calculator set up for just this fact or you're going to need some facility with a spreadsheet or you can ask your friendly economist. We now, and this is why we went through these computations, we now have a valuable opportunity to understand why the price of Treasury securities and the yields to maturity of those securities move in opposite directions. Price is up, yield's down. Price is down, yield's up. I'm going to make this point as simple as possible. So I'm going to revert back to the Treasury bill example. Remember that the market price in one pan of the scale was equal to the payment you will get 1 year later divided by the yield to maturity.

Well, wait a minute, how are we going to come to understand that? Only 2 things can change here. The final payment will never change. So if the market price goes up then in order to make the other side of the equation go up as well, you have to lower one plus the yield to maturity because it's in the denominator of the other side of the equation. So when market prices rise, the yield to maturity must fall. Conversely, when the market price falls, the yield to maturity must rise. It's a mathematical fact. The same is true for a bond that pays coupons. The decrease in the market price of a bond always implies an increase in the bond's yield to maturity but, don't worry, we're not going to go through that example. That is why the bond market overview presented previously shows opposite movements in the prices and yields for every maturity considered.

Now I'm going to introduce to you a new concept called the holding period yield of a Treasury security. I'm going to explain that the holding period yield of a Treasury security will not generally be the same as the yield to maturity. The yield to maturity is the x ante or before the fact yield that a bill, note, or bond purchaser will earn if he or she holds the bond from the date of purchase all the way to the date in which it matures. Put another way, the yield to maturity is the rate at which the purchaser's initial investment will grow between the date of purchase and the date in which the security matures but because there are active secondary markets, the purchaser may decide to sell the bill, note, or bond before it matures and holding period yield on the bond, on the bill, or on the note is another kind of interest rate concept. It's the rate of return that the purchaser earns on her financial investment between the date she purchases it and the date she sells it. Of course if she sells it one instant before maturity, those 2 yields are the same but they don't have to be because she can sell it earlier.

While the exact relationship between holding period yields and yields to maturity is extremely complex and really beyond the scope of our course, there are facts about holding period yields that are easy to understand and that I think you will find interesting. For example, if the yield to maturity of your bond rises between the time when you buy it and the time when you sell it, then your holding period yield will be smaller than the yield to maturity that you calculated when you bought the bond. Hold on, why is this so? This is so because the price of your bond will be lower when you sell it than you originally would have predicted. Why? Because that bond has to meet a market test for the new yield to maturity, and it does so by changing its price.

On the other hand, if the yield to maturity of your bond falls between the time when you buy it and the time when you sell it, good news, then your holding period yield will be higher than the yield of maturity that you calculated at the time you bought your bond. Why does this make sense? Again extremely intuitive, this makes sense because of the price of your bond will be higher when you sell it than when you originally thought. Your bond then is offering a coupon stream that's even more valuable relative to current market conditions. Market forces will bid up the price of that bond and you will benefit when you sell it.

Before we conclude today's lecture, I want to consider a practical problem, one that will allow us to also check our thinking about bond prices and interest rates, that is bond prices and yields. Suppose, for a minute, that you have purchased a 10-year U.S. Treasury bond that you expect to hold for 5 years and then sell. So there's some possibility that your holding period yield will not be the same as the yield to maturity that you know when you buy. The interesting question is what sort of economic news would likely create a capital loss for your bond holdings, that is, for you to sell it at a lower price than you bought it? What sort of news, presumably different news, would likely create for you a capital gain? Now happily, we now understand that the answer to this question depends on what has happened to the yield to maturity in the time between your purchase and when you sell the bond. If the yield to maturity has risen, you will experience a capital loss because the market price of the bond you sell will be lower in order to make the bond you are selling competitive with newer bonds that are promising higher yields. If, on the other hand, the yield to maturity has fallen, good news, you can expect a capital gain because the market price of the bond you will sell will be higher because it offers a higher yield to maturity than newer bonds, and the market will equate those 2 yields. So the question of capital gains can be restated.

What sort of economic events would make yields to maturity rise, and what sort of economic events would make yields to maturity fall? Here are a couple of economic events that might change yields to maturity. If economic growth increases beyond the expectations that were in place when you bought the bond then yields to maturity will have risen, and you will sell your bond at a lower price than you expected. Well why does this make sense? Well hold on a second. If the economy is growing very, very rapidly and in particular, more rapidly than the market predicted when you bought your bond then the market for credit is tighter. Many more individuals want credit than previously, and they're going to bid the price of that credit up. Indeed in a future lecture, we'll talk about that market process. You lent your money at a low rate and now the market demands a higher rate of interest and therefore, you must sell for a lower price in order to make your bond attractive to buyers.

Harkening back to our discussion of the debt ceiling in the previous lecture, if anything happens to make it more likely that the U.S. government would default on its bonds then the yield to maturity of newly issued bonds will rise. Why? Market participants will now demand higher yields as compensation for the higher risks that they face in lending to the U.S. government. If you think that that's an impossible outcome, remember the same rules we're talking about today would apply to corporate bonds. So if any news occurred that would lead us to believe that a corporation was more likely to default on its bonds, the same forces would be at work. Again you will realize a capital loss because a selling price for the bond you are selling is required to make it attractive to perspective buyers.

In this lecture, we have learned several important things. The present value equation provides the crucial link between bond prices and bond yields to maturity. The yield to maturity for a discount security like a Treasury bill or a strip is the rate at which the current market price for the security must grow so that the security is worth its face value on the day of maturity. A bond or note that has coupons provides 2 sources of payments to its owner. The first is the coupon payment. The second is the capital gain or possibly capital loss associated with paying the market price and receiving the face value at maturity. In this case, the yield to maturity is computed again using the present value formula to account for the amount and timing of all payments. Indeed the yield to maturity is the discount rate that makes the present value of the payments offered by the bond or the note or the bill exactly equal to its market price.

Someone who purchases a bond and sells it prior to maturity can receive a holding period yield different than the yield to maturity computed at the time of purchase. If interest rates fall after the purchase, the holding period yield will be greater than the yield to maturity at the time of purchase. If interest rates rise after the purchase, the holding period yield will be smaller than the yield to maturity at the time of the purchase. In this lecture, I have talked a bit about the connection between economic events and changes in the interest rate. In the next lecture, we will investigate more fully the connection between economic forces and market interest rates.

Thank you.

How Economic Forces Affect Interest Rates
Lecture 18

I n this lecture, you'll learn to think of interest rates in a new way: as market-determined "prices" that are set by the forces of demand and supply. What "good" is being priced when markets determine the interest rate? The answer is "early use of funds." In this conception, demanders are those who want to use funds earlier than their incomes justify, and suppliers are those who provide early use of funds to those who will pay sufficient interest. Equilibrium occurs at the interest rate that makes the plans of fund demanders and suppliers compatible. This lecture explains this idea of an interest rate as a market price in this lecture and learn how different long-run and short-run economic forces work on the rate of interest.

Interest Rates as Market Prices

- Let's begin by supposing that Jane wishes to purchase a new car for $20,000. We will assume that there is no inflation and that Jane pays the same interest rate to borrow that she receives when she saves.

- Jane has at least two options: (1) She can borrow $20,000 to purchase a car and repay the loan in equal monthly installments over 36 months, or (2) she can put an equal amount in her savings account every month for 36 months until the balance of the account is $20,000.

- The difference in cost of the two options depends on the rate of interest. Clearly, an increase in the rate of interest makes the borrowing option more expensive and the saving option less expensive when Jane's monthly payments are used as the measuring stick.

Figure 18.1

How Changes in the Interest Rate Affect the Cash Flow of Borrowers and Lenders When the Object Is to Purchase a $20,000 Automobile		
Interest Rate	Monthly Payment Required to Purchase Auto	Monthly Saving Required to Purchase Auto in 36 Month
2	$572.85	$538.62
6	$608.44	$505.91
10	$645.34	$474.72
14	$683.55	$445.03

Source: Michael Salemi.

- Economists take the view that relative prices matter for economic decision making and that relative prices adjust to clear markets. If a pound of apples costs $2.00 and a pound of pears costs $3.00, then the relative price of a pound of pears is 1.5 pounds of apples. This means that when a consumer chooses a pound of pears, he or she refuses 1.5 pounds of apples.

- If pears are scarce relative to apples, the relative price of pears should increase (say, to 2 pounds of apples per pound of pears). If pears become abundant relative to apples, then the relative price of pears should fall.

- The inflation-adjusted (or real) rate of interest measures the cost of goods today relative to goods in the future. If the real rate is higher, someone who buys goods now gives up more goods in the future. If the real rate is lower, someone who buys goods now gives up fewer goods in the future.

The Long-Run World

- In the long run, the real rate of interest is determined by the patience of the population and the productivity of the nation's capital. This important point was made by one of the great 20th-century economists, Irving Fisher.

- In Fisher's long-run world, the economy remains at full employment, government budgets are balanced, and the economy's current account is balanced. That means, approximately, that the value of goods and services imported in a year equals the value of goods and services exported. Clearly, the long-run world is one that we rarely see, but it is a world toward which economic forces propel us.

- When markets determine the rate of interest, the economic "good" that is being priced is "early use of funds." The interest rate is the price of that good.

Demanders and Suppliers

- Let's think of "demanders" as those who have some compelling desire to use funds in excess of their income. Examples include households that wish to buy a home or pay for a child's education, as well as business owners who wish to implement highly productive technologies or plans. The more productive, the higher the interest rate the demanders are willing to pay.

- For demanders, higher interest rates are a disincentive to borrow. Suppose you have an idea for a better mousetrap, but to buy equipment and obtain space for manufacturing and distribution, you must obtain startup funds. The interest you pay on these funds is a cost of realizing your business plan. The higher that interest rate, the greater the cost.

- There is another way to explain the role of interest rates in an investment decision: To invest is to spend money today and to receive in return a stream of future profits. An investment is economically rational only if the present value of the profit stream exceeds the current investment outlay. Higher interest rates imply higher discount rates for future profits and smaller values for present value.

- In this conception, it does not matter whether you must borrow the funds or you have them in hand. If you have them in hand, the interest rate measures your opportunity cost of using them to finance your mousetrap factory because you could lend them and earn the interest rate.

- Your investment plans must be sufficiently productive to justify all costs of implementation, including interest costs. As the interest rate rises, the plans of some entrepreneurs become unprofitable. The higher the interest rate, the greater the number of investment plans that are not profitable and will not be undertaken.

- "Suppliers" are patient in the sense that they are willing to lend from their current income. That is, they are willing to allow others to borrow a part of the income they have earned in exchange for interest payments. For demanders, higher interest rates are an incentive to lend.

- Patient people are more likely to lend than impatient people. Patience is likely to be higher when a household's income is more than sufficient to provide for food, clothing, and shelter. Patience is also likely to be higher when a household desires to make an expensive purchase in the future, such as a house.

- A higher interest rate is an incentive to supply funds because a higher interest rate implies a greater reward to saving. That is, a higher interest rate implies that one's savings will buy more in the future.

- In the long run, interest rates tend to the values that balance the plans of borrowers and lenders. If there is more credit demanded than can be supplied, those with the most productive projects will offer to pay a higher interest rate and will crowd out less productive projects. If there is less credit demanded than can be willingly supplied, the most patient savers will offer to accept a smaller interest rate.

The Departure of Interest Rates from Long-Run Values

- In the short run, interest rates depart from long-run values for several important reasons.

- For example, governments sometimes spend more than they earn in tax revenue; that is, they run deficits. When the government sector runs a deficit, it must borrow funds to balance its accounts. In doing so, government competes with private borrowers for scarce funds. If the government deficit increases (other factors unchanged), the demand for funds increases and interest rates rise. The rise in interest rates crowds out some investment projects.

- Interest rates may also depart from long-run values when a nation runs a current account deficit, which is the difference between the values of a nation's imports and exports (with some adjustments). When a nation runs a current account deficit, the value of its imports is higher than would be justified by its exports (and income flows).

- When the United States runs a current account deficit, the rest of the world "lends" it purchasing power. That is, our trading partners prefer to use some of the dollars they receive by selling us goods to buy financial assets issued by U.S. firms and the government. In effect, the trading partners are lending us funds.

- When the current account is in deficit, the supply of credit to the United States is higher than from domestic sources alone, which means that interest rates are lower, other factors unchanged.

- Finally, interest rates may depart from long-run values when the economy is in recession. In this situation, demand for credit is low in part because firms doubt that households will buy their products. Because demand for credit is low, interest rates are also low.

Figure 18.2

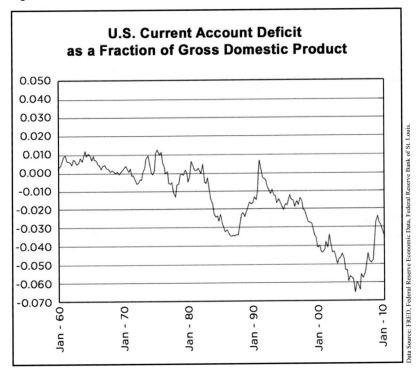

U.S. Current Account Deficit as a Fraction of Gross Domestic Product

Data Source: FRED, Federal Reserve Economic Data, Federal Reserve Bank of St. Louis.

Takeaways on Interest Rates

- Interest rates are important economic prices that are determined in the market for credit.

- In the long run, the saving and investment plans of the members of an economy jointly determine interest rates. In the short run, other forces are important, as well.

- Government deficits tend to raise interest rates because the government competes with private borrowers for scarce funds. Current account deficits tend to lower interest rates because the supply of credit is greater than it would be from domestic sources alone.

- When the economy is in a recession and resources are unemployed, interest rates tend to be lower both because demand for credit is low and because the Federal Reserve often lowers rates in an attempt to stimulate spending.

Suggested Reading

Federal Reserve Bank of New York, "Interest Rates: An Introduction."

Fisher, *The Theory of Interest*.

Kennedy, "Eight Reasons."

Mishkin, *The Economics of Money, Banking, and Financial Markets*.

Questions to Consider

1. What did Irving Fisher mean when he famously said that the (real) rate of interest was determined by the interaction between the patience of the nation's population and the productivity of its capital?

2. In what sort of nation would you expect the average real rate of interest computed over a century to be high? To be low?

3. Why do real rates of interest depart from their long-run values?

How Economic Forces Affect Interest Rates
Lecture 18—Transcript

Many of you know from your own experience the changes in interest rates have important effects on your household and business decisions. If you're my age, you remember the late 1970s when nominal interest rates exceeded 15%. As high as interest rates were then, they did not keep pace with the rate of inflation and real rates of interest were negative in those years. That was a time when borrowers did very, very well, and I can recall that many young householders, myself included, bought homes as soon as they could scrape together a down payment, or perhaps you remember the early 1980s when credit market conditions were very different. Nominal interest rates remain quite high, over 12%, and as high as 14% on Treasury bills but the rate of inflation had dropped by then in response to slower growth in the money supply engineered by Federal Reserve under the direction of Paul Volker. Then the real rate was very high, as high as 10% in some periods.

Today, I ask you to think of the interest rate in a new way. I ask you to think of interest rates as market-determined prices. Yes, interest rates are prices, and economists think of them in much the same way as they think about the price of a pound of apples, a bushel of corn, a gallon of gasoline, or a haircut. In particular, economists believe that interest rates are set by the market forces of demand and supply but what good is being priced when markets determine the rate of interest? The good in question is early use of funds. Let me elaborate a bit. What I mean by early use of funds is that a certain amount of money is allowed to be used earlier rather than later. A dollar, for example, or $1000, is allowed to be used say 1 year earlier. That situation occurs when demanders want to use funds earlier than their incomes justify.

Suppliers of that product provide early use of funds to those who will pay sufficient interest when they save and—and this is the important point—equilibrium occurs at the rate of interest that makes the plans of fund demanders who want to use funds early and fund suppliers who are willing to save compatible. Equilibrium occurs at an interest rate that make fund demanders' and fund suppliers' plans compatible. But interest rates are different than other prices in several important ways. First, a change in interest rate directly affects many economic markets while a change say in the price of corn directly affects only a few. Second, it is through interest rate changes that central banks attempt to stabilize the economy, keeping inflation low and steady and keeping output near full employment levels.

We'll talk about how they do that later, but it's important now to realize that these first 2 points are related. The Fed changes interest rates because it can, and because it knows that interest rate changes have widespread effects. Third, a change in the rate of interest must be viewed in the right way in order to be understood. In this lecture, I will begin by explaining why it is appropriate to think of an interest rate as a market price. I will then explain, in detail, as to how one should view interest rates. In this part of the lecture, I will reintroduce the important concept of the real rate of interest that we encountered in our earlier lecture. Finally, I will explain how different long-run and short-run economic forces work on the rate of interest, how they affected the rate of interest. In later lectures, we will see how changes in interest rates affect stock prices, how international differences in interest rates affect exchange rates, and how interest rate policies are at least in normal economic times, the backbone of central bank stabilization policies. The rate of interest is a very important market price.

To fix ideas, let's have an example. Let's suppose that our friend Jane wishes to purchase a new automobile for $20,000. To keep things simple, we will assume that there is no inflation and that a comparable automobile will be available in 3 years for the same price. That's a good assumption given no inflation. To allow for inflation would be possible and in our example, we would replace nominal interest rates with the real rates of interest. Also to keep things simple, I assume that Jane pays the same interest rate to borrow that she receives when she saves. I know that's not true, but it keeps things simple and it does absolutely no violence to the point I wish to make. My point is valid even when I make this simplifying assumption.

Let's take a look at 2 of Jane's options. Jane has lots of options, but I focus on these 2 because they're so instructive. Jane can borrow $20,000 to purchase an automobile and repay the loan in equal monthly installments over 36 months, or she can put an equal amount of money in her savings account every month for 36 months until the balance in that account is $20,000. Now the table you are seeing shows how the difference in cost of these 2 options depends on the rate of interest. So let me explain very clearly what you're looking at. In the left column, you see different potential values of the interest rate, 2%, 6%, 10%, and 14%. In the second column, you see the monthly payment required to purchase the auto now. So this would be Jane's monthly payment if she took out a loan, bought the auto now and made equal monthly payments. In the third and last column, you see the monthly saving required to purchase the auto in 36 months.

Now what you see is it's always more expensive to have the auto now than later but how much more expensive depends on the rate of interest. Clearly an increase in the rate of interest, and you can verify that by looking at the table, makes the borrowing option more expensive and the saving option less expensive when I use, as a measuring stick, Jane's monthly payments. Economists take the view that relative prices matter for economic decision making and that relative prices adjust to clear markets.

An example will help. Suppose that the price of a pound of apples is $2 and the price of a pound of pears is $3. The relative price of a pound of pears is 1.5 pounds of apples. This means that when a consumer chooses a pound of pears, that consumer refuses 1.5 pounds of apples. If pears are scarce relative to apples, say there's some blight, the relative price of pears should rise let's say to 2 pounds of apples per pound of pears. If, on the other hand, pears become abundant relative to apples, then the relative price of pears should fall say to one pound of apples per pound of pears. The inflation adjusted, we call it the ROI (rate of interest), measures the cost of goods today relative to goods in the future—let's say 3 years. If real rates are higher, someone who buys goods now gives up more goods in the future. If the real rate is lower, someone who buys goods now gives up less goods in the future. This is precisely what we saw in the example of Jane. As the interest rate rose, she had to give up more goods in order to have her car earlier. How do we know? Her interest payments increased, and she had to finance those higher interest payments by giving up other goods she could've purchased with those dollars.

This is supposed to be a story about how interest rates are determined by market forces and in the long run, the real rate of interest is determined jointly by the patience of the population in an economy and the productivity of the nation's capitol. This very important point, indeed that very sentence, was made by one of the great 20th-century economists, Irving Fisher, in his 1930s book *The Theory of Interest*. As an aside, that book is a good read even today and has one of the best first lines of any economics book ever written. Fisher said in the first line, income is a series of events. I love that line. It makes me think every time I read it. Fisher said in the long run, the real rate of interest is determined by the patience of the population and the productivity of a nation's capitol but what did Fisher mean, first by the long run?

Well, according to Fisher, in the long run, the economy remains at full employment. In the long run, government budgets are balanced. Why? Well if they stay perpetually in deficit, the governments go out of existence. In the long run, the economy's current account is balanced, and we'd better pause and see what that means. That means approximately that the value of goods and services that we import from the rest of the world in a year is just equal to the value of goods and services that we export to the rest of the world in that same year. Now to be precisely correct, we must adjust both imports and exports by allowing for income that we earn on our capital holdings abroad and also allowing for income earned by capital holdings of foreign citizens in the United States, but you get the idea. There has to be a kind of balance between outflow to the rest of the world and inflow from the rest of the world.

Clearly the long run world I describe is a world we rarely, if ever, see. Why is it we're thinking about it? Because that long run world is a world toward which economic forces propel us. We don't get there but we're always moving there. We don't get there because stuff is always happening, but it's a world worth thinking about, and it's a world that Fisher used to explain the market behind the real rate of interest. What good is being priced in this market? The economic good in question is early use of funds, right, the ability to use funds early. For the sake of discussion, early use of funds can be thought of as the right to use $1000 for 1 year, 1 year earlier. What do I mean? Well, you could use that $1000 a year later, or you could use it a year earlier. The right to use it a year earlier is the good, it's a valuable good, being able to buy things early is a valuable thing, and it's the good that we think that credit markets price.

I said that the forces of demand and supply matter. Who are the demanders? Demanders are those who have some compelling desire to use funds in excess of the funds that their income provides them. Examples include households that wish to buy a home or pay for a child's education. Examples also include owners and managers of firms that wish to build capital that perhaps implement highly productive technologies, ideas, and business plans. The more productive, the higher the interest rate those demanders would be willing to pay. For fund demanders, however, higher interest rates are a disincentive to borrow. That's very, very important. Suppose you want to build a better mousetrap and have an idea about just how to do it. Suppose further that in order to buy the equipment and obtain suitable space to manufacture and distribute your mousetrap, you must obtain $100,000 in start-up funds. The interest you will pay on these funds is a cost to you of realizing your business plan, of realizing your dream. The higher that interest rate, the higher are those interest rate costs.

There's another very useful way to explain the role of interest rates in an investment decision. To invest is to spend money today and to receive, in return, a stream of future profits. An investment is economically rational only if the present value of that profit stream that you hope to get is higher than the current dollar outlay for your investment and higher interest rates imply higher discount rates for those future profits and smaller values for present values. It does not matter whether you must borrow the funds or whether you will already have those funds in hand. The interest rate in both cases measures your opportunity cost of using your funds to finance your mousetrap factory. Why? You could always lend the funds you have in hand to someone else and earn the rate of interest. That means that the interest rate is important to you whether you have the money in your pocket or whether you must borrow it.

The other side of the market are suppliers of credit, and suppliers are those who are patient. Patient? Patient in the sense that they are willing to lend from their current income. That is they're willing to receive interest payments and allow others to borrow a part of the income they have earned. For suppliers of funds, for those who are patient, higher interest rates are an incentive to lend. Patient people are more likely to lend than impatient people. Patience is likely to be higher when a household's income is more than sufficient to provide for food, shelter, and clothing. Patience is also likely to be higher when a household desires to make an expensive purchase in the future, again such as a college education for its children or a house or purchase a retirement income. A higher interest rate is an incentive to supply funds because a higher interest rate implies a greater reward to savings. That is a higher interest rate implies that one savings will buy more in the future, the goods bonus to saving will be higher.

In the long run, Irving Fisher's long run, interest rates tend to those values that balance the plans of borrowers and lenders. If there were more credit demanded than could be supplied, those with the most productive projects would offer to pay higher interest rates. They'll crowd out the less productive projects, but the interest rates will rise. On the other hand, if there's less credit demanded than can be willingly supplied, the most patient savers would offer to accept smaller interest rates, and interest rates would fall. Well the long run is an ideal horizon.

What about the reality in which we live? Economists refer to that as the short run. John Maynard Keynes once quipped in the long run, we're all dead, and what he meant was we got to focus on the short run so let's do that. In the short run, interest rates depart from long run values for several very important reasons. Governments sometimes spend more than they earn in tax revenue. They run deficits. When the government sector runs a deficit, it must, as we've seen, borrow funds to balance its accounts. In doing so, the government competes with private borrowers for those scarce funds. If the government deficit increases, other factors unchanged, the demand for funds increases and interest rates rise. The rise in interest rates crowds out some investment projects. What do I mean? This is very, very important.

When governments borrow more, when their deficits are higher, interest rates rise and some investment projects no longer are sufficiently profitable to justify doing in the face of the higher interest rates. Governments are in competition with private investors for scarce funds. In the short runs, nations also run current account deficits. A current account deficit is the difference between the value of a nation's imports and the value of its exports. I've already explained there's an adjustment for income flows into and out of the country. There's also another adjustment for transfer payments between countries such as those associated with foreign aid but the point is inflow and outflow.

When a nation runs a current account deficit, the value of its imports is higher than would be justified by its exports and therefore income flows. When the U.S. runs a current account deficit, the rest of the world, in effect, lends it purchasing power. That is, the trading partners of the U.S. are in a situation where they prefer to take some of the dollars that they receive by selling goods to the United States and use those dollars to buy financial assets, say those issued by the U.S. Treasury and also those issued by firms, in effect, our trading partners lend us funds. When the current account is in deficit, the supply of credit to the United States is higher than from domestic sources alone, which means that interest rates are lower if we don't allow some other factors to change.

Let's look at some data and see how important that is for the United States. What you are seeing now is a timeline of our U.S. current account deficit as a fraction of our gross domestic product, and remember, we make it a fraction of gross domestic product because we want to normalize for changes in the size of the U.S. economy. The data run from 1960 all the way to 2010. We will see that for the first half of the period roughly the current account was either slightly in surplus or slightly in deficit. You'd have to say that basically that account was balanced. During the 1980s there was a sustained period of current account deficits. The rest of the world was lending us money. They were being patient for us but by the early 1990s, that situation had corrected itself. Then a very, very important change occurred. The United States entered a period of persistent current account deficits. We routinely got more imports than we sent the rest of the world goods in the form of exports. That situation has still not reversed.

There's good news, folks, and there's bad news associated with this. The good news is that that current account deficit has kept our interest rates lower. That means that we have been able to do more investment than we would otherwise have been able to do because the rest of the world was willing to lend us money. The bad news is that eventually the rest of the world will want to be repaid. The third reason that the short run departs from the long run, the current reality is different from Irving Fisher's ideal is that the economy is sometimes in a recession. When the economy is in a recession, demand for credit is low in part because firms doubt that households will buy their products. Therefore interest rates are low because demand for credit is low. In a recession, interest rates may also be low if the Federal Reserve uses monetary policy to lower them in an attempt to stimulate an interest sensitive spending. The Fed has in mind the idea that if it lowers interest rates, some investment projects would become viable.

In summary then, interest rates are important economic prices that are determined in the market for credit. In the long run, the saving and investment plans of the members of an economy will jointly determine interest rates. In the short run, other forces are important as well. Government deficits tend to raise interest rates because the government competes with private borrowers for scarce funds. It's one of the reasons why at various points in our history, we have worked so hard to balance the government budget. Current account deficits tend to lower interest rates because the supply of credit is bigger than it would be from domestic sources alone. When we run a current account deficit, the rest of the world willingly lends us funds. When our economy is in a recession and resources are unemployed, interest rates tend to be lower both because demand for credit is low and because the Federal Reserve often lowers interest rates in an attempt to stimulate spending. I have argued then that interest rates are an important market price balancing the plans of spenders and savers, of borrowers and lenders.

Thank you very much.

Glossary

asymmetric information: The condition when one party in a transaction has substantially more relevant knowledge than another. Often, the relevant knowledge is about the quality of the product being bought and sold.

balance sheet: A list of the assets, liabilities, and net worth of a firm or individual and that "net worth" is defined to be the value of the firm's assets minus the value of its liabilities.

bank runs: Situations in which depositors all try to withdraw deposited funds at the same time.

barter: Exchange without money.

bond: A certificate promising to repay money at a fixed rate of interest at a specified time.

bubble: An event in which the price of a financial asset grows more rapidly than justified by fundamentals for a substantial period of time.

capital stock: The cumulative measure of all past investment activity.

commodities futures contract: An agreement to buy a well-defined quantity and quality of a commodity at a specified future date.

commodity money: A particular commodity that is agreed upon in the society to be acceptable for exchange.

common stock: An ownership interest in a corporation.

Consumer Price Index (CPI): An index of prices of goods and services (a bushel basket of goods) purchased by the typical household in the United States.

deficit: When government revenues are less than expenditures. The deficit is a flow—its units are dollars per year or per quarter.

derivative: An agreement between two parties, the value of which depends on an underlying price or transaction.

discount rate: A positive number that defines the rate at which a future payment loses value as the date of the payment moves further into the future.

excess reserves: Reserves that were calculated to be beyond the amount required by law or prudence.

exchange rate: The market price of one currency in terms of another, a trading ratio between two currencies.

expected value (EV): The probability-weighted average of the game's payouts.

fiat money: Money that is valuable in exchange because a government has declared it to be.

financial intermediaries: Firms, such as banks, that channel funds from savers to investors and other decision makers who have decided to spend more than their current income permits.

financial investment: Stocks, bonds, and other financial products that individuals purchase as part of a financial plan.

gold standard: An agreement among participating countries to fix the price of each country's currency in terms of an ounce of gold. England adopted the standard in 1819, and the United States adopted it in 1834.

greenbacks: Paper currency issued in 1862; it was used as legal tender after the U.S. government suspended payment in gold in 1861.

house-advantage game: When the expected value is negative.

hyperinflation: Episodes during which the monthly inflation rate exceeds 50%.

inflation: Persistent increase in the general level of prices.

inflation rate: The rate at which the price index increases over time.

investment: The value of increases to a nation's capital stock, such as its factories, equipment, software, and other durable goods used as part of the production process, as well as human capital.

liquidity: A financial asset is said to be "liquid" if it can be rapidly converted to cash with no loss of value.

money: An asset that its owners rightly believe they can, quickly and without loss of value, convert to purchasing power; something that can be used as a medium of exchange.

national debt: The accumulation of deficits; it is a stock rather than a flow.

net worth: Is the value of assets minus the value of liabilities.

nominal rate of interest: Specifies number of dollars borrower must pay to borrow funds.

non-transactions deposits: Deposits in savings accounts, from which funds can be withdrawn at any time.

notes: Medium-turn debt instruments of the Treasury; the promise of the Treasury to pay the face value of the note at maturity and also to pay coupon payments every six months.

player-advantage game: When the expected value is positive.

policy discretion: The conduct of policy that is not bound by a policy rule.

policy rule: A formula for determining policy. It specifies what the policy instrument is and how settings of the instrument should respond to observable changes in the state of the economy. The policy instrument is generally meant to be the federal funds rate.

real rate of interest: The nominal rate minus the rate of inflation expected to occur.

real returns: The sum of percentage capital gains and dividends earned on the NYSE market portfolio minus the rate of inflation.

saving: The difference between a decision maker's income and consumption.

seigniorage: The revenue that a government obtains by deflating the value of its money.

STRIPS (Separate Trading of Registered Interest and Principal Securities): The result of stripping the coupon payments from a Treasury bond or note and using those coupon payments to create another government debt obligation that makes a single payment on its maturity date.

surplus: When tax revenues are greater than expenditures.

T-account: A graphical representation of the balance sheet of an economic entity. The T-account lists assets on the left side and liabilities and the asset's net worth on the right.

T-bill: Short-turn debt instruments of the Treasury; the promise of the Treasury to pay the face value of the bill at maturity.

time deposits: Deposits which have fixed maturity dates.

TIPS (Treasury Inflation Protected Securities): The principal of a TIPS increases with inflation and decreases with deflation, as measured by the CPI. When a TIPS bond matures, the owner is paid the adjusted principal or original principal, whichever is greater.

transactions deposits: Deposits against which checks can be written.

Troubled Asset Relief Program (TARP): Enacted by the Emergency Economic Stabilization Act of 2008, it provided funds for the bailout of troubled financial firms after the subprime mortgage crisis during the Great Recession. The Federal Reserve and the Treasury used TARP funds aggressively to keep banks and non-bank financial firms from failing.

volatile inflation: Inflation that oscillates between low and high rates.

yield to maturity: The ex ante yield that a bill, note, or bond purchaser will earn if the bond is held from the date of purchase to maturity.

Bibliography

Akerlof, George A. "The Market for 'Lemons': Quality Uncertainty and the Market Mechanism." *Quarterly Journal of Economics* 84, no. 3 (1970): 488–500. In this classic economic writing, Nobel laureate George Akerlof introduces the concept of "asymmetric information" and explains why and how information asymmetries can lead to market failures. Banks face asymmetric information when they contemplate loaning funds.

Akerlof, George A., and Robert J. Shiller. *Animal Spirits: How Human Psychology Drives the Economy, and Why It Matters for Global Capitalism.* Princeton, NJ: Princeton University Press, 2009. The authors depart from mainstream economic thinking in order to restore an idea first made popular by Keynes: that financial decisions are sometimes driven less by rational calculations and more by "animal spirits." Animal spirits are restored to theory by calling on modern research in human psychology that has led to the relatively new field of behavioral economics.

Alesina, Alberto, and Lawrence H. Summers. "Central Bank Independence and Macroeconomic Performance: Some Comparative Evidence." *Journal of Money, Credit, and Banking* 25, no. 2 (1993): 151–162. Alesina and Summers provide measures of central bank independence and argue that the data suggest that economic outcomes are better in nations where central bank independence is greater.

Armendáriz, Beatriz, and Jonathan Morduch. *The Economics of Microfinance.* 2nd ed. Cambridge, MA: The MIT Press, 2010. The authors study microfinance arrangements from an economic perspective. They make the case for intervention in traditional credit markets, explore a variety of microfinance models, and consider commercialization of microfinance and measurement of the impact of microfinance programs.

Barro, Robert J., and David B. Gordon, "A Positive Theory of Monetary Policy in a Natural Rate Model." *Journal of Political Economy* 91, no. 4 (1983): 589–610. Barro and Gordon set out a model of monetary policy that implies an inflation bias whenever the central bank acts with discretion. While the paper contains a mathematical analysis, it is accessible to those who are comfortable solving systems of equations and working with conditional expected values.

Beetsma, Roel, and Massimo Giuliodori. "The Macroeconomic Costs and Benefits of the EMU and Other Monetary Unions: An Overview of Recent Research." *Journal of Economic Literature* 48 (September 2010): 603–641. An overview of research about the costs and benefits of monetary union, with a focus on the euro area. The authors point out that unification entails the loss of independent interest-rate policies by individual union members and investigate the benefits that may offset this cost. The article emphasizes the importance to the union of fiscal policy coordination among union members.

Bernanke, Ben S. "Monetary Policy and the Housing Bubble." Paper given at the Allied Social Science Association Meetings, January 3, 2010. http://www.federalreserve.gov/newsevents/speech/bernanke20100103a.htm. Bernanke makes the case that low federal funds rates were not responsible for the housing bubble that ultimately caused the subprime mortgage crisis. He argues that a more likely cause was the inflow of savings to the United States from the rest of the world.

———. "Policy Coordination among Central Banks." Speech given at the 5th ECB Central Banking Conference: The Euro at Ten: Lessons and Challenges, Frankfurt, Germany, November 14, 2008. http://www.bis.org/review/r081118a.pdf. In this speech, given on the 10th anniversary of the euro, Bernanke emphasizes the importance of policy coordination among central banks. He also points out that during the Great Contraction, there has been a shortage of dollar funding not only in the United States but around the world.

Blume, Marshall E., Jean Crockett, and Irwin Friend. "Stock Ownership: Characteristics and Trends." Working Paper 12-74, Rodney L. White Center for Financial Research, The Wharton School, University of Pennsylvania. http://finance.wharton.upenn.edu/~rlwctr/papers/7412.PDF. A valuable source of data on stock ownership.

Bordo, Michael D. "Gold Standard." In *The Concise Encyclopedia of Economics*. Library of Economics and Liberty, http://www.econlib.org/library/Enc/GoldStandard.html. Explains how the gold standard worked and assesses its performance.

Cardoso, Eliana A. "Hyperinflation in Latin America." *Challenge* 32, no. 1 (1989): 11–19. An interesting and accessible account of the causes and consequences of hyperinflation in Latin America.

Cassidy, John. "Anatomy of a Meltdown: Ben Bernanke and the Financial Crisis." *The New Yorker*, December 1, 2008. http://www.newyorker.com/reporting/2008/12/01/081201fa_fact_cassidy. Cassidy presents a highly readable analysis of how events unfolded during the subprime financial crisis. He explains how Ben Bernanke took over the reins of the Federal Reserve during a period of relative calm but was faced with unprecedented challenges as the subprime crisis evolved.

Center for Medieval and Renaissance Studies, University of California, Los Angeles. *The Dawn of Modern Banking*. New Haven, CT: Yale University Press, 1979. Explains how modern banks developed from earlier institutions in a variety of settings. The chapter on medieval banks by Robert Lopez is particularly interesting.

Chomsisengphet, Souphala, and Anthony Pennington-Cross. "The Evolution of the Subprime Mortgage Market." Federal Reserve Bank of St. Louis *Review* 88, no. 1 (2006): 31–56. A highly readable account of the growth in the subprime mortgage market prior to the subprime crisis.

Christensen, Jens. "TIPS and the Risk of Deflation." Federal Reserve Bank of San Francisco Economic Letter, October 25, 2010. http://www.frbsf.org/publications/economics/letter/2010/el2010-32.html. This brief article compares the yields on TIPS with yields on government bonds that do not provide inflation protection to conclude that financial market participants considered the risk of negative price inflation to be low.

Bibliography

Congress of the United States. Public #43—63D Congress (The Federal Reserve Act of 1913). http://www.llsdc.org/attachments/files/105/FRA-LH-PL63-43.pdf. Includes the text of the original Federal Reserve Act.

Coval, Joshua, Jakub Jurek, and Erik Stafford. "The Economics of Structured Finance." Working Paper 09-060, Harvard Business School Finance, 2008. http://papers.ssrn.com/sol3/papers.cfm?abstract_id=1287363. Provides an intuitive explanation of collateralized debt obligations and the role they played in explaining the subprime mortgage crisis.

Crowe, Christopher, and Ellen E. Meade. "The Evolution of Central Bank Governance around the World." *Journal of Economic Perspectives* 21, no. 4 (2007): 69–90. Explains how central bank independence is defined and measured, then documents how measures of central bank independence have changed over the past 25 years. The article also studies correlations between measures of central bank independence and transparency, on the one hand, and inflation, on the other.

Dwyer, Gerald P., and R. W. Hafer. "Are Money Growth and Inflation Still Related?" Federal Reserve Bank of Atlanta *Economic Review* (Q2 1999): 32–43. The authors note that working economists seldom use money growth to predict inflation and question whether money growth and inflation are still related. They explain the theoretical basis for the relationship and look at cross-country data to answer their question, finding that a strong relationship is consistent with the data.

E. F. Schumacher Society. "Local Currencies." http://www.smallisbeautiful.org/local_currencies.html. The E. F. Schumacher Society, located in Great Barrington, MA, has supported many of the successful launches of local currencies and has commissioned several articles about local currencies in general and specific initiatives.

Eichberger, Jurgen, and Ian R. Harper. *Financial Economics*. New York: Oxford University Press, 1997. For those who are familiar with calculus and mathematical notation, this book provides an interesting analysis of decision making under uncertainty, risk aversion, and the expected-utility hypothesis.

Einzig, Paul. *Primitive Money in Its Ethnological, Historical, and Economic Aspects*. 2nd ed. New York: Pergamon Press, 1996. Einzig presents a fascinating account of the evolution of exchange from barter to the use of commodity money. He argues that a variety of reasons explain a society's choice of primitive money.

European Central Bank (ECB). "The Implementation of Monetary Policy in the Euro Area." ECB, 2008. http://www.ecb.int/pub/pdf/other/gendoc2008en.pdf. Explains how a single monetary policy is implemented for the nations of the euro area and provides authoritative facts, rather than an intuitive explanation, of how ECB monetary policy is undertaken.

———. *The Monetary Policy of the ECB*. ECB, 2011. http://www.ecb.int/pub/pdf/other/monetarypolicy2011en.pdf. A comprehensive overview of monetary policy in the euro area, the conduct of the ECB, and the economic and institutional background for ECB policy. The book is not meant to be read casually but, rather, to make ECB policy transparent.

Federal Reserve Bank of New York Public Information Department. "Interest Rates: An Introduction." 2004. http://www.newyorkfed.org/education/print.html. This fact sheet provides basic but useful information on interest rates and markets where interest rates are determined. The article is written in a question-and-answer format.

Federal Reserve Bank of San Francisco. "The Economy: Crisis and Response." http://www.frbsf.org/econanswers/portal.htm. This portal includes audio and video and provides an overview of the recent financial crisis, as well as materials describing the steps that Congress and the Federal Reserve have taken to avoid a similar crisis in the future. The materials have been produced as part of the education mission of the Federal Reserve and are highly accessible.

———. "U.S. Monetary Policy: An Introduction." FRBSF *Economic Letter* 2004-01, January 16, 2004. http://www.frbsf.org/publications/economics/letter/2004/el2004-01.html. Originally produced as a pamphlet, then converted to an online resource. The article explains how the Federal

Reserve is structured, the goals and tools of monetary policy, and how monetary policy affects the U.S. economy.

————. "What Makes the Yield Curve Move?" FRBSF *Economic Letter* 2003-15, June 6, 2003. http://www.frbsf.org/publications/economics/letter/2003/el2003-15.html. Researchers in finance have used statistical tools to determine that shifts or changes in the shape of the yield curve are attributable to a few unobservable factors. The article explains this analysis and provides an economic interpretation of forces that cause movements in the yield curve.

Federal Reserve Bank of St. Louis. "The Financial Crisis: A Timeline of Events and Policy Actions." http://timeline.stlouisfed.org/pdf/CrisisTimeline. pdf. Provides a chronology of events during the subprime mortgage crisis.

Fisher, Irving. *The Theory of Interest*. Clifton, NJ: Augustus M. Kelley Publishers, 1974. In this book, which originally appeared in 1930, Fisher explains how the rate of interest is ultimately determined by the interaction between the "patience of a population" and the productivity of a nation's capital. Fisher provides fascinating insights into the motives for borrowing and lending and how changes in the rate of interest make the plans of borrowers and lenders mutually compatible.

Frank, Robert H., and Ben S. Bernanke. *Principles of Economics*. 4th ed. New York: McGraw-Hill Irwin, 2009. An excellent textbook that has particularly good chapters on international economics and foreign exchange markets.

Friedman, Milton. "The Crime of 1873." *Journal of Political Economy* 98, no. 6 (1990): 1159–78. The U.S. Coinage Act of 1873 forbade the free coinage of silver and put the United States on the gold standard. Friedman argues that the act was a mistake that had highly adverse consequences for the country. Because the technical analysis is relegated to the appendix, the paper is suitable for a general audience.

———. *Money Mischief: Episodes in Monetary History.* New York: Harcourt Brace Javanovich, 1992. Friedman looks at a variety of episodes in economic history with an eye toward convincing the reader that inflation is always due to excessive growth in the supply of money.

———. "The Role of Monetary Policy." *American Economic Review* 58, no. 1 (1968): 1–17. In his presidential address to the American Economic Association, Friedman explains why monetary policy cannot hold the market above "natural" rates of employment for long periods of time. He also argues that the most important objective that well-designed monetary policy can accomplish is to keep changes in the stock of money from becoming a major disturbance to economic stability.

Friedman, Milton, and Anna J. Schwartz. *A Monetary History of the United States, 1867–1960.* New York: National Bureau of Economic Research, 1963. A modern classic, in which Friedman and Schwartz track the evolution of the money stock and financial institutions in the United States from the greenback period to the period after World War II. The chapter on the Great Depression is valuable reading for anyone who is interested in studying monetary policy during economic crises.

Friedman, Milton, and L. J. Savage. "The Expected-Utility Hypothesis and the Measurability of Utility." *Journal of Political Economics* 60, no. 6 (1952): 463–74. In this famous article, the authors address the question of how to explain a decision maker who buys both insurance and lottery tickets. The case is interesting because the former decision suggests risk aversion while the latter suggests risk loving.

Galbraith, John K. *Money: Whence It Came, Where It Went.* Boston: Houghton Mifflin Company, 1995. A highly readable history of money from the time, 4,000 years ago, when individuals began exchanging precious metals for goods. The book ends with an assessment of the state of the U.S. dollar in 1975, when Galbraith was originally writing.

Glover, Paul. "A History of Ithaca Hours." January 2000, http://www. paulglover.org/0001.html. The fascinating story of one of the longest-lasting and most successful local currencies—Ithaca Hours.

Bibliography

Greider, William. *Secrets of the Temple: How the Federal Reserve Runs the Country*. New York: Simon and Schuster, 1987. Although the book provides a history of the Federal Reserve under Paul Volcker, it also explores the implications of Federal Reserve power from the point of view that decisions about money and financial institutions are political and social. The book is highly relevant for anyone interested in questioning the independence of the Federal Reserve.

Hammond, Bray. *Banks and Politics in America from the Revolution to the Civil War*. Princeton, NJ: Princeton University Press, 1957. This fascinating book covers the history of banks and the interaction of banking policy and politics in the United States from the time of the American Revolution to the Civil War. It explains the debate that surrounded the First and Second Banks of the United States and how variations in the vision of the Founding Fathers found their way into debates about the appropriate monetary arrangements to be established in our nation.

Hanke, Steve H., and Alex K. F. Kwok. "On the Measurement of Zimbabwe's Hyperinflation." *Cato Journal* 29, no. 2 (2009): 353–364. The authors use the concept of purchasing power parity to estimate rates of inflation in Zimbabwe, an effort necessitated by a Zimbabwe government decision to stop reporting inflation statistics. The paper is interesting and the data are fascinating.

Hennessy, Elizabeth. *Coffee House to Cyber Market: 200 Years of the London Stock Exchange*. London: Ebury Press, 2001. This interesting volume is not about stock prices or volumes of shares. It is a history of the people and places who developed the exchange. Hennessy explains how the exchange got its start in a coffeehouse located at what was later called Exchange Alley.

Heyne, Paul. *The Economic Way of Thinking*. 9th ed. New York: Prentice Hall, 2000. One of the most interesting and readable principles-of-economics texts available. The chapter on the supply of money is particularly relevant for those interested in the basics of the process through which money is created.

Jackson, Kevin, ed. *The Oxford Book of Money*. New York: Oxford University Press, 1995. Provides reflections on the nature of money from such thinkers as Dante and Milton, as well as social philosophers, including Veblen, Smith, Marx, and Keynes.

Jevons, William Stanley. *Money and the Mechanism of Exchange*. New York: A.M. Kelley Bookseller, 1964. The source for Jevons's famous phrase that a successful barter transaction requires a "double coincidence" of wants.

Judd, John P., and Glenn D. Rudebusch. "The Goals of U.S. Monetary Policy." Federal Reserve Bank of San Francisco *Economic Letter* 99, no.4 (1999). http://www.frbsf.org/econrsrch/wklyltr/wklyltr99/el99-04.html. The authors provide a straightforward and clear statement about the goals of monetary policy implicit in the Fed's legislative mandate. They also discuss current debates about revisions to that mandate.

Kennedy, Peter E. "Eight Reasons Why Real versus Nominal Interest Rates Is the Most Important Concept in Macroeconomics Principles Courses." *American Economic Review* 90, no. 2 (2000): 81–84. The article does an excellent job of explaining the importance of the real rate of interest to an understanding of basic macroeconomics and monetary policy. Very interesting and clearly written.

Kolb, Robert W. *Financial Derivatives: Pricing and Risk Management*. Hoboken, NJ: John Wiley and Sons, 2010. If I were to keep but one book about financial derivatives on my shelf, this would be that book. It provides an overview of the types of financial derivatives, a description of the markets in which derivatives are traded, an explanation of how derivatives are used to hedge risk, and a series of chapters devoted to different derivative products.

Kolb, Robert W., and Ricardo J. Rodriguez. *Financial Institutions*. Cambridge, MA: Blackwell, 1996. The book includes very readable chapters on the stock and bond markets and chapters on depository institutions and other financial intermediaries. Unfortunately, this source has not been updated since 1996.

Krugman, Paul R., and Maurice Obstfeld. *International Economics: Theory and Policy.* 5th ed. Reading, MA: Addison Lesley Longman, 2000. A technically sophisticated textbook for courses in international economics.

Kydland, Finn, and Edward C. Prescott. "Rules Rather than Discretion: The Inconsistency of Optimal Plans." *Journal of Political Economy* 85, no. 3 (1977): 473–491. In this famous paper, the authors explain the advantages to a policy authority of adhering to a rule rather than maintaining discretion to react differently to each policy situation.

Malkiel, Burton G. *A Random Walk Down Wall Street: Including a Life-Cycle Guide to Personal Investing.* 6th ed. New York: Norton, 1996. Perhaps the most famous book ever written about the stock market. It explains the efficient market hypothesis, which holds that any information useful for predicting future stock price values is already built into the current stock price value.

Meulendyke, Ann-Marie. *U.S. Monetary Policy and Financial Markets.* New York: Federal Reserve Bank of New York, 1998. The volume is a detailed but highly readable explanation of how monetary policy works. It provides a short history of U.S. monetary policy, an explanation of how policy affects banks and financial markets, and a series of chapters that explain the Federal Open Market Committee and the Trading Desk at the New York Federal Reserve. The volume also considers international aspects of monetary policy.

Mishkin, Frederic S. "Global Financial Instability: Framework, Events, Issues." *The Economics of Money, Banking, and Financial Markets.* 8th ed. Boston: Pearson Addison Wesley, 2007. One of the best available texts used to teach undergraduate courses in money, banking, and financial markets.

————. *Journal of Economic Perspectives* 13, no. 4 (1999): 3–20. Provides an assessment of the causes, consequences, and transmission mechanisms associated with episodes of financial market instability that spread across countries. Mishkin focuses on Mexico and East Asian countries between 1994 and 1998.

————. "Symposium on the Monetary Transmission Mechanism." *Journal of Economic Perspectives* 9, no. 4 (1995): 3–10. Provides an overview of the special issue of the *Journal of Economic Perspectives* dedicated to a study of how monetary policy works. The paper explains various "channels" through which the effects of monetary policy are distributed to economic decisions. These include the effect of monetary policy on interest rates, asset prices, exchange rates, and the availability of credit.

————. "What Should Central Banks Do?" Federal Reserve Bank of St. Louis *Review*, November/December 2000: 1–13. Mishkin summarizes recent analysis that guides central bank practice and develops and explains a list of guiding principles for central banks.

Morgan, Donald P., and Kevin J. Stiroh. "Too Big to Fail after All These Years." Federal Reserve Bank of New York Staff Report no. 220, September 2005. http://www.newyorkfed.org/research/staff_reports/sr220.html. Looks at interest rate spread data for evidence that "too big to fail" leads to an erosion of market discipline. The paper is a preliminary technical study, but most of the analysis can be understood by non-economists.

Mundell, Robert A. "A Theory of Optimum Currency Areas." *American Economic Review* 51, no. 4 (1961): 657–665. In this famous article, Nobel laureate Robert Mundell investigates conditions under which a group of countries are better off adopting a common currency than they would be if they maintained currency independence.

Norris, Frank. *The Pit: A Story of Chicago*. New York: Doubleday, Page and Company, 1903. This classic work of fiction revolves around trading in the grain pits at the Chicago Board of Trade in the early days of the 20th century.

Obstfeld, Maurice. "The Global Capital Market: Benefactor or Menace?" *Journal of Economic Perspectives* 12, no. 4 (1998): 9–30. The effects of the Asian financial crisis of 1997 and 1998 were not limited to Asia but rebounded around the globe, because financial markets are more global in scope than ever before. In this article, Obstfeld examines the benefits and costs of global financial markets.

Orsingher, Roger. *Banks of the World*. New York: Walker and Company, 1967. Particularly interesting is the first chapter of this book, which provides a history of banking from Babylonian times.

Paulson, Henry M., Jr. *On the Brink: Inside the Race to Stop the Collapse of the Global Financial System*. New York: Business Plus, 2010. Paulson was secretary of the Treasury under President George W. Bush. This is his account of the steps taken by Congress, the Treasury, and the Federal Reserve in response to the subprime mortgage crisis.

Plenty Currency Cooperative. "About the Plenty." http://theplenty.org/about. Offers facts about the Plenty, a local currency that circulates in the Piedmont area of North Carolina.

Poole, William. "The Fed's Monetary Policy Rule." Federal Reserve Bank of St. Louis *Review* 88, no. 1 (2006): 1–11. In this article, Poole explains that the federal funds rate, the instrument of monetary policy, closely approximated values that would have been predicted by the monetary policy rule of John Taylor.

Radford, R. A. "The Economic Organization of a P.O.W. Camp." *Economica* 12 (November 1945): 189–201. In a classic and fascinating article, Radford describes his experiences as a prisoner during World War II and his observations on how markets, trading systems, and "cigarette money" sprung up in the POW camp.

Redish, Angela. "Anchors Aweigh: The Transition from Commodity Money to Fiat Money in Western Economies." *Canadian Journal of Economics* 26, no. 4 (1993): 777–795. Redish uses the metaphor of an anchor and its chain to represent the connection between gold and the world supply of money. She argues that limitations in the supply of gold led, on many occasions, to attempts to "lengthen the chain" but that finally the chain was broken when the United States abandoned the gold standard.

Rockoff, Hugh. "The 'Wizard of Oz' as a Monetary Allegory." *Journal of Political Economy* 98, no. 4 (1990): 739–760. Reading this article is as much fun as economics has to offer. Rockoff argues that Frank Baum's classic book is an allegory and links key features of the plot and key characters to figures, such as William Jennings Bryan, who were involved with the free silver movement at the end of the 19th century. Readers of Baum's book will remember that Dorothy's slippers are not ruby but silver; the plot thickens.

Russell, Steven. "Understanding the Term Structure of Interest Rates: The Expectations Hypothesis." Federal Reserve Bank of St. Louis *Review* 74, no. 4 (1992): 36–50. Clearly and intuitively explains the connection between short- and long-term bond yields implied by the expectations hypothesis and provides a clear interpretation of the shape of the yield curve.

Salemi, Michael K. "Hyperinflation." In *The Concise Encyclopedia of Economics*. Library of Economics and Liberty, http://www.econlib.org/library/Enc/Hyperinflation.html. Defines hyperinflation, provides 20th-century examples, and explains the causes and consequences of hyperinflations.

Sargent, Thomas J. "The Ends of Four Big Inflations." In *Rational Expectations and Inflation*. New York: Harper & Row Publishers, 1986. In this essay, Sargent argues that monetary reform alone is insufficient to end hyperinflations. What is needed is fiscal reform sufficient to make monetary reform credible. Sargent uses data for four hyperinflations that occurred during the interwar period to illustrate and support his thesis.

Sargent, Thomas J., and Neil Wallace. "Some Unpleasant Monetarist Arithmetic." In *Rational Expectations and Inflation*. New York: Harper & Row Publishers, 1986. In this essay, Sargent and Wallace argue that there is a fundamental connection between monetary and fiscal policy that is rooted in the accounting requirement that government budgets must balance. When fiscal authorities run persistent deficits, monetary authorities come under great pressure to monetize the country's debt. When monetary authorities credibly signal that they will not monetize, fiscal authorities realize that they must offset current deficits with future surpluses.

Schlossberg, Boris. "Common Questions about Currency Trading," Investopedia, http://www.investopedia.com/articles/forex/06/SevenFXFAQs.asp. The title says it all.

Sharpe, William F. *Investments*. Englewood Cliffs, NJ: Prentice-Hall, 1978. In this book, 1990 Nobel laureate William Sharpe sets out and explains the capital asset pricing model.

Shiller, Robert J. *Irrational Exuberance*. 2nd ed. Princeton, NJ: Princeton University Press, 2005. Alan Greenspan coined the term, but Robert Shiller made the case that world financial markets have all too frequently experienced irrational exuberance of sufficient magnitude to inflate asset price bubbles. In the first part of the book, Shiller argues that the United States has experienced bubbles in both equity and real estate prices. In the remainder of the book, he analyzes why bubbles inflate and what members of society can do individually and collectively about bubbles.

Smith, Adam. *An Inquiry into the Nature and Causes of the Wealth of Nations*. New York: The Modern Library, 1937. This is the classic of classics for economists. In the early chapters, Smith explains how specialization is the key to the creation of wealth, how trade is necessary for specialization to occur, and how money is essential for trade.

Smith, Gary. *Money and Banking*. Reading, MA: Addison Wesley, 1982. A money and banking text that did not endure in the marketplace; however, chapter 2 provides a nice overview of commodity and fiat monies.

Solomon, Lewis D. *Rethinking Our Centralized Monetary System: The Case for a System of Local Currencies*. Westport, CT: Praeger Publishers, 1996. Solomon analyzes the history of monetary institutions in the United States and concludes that serious reform is necessary. The type of reform he favors is to replace our national fiat currency with a system of local currencies.

Stat Trek. "Statistics Tutorial: Basic Probability." http://stattrek.com/Lesson1/Probability.aspx.

Stern, Gary H., and Ron J. Feldman. *Too Big to Fail: The Hazards of Bank Bailouts*. Washington, DC: Brookings Institution Press, 2004. The authors argue that not enough has been done to counter the market expectation that big banks are too big to fail and will receive special government support if a financial crisis should occur. The authors explain why the problem is serious and of increasing importance.

Stiglitz, Joseph E., and Andrew Weiss. "Credit Rationing in Markets with Imperfect Information." *American Economic Review* 71, no. 3 (1981): 393–410. A technically challenging paper that explains why banks may not respond to a shortage of lendable funds by raising the rate they charge to borrow. The paper builds on Akerlof's concept of asymmetric information.

Sundaresan, Suresh. *Microfinance: Emerging Trends and Challenges.* Northampton, MA: Edward Elgar, 2008. A collection of essays on current challenges and trends in microfinance. The essays study the integration of capital markets with microfinance, securitization of micro-credit-backed securities, technological innovations in microfinance, and regulatory challenges to recent developments in microfinance. There is also an essay on the impact of gender empowerment caused by microfinance.

Taylor, John B. "Discretion versus Policy Rules in Practice." *Carnegie-Rochester Conference Series on Public Policy* 39 (1993): 195–214. Examines how research on policy rules can be applied to a practical policymaking environment. This is the paper in which Taylor first presents the monetary policy rule that now bears his name.

———. "A Historical Analysis of Monetary Policy Rules." In *Monetary Policy Rules*, edited by John B. Taylor. Chicago: University of Chicago Press, 1999. Examines episodes of monetary policy from the perspective of research on the benefits of monetary policy rules. Taylor documents that the U.S. monetary policy rule for interest rates has changed dramatically through time and that those changes have mattered to the performance of the U.S. economy.

Unterguggenberger, Michael. "The End of the Woergl Experiment." Reinventingmoney.com, http://www.reinventingmoney.com/documents/worgl.html. The source of the famous story about the town in Bavaria that launched a local currency during the Great Depression.

Von Muralt, Alex. "The Worgl Experiment with Depreciating Money." Reinventingmoney.com, http://www.reinventingmoney.com/documents/worgl.html. Discusses a feature of the Wörgl experiment that was designed to ensure that the citizens who received the local currency would spend it quickly, thereby stimulating the economy.

Woodward, Bob. *Maestro: Greenspan's Fed and the American Boom.* New York: Touchstone, Simon and Schuster, 2000. Woodward does a nice job of chronicling Alan Greenspan's career as chairman of the Board of Governors of the Federal Reserve. Among the book's insights is that Greenspan was able to convince President Clinton that a tax increase would make it easier for the Greenspan Fed to keep interest rates low.

Wright, Russell O. *Chronology of the Stock Market.* Jefferson, NC: McFarland & Company, 2001. Provides an annotated chronology of the New York stock market that indicates important events of both a statistical and an organizational nature. It is useful for those who are searching for facts, such as when the NASDAQ first went over 500.

Credits

Music Provided By: Getty Images.

Sound Effects Provided By: Digital Juice.

Graphs and Charts Provided By:

Alesina, Alberto and Lawrence H. Summers, "Central Bank Independence and Macroeconomic Performance: Some Comparative Evidence," Journal of Money, Credit and Banking 25 (May 1993). Copyright 1993 by The Ohio State University Press. Reproduced with permission of Blackwell Publishing Ltd.

Bloomberg.

Bond Market Overview, WSJ, 11/18/2010. Reprinted with permission of The Wall Street Journal, Copyright © 2012 Dow Jones & Company, Inc. All Rights Reserved Worldwide.

CME Group.

Crowe, Christopher and Ellen E. Meade, "The Evolution of Central Bank Governance around the World, Journal of Economic Perspectives, 21, 4, 2007, 69-90. Figure 1 and Table 2. Used with permission.

Data based on OECD (2010), "National Accounts at a Glance", OECD National Accounts Statistics (database), http://dx.doi.org/10.1787/data-00369-en accessed 3/16/2011.

Data based on OECD (2011), "OECD Economic Outlook No. 89", OECD Economic Outlook: Statistics and Projections (database), http://dx.doi.org/10.1787/data-00539-en , accessed 3/16/2011.

Federal Reserve.

Federal Reserve Bank of Atlanta Economic Review.

Federal Reserve Bank of Philadelphia.

FRED, Federal Reserve Economic Data, Federal Reserve Bank of St. Louis.

Graph from International Finance: Theory and Policy. Some rights reserved. Used with permission of Flat World Knowledge, Inc. www.flatworldknowledge.com.

Market Breadth, WSJ, 11/18/2010. Reprinted with permission of The Wall Street Journal, Copyright © 2012 Dow Jones & Company, Inc. All Rights Reserved Worldwide.

Market Rates Online.

Michael Salemi.

Mishel, Lawerence, Jared Bernstein, and Sylvia Allegretto, The State of Working America 2006–2007. An Economic Policy Institution Book. Ithica, NY: ILR Press, an imprint of Cornell University Press, 2007.

Poole, William, "The Fed's Monetary Policy Rule." Federal Reserve Bank of St. Louis Review, January/February 2006, 88(1), pp. 1–11. Copyright 2006, Federal Reserve Bank of St. Louis.

Shiller, Robert J.; Irrational Exuberance, Second Edition. 2005 © Princeton University Press. Reprinted by permission of Princeton University Press.

Source of "Asset-backed Securities Market": Federal Reserve Bank of San Francisco. http://www.frbsf.org/econanswers/response_q3more.htm. The opinions expressed in this course do not necessarily reflect the views of the management of the Federal Reserve Bank of San Francisco, or of the Board of Governors of the Federal Reserve System.

Source of "Fed Lending to Primary Dealers": Federal Reserve Bank of San Francisco. http://www.frbsf.org/econanswers/response_q1more.htm. The opinions expressed in this course do not necessarily reflect the views of the management of the Federal Reserve Bank of San Francisco, or of the Board of Governors of the Federal Reserve System.

Standard & Poor's and FiServ.

© StockCharts.com. Chart courtesy of StockCharts.com.

Top Banks in the World: Bankersalamanc.com, December 31, 2010. © Reed Business Information Limited 2011. These bank rankings are compiled from balance sheet information included on Bankersalmanac.com available at December 31, 2010. All figures have been converted into US dollars at the rate applicable at the date of that balance sheet. Great care has been taken to ensure the information's accuracy but Bankers' Almanac can accept no responsibility for any losses or damages arising from any errors or omissions. For up-to-date rankings, go to http://www.bankersalmanac.com/addcon/infobank/bank-rankings.aspx.

USGS.

World Gold Council.